Routledge Revivals

Innovation in the Science Curriculum

Of all the subjects in the school curriculum, science has been a most common target of the reformer's zeal. As a consequence, school science has featured frequently in studies of change in evaluation exercises and has also attracted the interest of social scientists. There have been others who have studied the effects of innovation in this field not as evaluators, nor as scientists, but as students of curricular problems. Such work is represented in this book, originally published in 1982.

It is particularly concerned with the way in which teachers use innovation and how this can assist policy making in the curriculum field. By focusing on the science curriculum the contributors examine in detail the way in which teachers cope with daily problems and with the demands that new ideas make on the systems to which they are accustomed.

The relationship between the school and the community is also dealt with in these case studies, all of which have implications for policy and research in the curriculum field.

T0383747

Innovation in the Science Curriculum

Edited by
John Olson

Routledge
Taylor & Francis Group

First published in 1982
by Croom Helm

This edition first published in 2018 by Routledge
2 Park Square, Milton Park, Abingdon, Oxon OX14 4RN

and by Routledge
711 Third Avenue, New York, NY 10017

Routledge is an imprint of the Taylor & Francis Group, an informa business

Publisher's Note
The publisher has gone to great lengths to ensure the quality of this reprint but points out that some imperfections in the original copies may be apparent.

Disclaimer
The publisher has made every effort to trace copyright holders and welcomes correspondence from those they have been unable to contact.

A Library of Congress record exists under ISBN: 0893971278

ISBN: 978-0-8153-6916-5 (hbk)
ISBN: 978-1-351-25308-6 (ebk)
ISBN: 978-0-8153-6913-4 (pbk)

Innovation in the Science Curriculum

Classroom Knowledge and Curriculum Change

EDITED BY JOHN OLSON

CROOM HELM
London & Canberra

NICHOLS PUBLISHING COMPANY
New York

Croom Helm Ltd, 2-10 St John's Road, London SW11

British Library Cataloguing in Publication Data
Olson, John
    Innovation in the science curriculum. -
    (Croom Helm curriculum policy and research series)
    1. Science - Study and teaching
    2. Curriculum planning
    I. Title
    507   Q181
    ISBN 0-7099-1900-X

First published in the United States of America in 1982 by
Nichols Publishing Company, Post Office Box 96, New York,
NY 10024
All rights reserved

Library of Congress Cataloging in Publication Data
Main entry under title:

Innovation in the science curriculum.

    1. Science - Study and teaching.
    2. Curriculum planning. I. Olson, J.K.
    Q181.I653   1982   375'.5   81-18966
    ISBN 0-89397-127-8   AACR2

CONTENTS

Foreword

This book takes up an important general issue in curriculum
policy and planning and studies it in relation to an area of the
curriculum which is of particular current concern - science education.
The general issue is the question of the kinds of understandings of classrooms and how they function that are needed in
order that effective action for curriculum improvement can be
undertaken. The first wave of post-war efforts to renew the
science curriculum - the Nuffield Projects in England, PSSC,
BSCS and Chem Study in the United States - tended to proceed
on the assumption that good ideas were capable of making their
own way: if a curriculum plan was advocated on grounds that were
rationally respectable, then schools would not only take it up,
they would also perform the work of translating it into a practical form that its proponents would recognise as fully adequate
to their original conception. Experience with the science projects,
and later with initiatives in other areas of the curriculum, soon
showed that this was an unrealistic expectation. Some ideas stuck
better than other, but most had problems making headway in
classrooms, and some foundered completely.
The first attack on this problem consisted of efforts to refine
further the process of planning and implementation itself and in
advocacy of greater resources for 'teacher education', for 'follow
through' and 'after care'. Apart from being expensive, this was
a solution which seemed not to go to the heart of the matter.
More recently, a different and more fundamental kind of investigation has been made of the awkward gap between intention and
realisation in curriculum planning. This has stemmed, on the
one hand, from an increasing concern on the part of curriculum
theorists with the nature of 'the practical' as a key to the understanding of curriculum issues and classroom processes, and on
the other hand, from the tradition of 'illuminative' and 'case
study' approaches to curriculum research which established
itself through the 1970s. Both styles of working have led in
their separate ways to an emphasis on the need to take seriously
the language and practices of the classroom - to regard them as
functional and rational given the ways in which schools and
teachers must get their work done. Hence, the problem of how
to manage the gap between intention and realisation is seen in
terms of a need to develop adequate ways of understanding and
discussing how and why teachers do what they do. These understandings can then become the basis of realistic change strategies

1

which recognise that curriculum improvement of a durable kind has to come about through a true partnership and dialogue between teachers and outside agents.

The papers commissioned for this book all report important recent research directed towards the elucidation of the practical knowledge of the classroom in the context of science education. Together, they pinpoint and explain the major issues which research is identifying, and also the techniques which have been evolved in order that questions of 'classroom knowledge' can be addressed. They provide an up-to-date source book of thinking on the nature of science classrooms and on how that thinking can be put to use by teachers, administrators and curriculum specialists who want to ensure that science teaching in our schools is as good as we can make it.

William A. Reid,
University of Birmingham

Ian Westbury,
University of Illinois

Editors

1 CLASSROOM KNOWLEDGE AND CURRICULUM CHANGE: AN INTRODUCTION

John Olson

INTRODUCTION

School Science and the Science Watchers

Of all the subjects in the school curriculum, science has been the most common target of the reformers' zeal. As a consequence school science has featured frequently in studies of change in evaluation exercises; social scientists, attracted by the upsurge of interest in the subject by funding agencies, have also joined the wave of science watchers.[1] There have been others in this wave who have studied the effects of innovation not as evaluators, nor as scientists, but as students of curricular problems. Such work is represented in this book.

The focus here, as it happens, is on the science curriculum; much of the money devoted to reform went to science and it is not surprising that there too went follow-up research. However the book is also about curriculum change, and the curriculum projects, whose fate in schools forms the substance of the accounts, are sources for a better understanding of the process of change itself: how teachers cope with innovation; how they cope every day; and how outsiders might better appreciate life in schools, and the demands that new ideas make on the stable systems that allow teachers to cope. These case studies have implications for policy and research in the curriculum field.

It is not an accident that the research reported here has been based on case study. As I shall argue later, it is only by getting close to the events of classroom life as teachers see them that we can properly appreciate what we observe there. Rob Walker's chapter brings us immediately to the nature of case study itself as he reflects upon his work for the Case Studies in Science Education project. His chapter comes first because it provides us with a vivid sense of the way case studies actually happen, how the researcher and the setting interact, and how insight is gained. Some of the problems endemic to the method are treated in his chapter and the reader is reminded of the virtues and limitations of the case method.

Edward Smith and Neil Sendelbach's close-up study of teachers' planning for activity-based science looks at the antecedents of teacher classroom activity in their plans, and in the recommendations of the teacher guides. Using the concept of 'problem space' defined by various frames, they have isolated significant differences between the frames of the guidebooks and those of the teachers. Their work has important implications for writers of curriculum guides.

Sally Brown and Donald McIntyre consider the costs and rewards of innovation from their readings of extensive interviews with teachers. Their work provides a rich framework with which to appreciate why teachers do not always use new ideas in ways that were intended. They conclude their chapter by suggesting that curriculum planning must be done using a more sophisticated appreciation of how teachers account for the costs and rewards of innovation.

The last chapter, my own, looks at the concept of teachers' classroom influence as it is involved in change. The way an integrated science curriculum was modified is explained in terms of teacher conservation of influence at the expense of conformity to project plans. This chapter, like the others, ends with proposals for curriculum policy and research; innovators, I argue, need to know more about the theories teachers have about their work, and to learn the language teachers use to describe and explain their actions. Such knowledge can then become the starting point for effective curriculum renewal - by paying attention to problems of communication which lie at the heart of curriculum renewal.

These accounts are not evaluation exercises, nor are they excursions into education from the social sciences to gather booty for the mother disciplines; they are rooted in curriculum problems and are of an anthropocentric cast. They are intended to be useful to those wishing to understand better how schools cope when faced with innovative curricula. School practice, we hope, is illuminated in a way that might help policy makers treat problems of reform with a greater respect for the complexity of the systems to be reformed; help teachers launch efforts at self-criticism through a better sense of the problems that confront them; and inform others about life in schools, and how we might better understand that life.

In this introductory chapter some of the issues that these accounts raise are discussed within a framework which I have called a humane perspective on change. My intent here is not to recast the studies in a perhaps alien mould, but to provide a way of looking at them all that I sense finds resonances with each, albeit somewhat differently in each case.

In the first part of the chapter I suggest that the expectations that reformers have had for change in schools in recent decades reflect an inadequate, mechanistic conception of institutional life. In its place a more humanistic frame is proposed, four elements of which are discussed in more detail: the diffuse nature of teaching as work; teaching and planning as the resolution of dilemmas; curriculum research as a form of hermeneutics; and curriculum change as a problem of communication. Fundamental to all of these elements is the idea that we cannot understand school change unless we understand what teachers are trying to accomplish by their actions in classrooms. It is with this idea that we begin. [2]

Appreciating the Views of Teachers

The accounts of science curriculum change which form the chapters of this book have started, as I see it, from a common approach to problems of curriculum research, namely: in order to understand the events of the classroom, it is necessary to appreciate what the teacher is trying to accomplish - to see things, at first, from the teacher's point of view. Certain important features of the accounts here follow from this way of setting the research problem. First, attention is given to events of importance to teachers relatively free from particular reductionistic prior-commitments. These reports, as I have said, are not exercises in the reduction of classroom complexities to particular languages selected from currents in the social sciences. As a consequence, the contributors have not had to shape their data to conform to the formalisms of this or that social science, or to reflect particular theoretical formulations like distorting mirrors.[3] In part, this avoidance of discipline can be interpreted as a response to a suspicion that reducing curriculum problems to 'scientific' problems has not been helpful in the policy field of curriculum. These reductions have simply dessicated and distorted rather than illuminated the problem. The lack of success of the 'scientific' approach to curriculum problems can be traced, I believe, to a failure to take seriously, as sources of description and explanation, the intentions of teachers as important actors in the field.[4] In an effort to mimic the pure sciences, causes have been preferred to reasons, although there is no obvious justification for this.

The reports in this book can be seen as travellers' tales from the region of teachers' intention. They all reflect this concern, and, as a consequence, tread warily in seeking to explain what was seen; showing respect for the complexity of the landscape traversed. Taking seriously the intentions of teachers has led to a sensitivity to teacher language; these are reports in the vernacular, not simply efforts to substitute teacher words for theoretical ones within the unchanged disciplinary language, but efforts to find out what words mean in the system of thought used by the teachers.[5] These reports reflect an awareness of the system of teacher thinking, and, as a consequence, we are placed in a better position to understand what teachers mean by what they say.

If we want to understand the meaning of teacher action in the classroom, we have to understand the system of thought teachers bring to bear on their work. What are the 'rules' they are using?[6] How are these rules organised? The accounts that follow here, based on conversations with teachers, begin to give us a picture of the complex systems, and the theories which lie behind them, that teachers have for coping in the classroom. These theories are tacit, and one of the advantages

of extended conversation with people, which is characteristic
of the case methods used here, is that the tacit can be revealed
and the emerging sense of it can be checked. These accounts
show how this can be done and suggest what the fruits are
like.

With these general comments in mind, we can now move to a
more detailed discussion of the humanistic frame which, I
believe, might usefully illuminate the importance of these studies
We begin with a discussion of the dominant conception of
teacher behaviour – what I have called, the mechanistic conception. The talk about this conception will form the backdrop
to a discussion of a more preferable frame.

MECHANISTIC CONCEPTIONS OF TEACHER BEHAVIOUR

Great Expectations

Before delving into the details of the mechanistic conception,
we should look briefly at why efforts to alter radically school
practice failed and why as a consequence, faith in mechanistic
conceptions has waned. As a working idea at this point, the
mechanistic conception locates control and explanation of
teacher behaviour in relation to system plans which teachers
are expected to implement, or to a system of environmental
variables which are seen to shape teacher behaviour. The
former conception, particularily, has dominated research and
development in the curriculum field. Its fruits have been
disappointing. [7]

In the last decade, there has been increased study of the
classroom; what these studies have revealed is an interesting
resistance by teachers to the use of innovative ideas as intended. As House put it, teachers have been unwilling to
'reorient' their practice. Studies of the role of the teacher in
curriculum development document the extent of this unwillingness to reorient, but say less about why this happens, and
what should be done about it. [8] Some of these studies bear
directly upon the research reported here because they were
conducted largely by observing teachers using innovative
curricula and, although generally not concerned to explore
what teachers considered salient about their efforts to change,
gave glimpses of the underlying concerns of teachers which
appear to have influenced their use of the new ideas. A brief
comment on three major studies on school changes will illustrate
the emerging awareness of the problems teachers face in coping
with innovative doctrine.

Marshall Herron, in interviewing users of the Biological
Studies Curriculum Study (BSCS) materials, found that, in
general, teachers using the materials did not have the same
degree of understanding of the nature of science as the
designers of the project did; in spite of the fact that many of
these teachers had been to institutes at which the philosophy

of the project was discussed. Such institutes had apparently failed to do the job. Herron concluded that: 'Teacher perception of new course material . . . is a problem that lies at the root of resistance to curricular change.'[9]
Similarly, Shipman (1974) found that the definitions of the humanities project he studied were at 'different levels for different groups. The teachers were involved in their own problems, and defined the project out of their experience in their classrooms. As a consequence, the basic principles behind the project were usually misunderstood, and often unconsidered.'[10] Shipman concluded that this narrow focus of the teachers was the main barrier to genuine implementation, and he proposed secondment of teachers to research and development teams to learn about the problems associated with innovation in schools. He did recognise the importance of understanding the status quo: 'But every change in routine is a threat to teacher pupil relations, and to standards of work . . . (maybe teachers) would be more effective and happy with conventional teaching.'[11]
Perhaps most revealing was Richard Carlson's finding that teachers using programmed instructions involving independent rates of progress acted to keep students moving more or less at the same rate.[12] Teachers gathered the class together periodically to teach them, even though this was not necessary, since they did not see the use of the programmed instruction as 'teaching'. Carlson concluded that, for some reason, teachers were not prepared to abandon the ways in which they normally organised their teaching.
What do these studies tell us? First, they illustrate the notion that proposed reorientation (major changes) often end up being variations (small scale changes within existing practice), or no change at all: proposed discovery approaches become didactic and individualised rates of progress were homogenised. Curriculum innovators appeared to have underestimated the conserving tendencies of teachers and schools. Researchers following the innovations into schools could only marvel at the extent to which teachers continued to do what they always did. Secondly, the studies I have reviewed above raise the question of what is an adequate conception of the interaction between innovative doctrine and school practice. Are teachers who do not innovate to be considered unimaginative and conservative? Is their unwillingness to change to be thought of as evidence of lack of professionalism? Shipman's comment about the possibility that teachers would be more happy with conventional practice captures the perplexity that exists about the failure of schools to adopt many innovations. These studies suggest that we need to look again at our assumptions about the work that teachers do, and how new ways of working can come to be. These studies hint at complex, underlying systems of coping that teachers operate for reasons we do not understand. Until now we haven't understood them

because our conception of teacher activity has been inadequate.

Mechanistic Conceptions: Two Forms

Some of the perplexity about change which is expressed in
the literature of curriculum implementation concerns the
'failure' of teachers to conform to expectations based on
rational models of change. Such models assume that teachers
would naturally understand and conform to central prescriptions for action; no ambiguities in the communication
process were envisaged. Failure on the part of curriculum
developers to appreciate the complexity of the teachers'
work setting, and to understand their language, has more
recently been seen as an important deficiency of 'rational'
models;[13] recent attempts to understand how teachers use
innovations have stressed the importance of the immediate
teaching environment - classroom 'ecology' - as a source of
explanation.
   In the former, 'the relationship between the elements of
the system are assumed to be known and the manipulation
of one element assumed to have predictable consequences for
the other elements . . . programming in this context can
only mean programming the teacher'.[14] The other conception
is advanced by Dreeben, who notes: 'The most obvious
characteristic of the school is the division into isolated
classrooms under the direction of the teacher. This fact in
itself determines much of what happens in schools.'[15] According to this view, what teachers do can be seen as a consequence of the 'properties of their classrooms'.[16] Both of these
views, which I call mechanistic, have limitations for understanding the work of teachers, and particularly the fate at
their hands of innovations in schools. Examples of each type
of approach will be discussed briefly to illustrate the nature
of these limitations.

The Rational View

Sieber, in his paper on curriculum change, uses images of
people at work in complex organisations to describe manipulative strategies for procuring allegiance and compliance with
change directives from above.[17] Such an approach is limited
on two grounds. First, the underlying theory of the functions
of curriculum development is inadequate. Teachers do not
stand in relation to innovative ideas as employees in a
bureaucracy stand in relation to policy directives. This is to
say that the image of compliant teachers does not well reflect
what exists, nor, more importantly, does it reflect what
ought to exist. Given the nature of education, it is not the
task of outsiders to manipulate the conformity of teachers to
policy directives concerning the operation of the curriculum.

People outside the school, and those inside, have related but different functions which do not stand in a relation of super- to sub-ordinate, and the teacher can be seen as an arbitrator between the demands of the curriculum materials and the instructional situation. Only rarely will arbitration lead to a settlement exclusively favouring the developer's intentions. [18] Furthermore, the complexity of the tasks of the school which Perrow calls a 'nonroutine type of firm', leads to 'unanalyzable search procedures and the need to deal with many exceptions'. [19] In view of the complexity of the tasks and differing value positions associated with education, it is hard to see how the image of teacher as target of manipulation can serve curriculum theory.

The Ecological View

The second version of the mechanical conception recognises the complexity of the teacher's setting. This setting is seen to influence what teachers do, and, accordingly, this view is often referred to as 'ecological'. [20] This conception of the teacher uses the biological analogy of an ecosystem to characterise the response of teachers to their environment. Such responses are seen as adaptive in the same way particular organisms fit into ecological niches. In this view, the environment controls the behaviour of the teacher in some unexpressed way, and the mind of the teacher is seen as a 'black box', interpreting signals from the environment and responding: to know the teacher is to know the environment where he or she works. While ecological conceptions remind us of the importance of the conditions in which teaching occurs, there are problems in using such conceptions as a basis for research and curriculum policy making. In practice, the teacher is manipulated by others who use an understanding of the classroom environment to find ways of gaining teacher compliance with plans from outside.

In short, neither form of the mechanistic conception of teacher behaviour commands respect. Both fail on moral grounds; the teacher is ignored as a moral agent. Both fail because they remain isolated from the meaning of events in classrooms as construed by those involved: the important actors. Mechanistic conceptions are ineffective platforms for change because they lead us to ignore the systems of thought that teachers bring to bear on problems by treating teachers as objects of manipulation. Rather than seek more sophisticated methods of manipulation, we need to find out what those systems of thought are like and to do this we have to pay attention to what insiders tell us. In this way we can pursue the goal of curriculum change through education rather than manipulation.

HUMANISTIC CONCEPTIONS OF TEACHER BEHAVIOUR

The Global and the Personal

One particular observation of Dan Lortie, provides a key of how we might better understand teacher behaviour:

> Educational goals are often stated in global even utopian terms . . . (We) observed that teachers 'reduce' such goals into specific objectives they use in their daily work. This reduction apparently involves two conservative tendencies; relying on personal convictions and obtaining high satisfaction from outcomes that are less than universalistic. When teachers cannot use stated goals to guide their actions, organizational objectives give way to personal values; the personal values, as we saw . . . are heavily influenced by past experience. [21]

Lortie suggests that teachers 'reduce' the global to the personal because the personal makes more sense and is satisfying. I would argue, in view of this, that if we want to understand the fate of innovations, we have to understand what teachers take to be satisfying and meaningful. My own work leads me to suggest that teachers 'conserve' personal values and satisfaction in the face of more universalistic expectations because they are coping with work demands which are difficult to understand, and with consequences of actions which are hard to foresee. Thus, for example, teachers I talked to construed giving notes as productive (good for exam passing), but discussing ideas as unproductive (not good for exam passing), and chose to give notes in spite of the innovative doctrine's call to do otherwise. The anticipation of the effects of a particular teaching approach on success at exam passing allowed the teachers to assess and make choices. The significant point is that these choices tended to preserve the more delimited and satisfying elements of teaching science at the expense of the more universalistic expectations of the curriculum developers, which had to do with goals such as fostering social responsibility and particular types of intellectual skills.

What I am suggesting by this example is that we must consult the views of the teacher if we want to understand why they make the choices they do. In this way we can understand what the actions mean within the system of thought of the teacher. We have to know the system as a whole, if we are to understand the meaning of the act. [22] This approach to understanding how teachers work in classrooms is valid because it is, in the end, more appropriate to the nature of education itself. Those involved in educating others are engaged in a morally bound pursuit and act as moral agents, and it does not seem possible on the one hand, to accept that what teachers do is bound up in the resolution of issues whose roots are moral, and on the other, to ignore the views of the teacher in an attempt to understand how that agency is accomplished. Besides this point, there is the further one that we simply cannot understand why humans act the way they do unless we at least consult their intentions; humans are not machines. [23] Problems teachers face in implementing innovation are inadequately understood, and, combined with an inadequate conception of the meaning of teacher behaviour, there have been unrealistic expectations of rapid change in school practice. These expectations have been based on a 'mechanical' model of the interaction between teachers and forces which either press for change, or inhibit it. However, educators tend not to do the kinds of things for which a 'mechanical' model of their work is appropriate. What teachers do is sufficiently complex ethically and practically to require a more humane perspective. What might this perspective look like?

Elements of a Humane Perspective

The Functions of the School and the Thoughts of Teachers. Innovations in schools occur in institutions, obviously; their fate is determined by how teachers think about their work. We need to understand that thinking, but we have also to locate that thought within some useful model of institutional life. The model selected has been adapted from the work of Taylor [24] and Reid. [25] In that model, the intersection of the social system, technology and goals, denotes the point where teachers do their work in the classroom. The model identifies these as the three major elements of institutional life with which teachers have to deal. It is the conflicting demands emanating from these three elements of school life that create dilemmas for teachers. How these domains of the teacher's world impinge on him or her is reflected in the dilemmas which they experience as they go about their work. Awareness of dilemma occurs especially when teachers are asked to change habituated practice, and learning more about how teachers perceive dilemmas is an important problem for research into curriculum change.

What the teachers do with an innovation can be interpreted as an accommodation between the various demands of the innovative doctrine in the three main domains of the teacher's work and the preferred solutions teachers have already adopted to cope with the demands of their work. Innovative doctrines require, by definition, reformulations of relationships between social systems, technology and goals. They are pressed upon teachers as visions of what might be, and they implicitly, if not explicitly, criticise the existing practices they seek to change. Innovative doctrines propose resolutions amongst the domains of teacher's work different from those that exist. The demands of innovation recreate consciousness of, and highlight already existing, but submerged, perceptions of the satisfactory and unsatisfactory consequences of existing resolutions of dilemmas. Examples of the 'surfacing' of dilemmas in the context of discussion of innovation with outsiders can be seen in the reports here. Brown and McIntyre, for example, found that teachers were concerned about the effects of guided-discovery on their relationship to their classes. They document some of the dilemmas teachers faced associated with the guided-discovery methods and integrated subject matter of Scottish Integrated Science. Smith and Sendelbach also found that teachers using new materials faced perplexing dilemmas. They observed that teachers departed from guidebook prescriptions in systematic ways, and that the divergent written plans teachers made – although apparently minimal – were, on talking to teachers, found to be cues or reminders which lead back to undocumented but extensive plans in the teachers' memories. Through talking to teachers about their planning, they were able to appreciate the role 'plans-in-memory' played in the way teachers dealt with dilemmas associated with discovery vs. control in the classroom.

Innovative doctrines, in so far as they create increased awareness of the consequences of the diffuseness of teaching, recreate dilemmas for teachers by forcing them back to choices once made and now forgotten. The case for A or B is reopened and must be resolved again. Clearly teachers will vary in the extent to which attempts to follow the policy dictates of an innovation will generate the kinds of experience described here. Many factors can be imagined to influence the degree of awareness of dilemma, but the general point stands. Innovations have potential, because of what they are and how they are perceived, to evoke at least some reflection - to provide a starting point for a reconsideration of practice through discussion with outsiders, and a basis for systematic reconstruction of the rules that guide practice. Study of innovation thus provides an arena for the understanding of school life itself.

The dynamic interaction amongst the elements of teaching life we began with (social system, technology, goals), conceived of as a source of dilemmas, provides a functional frame for understanding how existing practice and innovative doctrine might interact inside the minds of teachers. The link between mind and environment is provided by the concept of dilemma. Understanding the dilemmas teachers say they experience in their work gives us a basis for reconstructing and understanding the practical theories which inform the decisions teachers make.[26] These theories can be thought of as functional ones: directed to accomplishing a stable arrangement of the elements of teaching life. How do these theories function?

If we are going to understand how teachers cope with innovation then, most fundamentally, we need to understand what they are trying to accomplish. One important function, I would argue, is the control of the effects of task diffuseness.

Before returning to the concept of dilemma, we must first
explore the significance of the diffuseness of the teacher's
work.

Teaching as the Control of Diffuseness. Bryan Wilson, in
his analysis of the teacher's role, suggests that in teaching:
'The role obligation is diffuse, difficult to delimit, and the
activities of the role diffuse . . . (there are) conflicts intrinsic
to the teacher's role and the circumstances in which it is per-
formed.' Wilson defined a diffuse role in contrast to a specific
one which he notes has the following characteristics: 'There
are set tasks which can be defined in terms of the exact
manipulations involved . . . there is a precise content change
in the material handled which results from the role performance.
The role player has a specialized and easily defined expertise.
There is a formal limitation to the competencies which the role
player exercises in his role. The role player's commitment is
delimited.'[27]
     The main thrust of his argument is that diffuse roles carry
with them the potential for conflict and insecurity.[28] The significance of this relationship has not been probed, as Delamont
has observed: 'Teachers are balancing contradictory aims all
the time, but we know little of how they go about it, or how
they view this necessity. This is odd when so many have
argued that the teacher's role is so diffuse, because it
involves the constant reconciliation of the unreconcilable.'[29]
Brown and McIntyre, for example, speak of such contradiction
inherent in the teachers' role: they note that teachers value
autonomy, and yet they want personal support for trying new
ideas; these tend to conflict and create dilemmas in practice.
     The term diffuse does not quite capture Wilson's own
characterisation of the work of the teacher, but will be retained and used here with a richer connotation. If we think
of the teacher acting in a play whose curtain times are
variable, whose props and scenery do not always work,
whose actors are never quite sure of their lines and whose
audience might have come to the wrong play, we have some
of the sense in which the term diffuse is being used here. It
isn't just that the work spreads out over a number of kinds
of human interaction (e.g. cognitive and affective), but
that there is a lack of clear evidence of efficacy, of acceptance and of task completion.
     One of the consequences of diffuseness of the teaching
task is that teachers are often faced with having to make
choices without adequate information, and with the likelihood
that, whatever they do, they will not be able to please everyone, not even themselves. In such a way are dilemmas
created. Edward Smith and Neil Sendelbach pursue this idea
in their work. Teachers they talked to were expected to
develop in students quite complex cognitive skills which were
difficult to delimit. Where they needed help most, it was least

available; the 'Teacher's Guide' was not effective in communicating what was intended to happen and why, and teachers departed from the intended plan in order to delimit their task. Similarily Rob Walker observed a teacher who taught from the text. Now teaching from the text was not something that the projects funded by the National Science Foundation have promoted; yet this teacher had good reason for using the text the way she did. Walker found that teaching from the text helped her accomplish certain objectives; helped her delimit the task. In my own study, teachers worked from a syllabus of content to be covered during the year even though this was not part of how the project they were using was to operate. In this way the teachers were able to maintain the examination preparation system; a system which did delimit their work.

To put this another way, dilemmas that teachers experience in their working life stem from the diffuseness of the work they do. If we want to understand teaching and how teachers change, we have to pursue those dilemmas back to see how teachers cope, and in this way the concept of a dilemma becomes central to a humane conspectus for understanding innovation in schools. More needs to be said about the concept of dilemma itself and how dilemmas are resolved.

Teaching as the Resolution of Dilemmas. The concept of a dilemma has been developed from the work of the Berlaks.[30] In their study of English primary schools, they noticed that at times teachers did not adhere to the doctrinal requirements of the 'open education' movement. This 'inconsistent' teacher behaviour was taken to be problematic by the Berlaks, who explained the apparent inconsistencies by hypothesising that teachers were drawn to some degree to both poles of a dilemma. They identified three major categories of dilemmas reflected in the teachers' behaviour: those associated with - child and society, teaching-learning process and justice. The dilemmas they identify are similar to what Egan calls the presuppositions that underlie curriculum decisions.[31] Such presuppositions are fundamental commitments, analysable into dichotomies which are inherent in actions; they are the fruits of the logical reconstructions of people's behaviour.

While it is useful philosophically to understand the logic of people's behaviour, functionally we need to understand how those dilemmas are perceived by the people involved. Rather than a reduction of the perplexity of the issues to a logical analysis of polar positions at the level of fundamental commitments, the search, from a curriculum point of view, must be for terms and expressions in the language of those who have experienced the dilemma. Sally Brown and Donald McIntyre, for example, have isolated clearly some of the dilemmas Scottish teachers faced in trying to use guided-discovery methods. Their comments make it clear that the Working Party which developed the scheme had not considered what it meant to use it in a less than perfectly equipped class-room. The dilemmas of the teachers using the materials and, interestingly, the dilemmas faced by the teachers on the Working Party, are seen as partially responsible for the way the scheme fared in the schools. The teachers on the Working Party, for a variety of reasons, were not able to exert much influence over the way the scheme was designed.

The nature of the dilemmas teachers face in their work can be inferred from what they say about their experiences; about what perplexes them. To understand what teachers are coping with, it is necessary to study what the teachers say, to understand the nature of the dialectical issues they face, and thus to understand the meaning of their consequent patterns of action. Instead of a logical, or mechanical, analysis of the actions of innovating teachers, we discover the viewpoints of teachers in their own terms. Rather than sit in the back of the room, and then go away and reconstruct what the teacher was coping with, we must talk to the teacher at the very least; otherwise, how are we to know what the behaviour of the teacher means?

Coping with dilemmas associated with innovation is a common thread in the reports here. Of particular importance is the dilemma created when the new way upsets the stable patterns of classroom interaction that teachers have created. All report on the importance teachers place on the management of class-room activity and the dilemmas which stem from problems of management. In their study of how teacher planning intentions might be framed, Smith and Sendelbach found that the teacher's dominant concern and focus of attention was on engaging the students in manipulation of materials and associated classroom management requirements. However, the organisation of the guide to the materials differed significantly from how teachers organised their planning, and this dis-sonance created dilemmas for the teachers. Rob Walker also found science teachers concerned about management. Walker pursued what the teachers had identified as the key issue in curriculum and teaching - the problem of motivation. Teachers, he found, had concerns quite different from those of science reformers.

Similarily, I found that teachers were concerned about class-room influence; a dominant factor in explaining the way they construed their experience with the Schools Council Integrated Science Project ('Patterns'). Like Smith and Sendelbach, I found that the guide to the materials focused on concerns quite different from those of the teachers. Brown and McIntyre also found that teachers were hesitant about their ability to teach an integrated course and considered it unlikely that they could present the whole range of material in an interesting form. The virtues of integration were, for teachers, the very sources of <u>dilemmas in practice</u>.

Teacher concerns about classroom management and subject

matter presentation are not new; the studies in this book
have located them within frameworks of teacher thinking
which allow the reader to make sense of those concerns. These
frameworks reflect some of the complexities of the work of
teachers which I have conceptualised here in terms of teaching
as a diffuse activity, and teacher decisions about teaching as
a way of coping with the dilemmas that emerge because teaching is a diffuse task.

Given the central role the concept of dilemma plays in the
process of understanding teacher theories of practice, we
need appropriate research methods for discovering what these
dilemmas are. Without this kind of research it seems clear that
outsiders are more likely to propose innovative ideas which
will increase the dilemmas that confront teachers in their work,
rather than give useful advice and help teachers do a better
job.

The reports here do not conform to a single conception of
case study. Each has been based on a particular approach to
cases; nonetheless all, it seems to me, have been able to
illuminate for us the world of innovation in schools by approaching the view of teachers closely and treating their words as
text for interpretation.

Curriculum Research as a Form of Hermenuetics

A central concern of research in curriculum is to understand
how teachers make sense of and use innovative ideas. To do
this, I have argued that it is necessary to study the 'phenomena of innovation in use' from the point of view of the
teacher and others involved. How can this be done?

As we saw, when schools adopt an innovation, they do so in
a context which is already functioning to accomplish goals.
Organisations tend to stabilise around practices which permit
a balancing between goals, social relationships and techniques.
The fate of an innovative project will depend, in important
measure, on how its proposals, as understood by the teachers,
affect that balance. For purposes of understanding change in
schools and for policy formation, understanding the way in
which the stable systems of the school operate is important.
Brown and McIntyre, for example, talk about the personal
costs and rewards that teachers assess in their use of innovation. They argue that science teachers will preserve
classroom autonomy at the cost of a lack of control over how
the science curriculum is organised. Lortie makes a similar
point in relation to assessing the effects of CAI:

> It is one thing to make assertions about the differences
> between human and man-machine interaction, but quite
> another to identify and measure their effects on students.
> To do so we must dig deeper into previously ignored
> aspects of the conventional system, thus probing aspects

of schooling which were previously ignored. This is
indicative of the general tendency of change to increase
our interest in the status quo. [32]

How are we to understand the status quo? House has suggested that in order to understand the fate of innovative
ideas in schools it is necessary to understand the phenomenology of the teacher's world. [33] While House does not define
phenomenology, here the term is taken to mean a representation and interpretation of the viewpoint of the person involved
in the action being studied. This viewpoint is considered to
be important in <u>understanding</u> the actions of people. As Kelly
put it: 'Two people can act alike even if they have each been
exposed to quite different phenomenal stimuli. It is in the
similarity in the construction of events that we find the basis
for similar action and not in the identity of the events themselves.' [34] The key point here is that the explanation of the
action lies in the construction placed upon the context of the
action by the actor, not in the context itself. Thus one has to
understand the other person's <u>experience</u> of the context. This
is not to say that understanding the context is not important.
Clearly, understanding context is important, for it is that
context which provides the actor with problems and possibilities. Within the idea of context must also be included the
context of the research activity itself. The responses people
make to being researched are importantly affected by people's
perceptions of the research's purpose and status.
   Research on curriculum innovation, however, has tended to
look at school and classroom events associated with innovation
from the viewpoint of the innovative doctrine, or the conditions
of implementation. The goals, related technology and implied
social system of the innovation may, in practice, have limited
points of contact with those of the teachers. Outsiders may
simply not be in a position to understand what the innovation
<u>means</u> to those who are using it, nor what the teachers are
expected to give up means. Scriven's programme of goal-free
evaluation goes some way to recognise this problem, although
he seems to assume that a language exists common to insiders
and outsiders for talking about goals and procedures. [35] He
speaks of the contaminating effects of the developer's goals
more as a source of bias than as a source of difficulties in
communicating with the teachers. The kind of arrogant
acceptance of the view of the developer that Scriven is
trying to avoid is also suggested by Reid, who notes: 'Research is something done by the expert to the in-expert.
(In such a process) people who are the actual objects of
research are the last to be consulted.' [36] Clearly the views of
the 'insiders' must be consulted.
   As an approach to understanding the view of 'insiders',
Hudson argues for a 'hermeneutic' approach to evidence. Such
an approach, he notes, involves different kinds of interpretive

activity in which the interpreter reconstructs another person's intentions using that other person's terms, or another person's intentions are restructured in some new terms.[37] Both of these interpretations start with the other person; that is, the teacher. Initially the person's situation can be viewed in their own terms; efforts can be made to understand their language. The investigator can become familiar with those things that are important to the teachers and to the school; school prospectuses can be read; professional development material aimed at the teacher studied; staff meetings attended. Later, what has been learned can be transformed by the investigator into more general terms; the individual reports can be used to develop an interpretation of teacher perspectives in a language other than that of the teacher, but adequately translated from it; a key point to which we will return later.

There are, however, uncertainties associated with this 'hermenuetic' research method. Following Hudson, three can be identified which deal with important problems associated with the analysis of reports of other people. They are: context, self-deception and preferred metaphors. A fourth, the problem of generalisation, is added to these.

Context. The first has to do with context. The meanings the person perceives are embedded in the contexts that surround him. Because of the importance of context, the researcher is faced with the problem of simultaneously sharing the perspective of the other person and remaining detached. Although the researcher must have some basis for appreciating the context being studied, he or she has to remain sufficiently detached in order not to take for granted common practice and common understanding shared by the teachers. As Rob Walker suggests, the case study reassembles ideas, information, insights and understanding into a human and institutional whole.

There are two sides to the context pitfall, however. On the one hand, failure to consider the context of meaning limits one's ability to make sense of what people are saying; on the other hand, as Parsons argues: 'excessive attention to the participant's views can lead to a 'disembodied' sort of reasoning . . . The opinions of the participants or groups are themselves context bound not just within a contemporary situation vis-à-vis a particular innovation, but within a personal developmental field; within organizational and cultural fields which have histories'.[38] What Parsons urges is the treatment of the cases within a larger framework. Such a caution needs to be heeded to avoid the dangers of ahistoricism; one way of doing this is to locate the research in a particular school in its historical context; in the context of trends in science education; in relation to the personal histories of those involved.

Self-deception. Turning to the second source of uncertainty, it is clear that all of us are prone systematically to protect ourselves from inconvenient truths; we deceive ourselves. As a remedy, Hudson suggests that: 'It is not enough for the psychologist to construe another's experience as that other person experiences it; he must construe in the light of evidence about what actually occurs.'[39] It is well known that the self-reports of professional groups suffer from their tendency to overplay the work; they tend to show the investigator and the public a face which reflects well on the profession and on the person. The content of a self-report in the interview situation is to some degree an artifact of the encounter itself and informative of how the person handles such encounters. Clearly, there are many ways of avoiding the pitfall of taking things at face value; the significant problem is to know when the masks have been penetrated. Sustained presence of the researcher in the school may help only if the researcher is sensitive to the 'drama' of the research encounter.

Preferred Metaphors. The third source of uncertainty comes from the use of one's own preferred metaphors. These control how one interprets data and are in turn controlled by that data. There is a two-way relationship between data and interpretive metaphor which may become dominated by the metaphors, insulating the investigator from critical information. The importance of exposing the interpretive perspective in hermeneutic research is clear; as is the need to avoid the treatment of data uncritically in terms of preferred images. The contrapuntal use of different types of data, as can be seen in the reports here, can help avoid uncritical acceptance of a favoured point of view. Whatever picture emerges of the teacher's view, it is bound to be partial; however, as Hudson has suggested, one has a choice to make between building bridges over voids of ignorance through exclusive attention to what can be observed or walking into such voids in search of the wellsprings from within. Rob Walker talks about the 'biases' of the site visitor being checked by having others look at what is happening. In the end, he finds control of preferred metaphor in being able to prompt people to tell him what really is on their mind; that is, in being able to listen without signalling what he expects to hear.

Generalisation. There remains an uncertainty beyond the three identified; that is, the matter of generalisation. The people whose ideas form the substance of these case studies are not a sample from which generalisations can spring in the sense of moving from sample to population through the use of inferential statistics. What can be learned from the few people typical of case studies? First of all, the reports can be aggregated in various ways; some qualitative, some quantitative. The people often face similar problems in similar settings and their views in aggregate can reveal something of what it was like to confront similar problems in similar settings. On

the other hand, the schools do differ; there are variations in
how teachers perceived the abilities of pupils, the suitability
of curriculum projects for their schools, the reaction of their
peers to their work with innovations. Often commonalities are
great and differences are less so. What emerges from interpretation of case reports and other data are threads of
common experience, commonly interpreted; there are detec-
table perspectives that teachers and their pupils share in the
contexts where similar problems are grappled with. These
perspectives can represent limited steps towards pinpointing
critical processes and identifying common phenomena. DuMas
calls such a process 'ideographic nomothesis': 'The study of
many single cases may be summarized to yield generalizations
about the populations.'[40] Case data can provide the basis for
limited nomothesis in the form of generalisations about the
dilemmas teachers face in their work. Interpreting these
dilemmas becomes the basis for understanding the fate of
innovative doctrines; a central goal for curriculum research.

Curriculum Research and Communication

The Teacher's Point of View. Taking the teacher's point of
view seriously leads us to forms of inquiry and to particular
problems not typically characteristic of current curriculum
research. In the end, use of these methods and attention to
these problems will give us a better idea of how teachers
organise their thinking – their practical theories – and how
they act in the light of their rendering of the tasks at hand
and the resources available to accomplish them. For those who
wish to guide teachers, such understanding is invaluable
because the person who wishes to communicate ideas to
teachers is going to have to understand the network of
beliefs that teachers hold and what particular terms mean
within such networks.

One of the most important problems for curriculum, I would
argue, is that of communication. The accounts in this book
are based on studies of people outside schools seeking to
influence what those inside do and in various ways failing to
communicate their ideas. Why do these failures occur? They
occur, I think, because outsiders fail to understand what
teachers are trying to do, and, as a consequence, a gap exists;
what one person means to say, the other does not understand. This issue is at the root of the problems identified in
this book. These accounts illustrate the difficulties faced by
outsiders trying to communicate ideas to teachers mainly
through written documents, and the difficulties teachers face
in trying to understand what is meant by the documents they
read.

Sally Brown and Donald McIntyre treat this issue at length.
They argue that curriculum makers must pay attention to how
teachers talk about their work. They have used, as an example

of what can happen by default, the differences between the way teachers viewed guidance (in guided-discovery) and the Working Party's view. Using a stimulated recall technique they probed teacher conception of guidance and found teacher conceptions at variance with the 'official' view of the curriculum makers. Similarily Ed Smith and Neil Sendelbach have found that one of the reasons elementary science teachers departed from procedures suggested in the teacher's guide was due to the inherent difficulties in communicating to teachers why certain procedures were desirable. They noted that the most reliable influence of the programme material appears to have been on the kinds of activities carried out and lower level knowledge addressed. Less reliable was their influence on higher level knowledge addressed and the overall instructional strategy. They concluded that people trying to communicate ideas to teachers need to consider how teachers organise their teaching approaches; that is, they need to know more about the practical theories of teachers.

What can we learn from these studies about communication in curriculum? First, they suggest that we need to pay attention to how teachers construe their work and the nature of the language they use to talk about that work. More specifically, we need to find out what their theories of practice are as part of the process of developing guides to curriculum practice. If we adopt the idea that the role of the outsider is to offer the insider guidance, not orders, then we are led to consult the insider by the very nature of the guidance act itself.

The notion of a curriculum guide begs comparison with the sort of guides we go to to help us understand unfamiliar territory. The classical guide of this kind is the Baedeker's guide. How do these guides work? Consulting my 1910 Baedeker's 'Great Britain', I learn, for example, that 'Salisbury Cathedral, a splendid example of pure Early English, enjoyed the rare advantage of having been begun and finished within a period of forty years and is remarkable for the uniformity, harmony and perspicuity of its construction.' These are the sorts of statements I expect to find in a guide. The guide helps me interpret what I see around me; it offers advice on how best to spend my time and money. The things I find in a guide are what I expect to find there. The guide is written according to conventions which both the guide writer and the reader understand. Thus, in the case of my Baedeker, the way the landscape is treated is not unexpected; it conforms to the conventions of guide writing of the Baedeker tradition: the landscape, normally perceived by most as relatively undifferentiated, is in the Baedeker's guide almost insanely detailed and particular. One looks to left and right almost every other second; objects of note are everywhere and are to be thoroughly savoured.

The Baedeker guide can be likened to what Walker calls: 'curriculum documents . . . the writings teachers and students

use'. [41] He notes that such documents need to be clear and
specific so that those who 'are supposed to be instructed by
the document know exactly what they are being advised to
do'. [42] The travel guide has to live up to the same demands, but
there is more than the matter of clarity and specificity at stake
here. The guide writers are relying on the reader to understand the intention of the guide writing act itself; that something special is happening. What is being offered isn't just
information, or description, but something that will be of
benefit. The guide writer offers advice. The guide writer
relies on the reader to take what is written in this way. The
particular activities of the innovator attempting to communicate
with the teacher can be more clearly understood when taken
as part of the larger <u>linguistic</u> activity of advising.

The Innovator as Adviser. An approach to understand such
an activity can be found in Searle's analysis of speech acts in
which he shows how such acts might be successfully per-
formed. [43] This analysis allows him to isolate rules which
govern how statements are to be taken. These rules he likens
to those of games in which certain preparatory and essential
conditions must obtain. Thus, in the case of chess, in order to
move it must be one's turn to move, and the move must be
one permitted by rules governing a particular piece. Further,
one is expected not to cheat, or lose on purpose. It is the
<u>preparatory</u> rules that are of particular interest here.
    Preparatory rules are those rules which give the act point;
if the act is to be understood as the kind of act it is, then
people expect the actor to conform to certain prior conditions.
So, for example, in the case of advice, I would not advise
someone to do something they were already doing, and I
should have reason to believe that the person would benefit
from the future act that is being advised. The point of these
rules is that they permit us to isolate those elements of the
advising activity which give it its particular force; that is,
which enable the hearer or reader to understand what is
meant. So, in the case of advice, I would not expect to go
to a guide and find that I am advised to do what I am already
doing. Advice is something new. How difficult I might find
the advice to understand depends on the novelty of the
proposal. I would also take it that what I am being urged to do
is well founded. The person who advises me presumably has
reason to believe that it will be in my interest to do what is
being advised.
    We can now use rules of advice-giving to look at an example.
I take as a case in point a statement in the teacher's guide to
the English Schools Council Integrated Science Project (SCISP):

> There will be a partnership between teacher and pupil in
> learning . . . Teachers are often worried about the danger
> of imposing their attitudes on pupils. It is suggested that

class discussion be based on the materials provided . . .
and that they should not become the basis of disagreement
between pupils and the teacher. Direction will sometimes
need to be given and the teacher selects the material to be
discussed.[44]

How effective is this as a piece of advice? Clearly, the writers
had reason to think that teachers would not normally think of
their work as a partnership. The advice is thus well founded in
this respect. But what about the other preparatory rule: the
writer has some reason to believe that the teacher will benefit
from this advice? It is here that one begins to worry about the
adequacy of the advice. As we have seen, one of the rules of
effective advising is that the writer has good reason to offer
such advice. What might count as good reason? What do the
innovators know about how teachers conceive of partnerships
in the classroom? What do they know of how teachers cope with
disagreement? The act, if it is to have the force of advice,
supposes that the guide writer knows something about how
teachers construe their influence in the classroom. For the
advice to be advice at all, we have to suppose that the innovator knows something about the problems teachers have in
exercising influence in the classroom.

Unless the innovator has some idea about what the teacher is
already doing, and about what the teacher intends to do, how
can the writer give advice? This seems a trivial point, but it
isn't. The rule requires, I would argue, that the innovator
find out about the intentions of the teacher. The innovator
isn't just talking off the top of his or her head; he or she
knows something about the context in which his or her advice
is to be taken. Returning to the example taken from the
curriculum project, it became clear to me from talking to
teachers that the advice offered did not speak to the problems
the teachers actually faced in trying to operate the project.
From what I could determine, the statements in the teacher's
guide did not add up to a successful act of advice giving.

As we will see in the accounts in this book, the problems
teachers have in using innovative ideas can be traced to a
failure of the innovators to take seriously one of the rules of
advice giving: they did not find out about the life of the
people they presumed to advise. Instead of advising, they
exhorted, they advocated, they enjoined: each of these quite
different acts from advising and each supposing a different
set of communicative rules. They failed to do the research
that advice giving requires. An appropriate agenda for
research has been suggested by Fenstermacher using an
intentionalist account of action. He suggests that the researcher of teaching find out more about what teachers intend
by their classroom actions: what are teachers trying to
accomplish by their acts? How do the belief of teachers come
to be formed? What is the influence of the institution on the

formation of beliefs? These are useful preliminaries for the
guide writer to undertake or study. As Fenstermacher notes:
'The researcher of teaching cannot do research without in some
way participating in the education of teachers, nor can teacher
education transform beliefs without participating in the study
of teaching.'[45] Communicating with teachers calls upon the writer
to be both researcher and educator; and in both roles, he or
she will have to pay attention to the intentions of teachers. Why
is this so?

To pursue social science knowledge, we may well invoke causes
outside the teacher to account for practice, but if we wish to
advise the teacher we will have to study practice from the
teacher's point of view. If we didn't, we would have no reason
to think that our advice was potentially helpful, because we
would not know what the teacher was trying to accomplish. If
we ignore the intentions of the teacher, we have no gounds
for offering advice; what we offer is only gratuitous and ran-
dom. We could, of course, simply tell the teacher that some
action A is good for him or her because research says it is so.
If we did this we would not be guiding, but doing something
else like mandating; a different sort of act entirely. And in
fact many documents which we might think of as guides have
the force of mandates. A guide to some new practices in teaching can be written effectively only if the author knows something about the existing practices of those he or she wishes to
influence. In the case of the project I studied, the writer of
the guide to the curriculum project simply did not pay attention to the pedagogical implications of what they were proposing. Had they done so, they might have hesitated to advise
what they did. The guide writers apparently were not interested in pedagogy, ironically; instead they took it as their
task to instruct teachers in the nature of a hierarchy of cognitive operations, and show how the activities selected in the
texts functioned in terms of the psychological theory. Advice,
useful to teachers, was mostly absent; exhortation to adopt
the new practices was more common.

It is not surprising that the teachers did not use the guides;
when they went for guidance, they most often got a lecture.
This put teachers in an untenable position. The students who
took the course wrote externally set examinations, and the
teachers were expected to prepare them to do well. But how
to do well when it was difficult to know how to operate the
project in the absence of guidance? The teachers, I found,
rewrote the lectures of the handbook into a guide they could
use. Their 'guide' was a translation of the theoretical language of the handbook into a familiar language of practice. In
this way they 'found' information which could be used to
operate the project in the minimal way they did. They extracted and reshaped elements of the project plan to suit how
they normally operated. Normal operation allowed them to
get on with the job of preparing students for external examina-

tions. They created a guide by giving themselves advice which made sense in their own context.

An example of how teachers constructed their own guide out of the handbooks can be seen in their fabrication of a syllabus to use in preparing students for examinations. It was here that teachers sought advice from the handbook. What was the syllabus of content they were responsible for? The answer from the project team was that the project did not have a syllabus in the teachers' sense of that word; only a limited number of cognitive skills which were to be nurtured by the teacher; and to be locked in the heads of their students, and not to be found in the notebooks to be reviewed and learned for the examination.

Where the handbook writers went wrong was in not appreciating why a syllabus was important to teachers; how such an institution functioned in the classroom. Teachers pointed to the syllabus as an authoritative text to be used in disputes with pupils and outsiders on whether this or that should be taught. The syllabus, they said, provided a measure of ground covered and formed a contract between teacher, pupils and examining board. SCISP had no syllabus, but there was a list of concepts and generalisations given to illustrate one of the three unifying themes, 'building blocks'. The teachers construed this list as a 'syllabus' and proceeded to translate it into the basis of a 'syllabus' system.

To tell teachers that there was no syllabus was like an architect saying to a builder that there are no plans for the building, but perhaps a lecture on prestressed concrete might be of interest. Without an understanding of the pedagogical theories of teachers, in which the syllabus was an important term, the handbook writers, in their efforts to guide, failed to provide the kind of advice that would have been helpful in the circumstances.

The Innovator as Translator. Innovators writing about their ideas have an obligation to their readers beyond familiarising themselves with the intentions of the people they hope to guide; beyond conceiving of the practice of teachers, they have to be able to give advice in a way that others can understand it. In everyday language, there may not be a problem about advising: advice about how to keep healthy, about how to tend one's garden may not be difficult to communicate; however, that may not be the case in communicating innovative ideas about teaching. Much of such advice is given on the basis of prescriptions drawn from research and communicated in a language of the research field itself or idealisations of practice. Examples of the problems teachers have in translating such 'foreign' languages can be seen in all of the reports in this book. In my own case, teachers had to translate a language derived from a particular brand of cognitive psychology. Thus, students were meant to engage in 'problem

solving' and 'pattern finding'; these words had quite precise
technical meanings in the theoretical language of the planners.
The teachers did not understand these words that way. When
asked, they could give no more than their everyday meanings.
Pattern finding was seeing patterns in things, like patterns
in a painting; problem solving was solving problems, like
starting a stalled car. What the project planners meant by
these terms was not communicated; the teachers were not able
to translate them into classroom relevant terms. Thus the
guide writer is faced with a problem of communicating his
meanings to others, and it is to this central problem that we
now turn.

The problem of being understood was brought home to me in
one of the interviews with a teacher involved in the curriculum
project which I studied. When asked about the difficulties
involved in operating the project, the teacher said that it had
been difficult to <u>revise</u>. For the next ten minutes I quizzed
him on the assumption that he meant that he had had trouble
deciding what to change in the course when he again taught it.
This isn't at all what the teacher meant. He meant that it was
difficult to review with the students the material they should
know for the examination; a major criticism of the project, as
it turned out. What the teacher had done, in his brief complaint, is mean more than he said. He expected me to appreciate the <u>implications</u> (the reverberations within his system of
beliefs about teaching) of saying that revision was difficult.
For the sake of brevity, and of not stating the obvious, he
had telescoped his complaint, a fundamental one, into a brief
sentence loaded with freight. I had to scramble to find out
what the teacher meant by what he had said. I had to find out
what the term 'revise' meant in his theoretical system. What
he meant was 'Look, I don't want to complain, but in this
project it is difficult to accomplish one of the most important
tasks I am asked to do.' If I hadn't been able to see that
we were at cross purposes we would have never talked about
a central issue for that teacher. His idea of course revision
and mine were different. These terms have different means
in our respective conceptual systems. Both were what Churchland calls 'systemically' important. [46] Innovators run similar
risks in talking to teachers as the accounts in this book
witness.

Curriculum Change as a Problem of Communication. What is
the significance for innovators of the cases in this book? The
significance is that innovators must not only appreciate the
<u>intentions</u> of the teachers, they need to understand the <u>lang-
uage</u> used to talk about those intentions. In all of the accounts
that follow teachers were concerned to use their influence to
prepare students for examinations, for the next grade, for
the work next month. The way they talked about their work

reflected these concerns and the theories teachers espoused were related to them. The innovators, whose ideas these teachers were attempting to translate, recommended ideas which these teachers had difficulty understanding and, to the extent that they did understand, practicing. Guides to the innovations studied here were written in one language; teachers spoke another: that is one clear message which emerged from the case studies.

Clearly, the innovator must be concerned about how the terms of one language are going to be translated in another. Is it up to the teachers to translate the language of innovation into their language? I think not; surely the onus is on the guide writer? It is he or she who wants to communicate new ideas about practice.

Take the case of discovery or inquiry teaching discussed in this book. At times this involves classroom discussion which is constituted by a number of rules. The accounts here suggest that this particular kind of classroom activity was not familiar to teachers. They did not know the rules governing discussion, but they did know that allowing pupils to talk freely in class undermined their influence. Teachers did not understand that 'not dominating the class' could count as a form of influence. It was here that they could have been offered some advice about how it might be that influence and discussion were compatible, and that discussion did not involve the abdication of influence. However, the innovators did not talk about discussion in such a way that teachers could understand what was meant in their own terms. To make this translation the innovators would have to know something about the nature of the theories about teaching that teachers have, and how classroom influence figures in those theories.

Churchland, in his discussion of theoretical and non-theoretical concepts, argues that the distinction between theory and common sense is a false one: 'If viewed warily, the network of principles and assumptions constitutive of our common-sense conceptual framework can be seen to be as speculative and as artificial as any overtly theoretical system. . . In short it appears that all knowledge. . . is theoretical; that there is no such thing as non-theoretical understanding.'[47]

The import of this view for communication is that we do not distinguish between the theories teachers have about their practice and theories about practice based on the disciplines. Both share the same properties as theories and, for both, attempts to convert the terms of one into the terms of the other takes us into problems of translation as much as in any other case of translating from one conceptual domain into another; within science, for example. The accounts in this book give us reason to think that the language in which most innovative ideas are couched, at least those institutionalised as funded projects, is in need of translation into practitioner language if the innovative ideas are to be understood.

Churchland offers advice on how this might be accomplished. He says: 'An individual's understanding of a term can be decisively specified only against the background provided by the entire interlocking network of (systemically more important) sentences he accepts. Therefore if we wish to speak of (sameness of understanding) across idiolects, we must again think in terms of corresponding modes in sufficiently parallel networks. In this way we are led to a holistic conception of both meaning and understanding.'[48]

This means that the person who wishes to communicate ideas to teachers is going to have to understand the network of beliefs that teachers hold and what particular terms mean within such networks. This is commonly known as the 'Principle of Charity', and it ought to be a fundamental concern of innovators.[49] The burden on the innovator is clear if he or she wishes to guide practitioners - the guides have to be written in a language teachers understand: the translator has to understand the important uses of terms in other people's languages and to do that their whole system of beliefs must be understood. The outsider has to translate the new ideas into the insiders' language.

If the innovator wishes to communicate his or her ideas to teachers, he or she has to find some way of translating current practices into new formulations in a way that preserves the meaning of the words used by teachers to describe the old practices; the guide writer must be a speaker of the practical languages of teachers and be able to express the new intentions in such a way that new meanings are possible, but with a maximum of shared meaning retained. Brown and McIntyre, in their account of teacher translation of innovative ideas, suggest that teachers come to understand the meaning of innovative proposals through coping with their practical implications. Over time teachers might also consider more general ideas associated with the new practice. The interesting point here is that the new understanding emerges from an initial engagement in the old terms. In this translation process some statements are more important than others; the writer has to know what the important sentences are in the teachers' theories, and work to preserve the meaning of these in the translation. To know what those sentences are he has to know the rationale of the overall system of beliefs. [50] We can't know this unless we take the views of teachers seriously. The accounts that follow represent efforts to find out more about the belief systems of teachers; they represent new directions in curriculum research, based on a conception of change which is generous to, and respectful of, the common-sense theories of teachers, and sensitive to the problems that inhere in the communication of new ideas in teaching.

NOTES

1. National Science Foundation, 'Case Studies in Science
   Education' (Centre for Instructional Research and Curriculum Evaluation, University of Illinois at Urbana-Champaign,
   1978), p. 16:6.
2. See R. Harré and P.F. Secord, 'The Explanation of Social
   Behaviour' (Blackwell, Oxford, 1972), p. 1.
3. The limitations of the theoretic have been laid out by
   Schwab. See J.J. Schwab, The Practical: A Language for
   Curriculum, 'School Review', vol. 78 (1969), pp. 1-24.
4. For an extended discussion of this point, see G. Fenstermacher, A Philosophical Consideration of Recent Research
   on Teacher Effectiveness, 'Review of Research in Education', vol. 6 (1978), pp. 157-85.
5. I am indebted to George Hills here for directing me to:
   J. Searle, 'Speech Acts' (University Press, Cambridge,
   1969).
6. Ibid., p. 52.
7. See for example, M. Hanson, Beyond the Bureaucratic
   Model: A Study of Power and Autonomy in Educational
   Decision Making, 'Interchange', vol. 7 (1976), pp. 27-38.
   See also note 13.
8. The term 'reorient' is taken from E.R. House, 'The Politics
   of Curriculum Innovation' (McCutchan, Berkeley, 1974).
9. M. Herron, On Teacher Perception and Curriculum Innovation in J. Weiss (ed.), 'Curriculum Theory Network Monograph Supplement' (Ontario Institute for Studies in
   Education, Toronto, 1971), p. 48.
10. M. Shipman, 'Inside a Curriculum Project' (Methuen,
    London, 1974), p. 47.
11. Ibid., p. 172.
12. R.O. Carlson, 'Adoption of Educational Innovations' (Centre
    for the Advanced Study of Educational Administration,
    University of Oregon, 1965).
13. See, for example, A. Wise, Why Educational Policies often
    Fail: The Hyper-rationalization Hypothesis, 'Journal of
    Curriculum Studies', vol. 9 (1977), pp. 43-58.
14. Ibid., p. 47.
15. R. Dreeben, 'The Nature of Teaching: Schools and the
    Work of Teachers' (Scott, Foresman, Glenview, 1970),
    p. 51.
16. Ibid., p. 102.
17. S.D. Sieber, Images of the Practitioner and Strategies of
    Educational Change, 'Sociology of Education', vol. 45
    (1972), pp. 358-62.
18. Here, I have drawn upon an extensive treatment of this
    by F.M. Connelly, The Functions of Curriculum Develop-
    ment, 'Interchange', vol. 3 (1972), pp. 161-77.
19. C. Perrow, 'Organizational Analysis: A Sociological View'
    (Wadsworth, Belmont, 1970), p. 80.

20. See S. Sarason, 'The Culture of the School and the Problem of Change' (Allyn and Bacon, Boston 1971); W. Doyle
and G.A. Ponder, The Practicality Ethic in Teacher
Decision-Making, 'Interchange', vol. 8 (1977), pp. 1-12;
and R. Barr and R. Dreeben, Instruction in Classrooms in
L. Shulman (ed.), 'Review of Research in Education',
vol. 5 (1977), p. 163-98.
21. D. Lortie, 'School Teacher' (University of Chicago Press,
Chicago, 1975), p. 212.
22. I have drawn here upon the section Meaning and Understanding in G. Churchland, 'Scientific Realism and the
Plasticity of Mind' (University Press, Cambridge, 1979).
23. See R.S. Peters and J.P. White, The Philosopher's
Contribution to Educational Research in W. Taylor (ed.),
'Research Perspectives in Education' (Routledge & Kegan
Paul, London, 1973), p. 104.
24. P.H. Taylor, W.A. Reid, B.J. Holley and G. Exon,
'Purpose, Power and Constraint in the Primary School
Curriculum' (Macmillan, London, 1974).
25. W.A. Reid, 'Thinking About the Curriculum' (Routledge
& Kegan Paul, London, 1978).
26. For a discussion of the concept of theory, see Churchland,
'Scientific Realism and the Plasticity of Mind', pp. 46-54.
27. B. Wilson, The Teacher's Role: A Sociological Analysis,
'British Journal of Sociology', vol. 13 (1962), p. 22.
28. For a discussion of Wilson's work, see F. Musgrove,
Research on the Sociology of the School and Teaching in
W. Taylor (ed.), 'Research Perspectives in Education'
(Routledge & Kegan Paul, 1973), p. 159; and C. Lacey,
'The Socialization of Teachers' (Methuen, London, 1977),
p. 410.
29. S. Delamont, 'Interaction in the Classroom' (Methuen,
London, 1976), p. 60.
30. H. Berlak and A. Berlak, Toward a Political and Social
Psychological Theory of Schooling: An Analysis of English
Informal Primary Schools, 'Interchange', vol. 6 (1975),
pp. 11-22.
31. K. Egan, Some Presuppositions That Determine Curriculum
Decisions, 'Journal of Curriculum Studies', vol. 10 (1978),
pp. 123-33.
32. D. Lortie, Observations on Teaching as Work in R.M.
Travers (ed.), 'Second Handbook of Research on Teaching'
(Rand McNally, Chicago, 1973), p. 478.
33. House, 'The Politics of Curriculum Innovation', p. 168.
34. G. Kelly, 'The Psychology of Personal Constructs', 2. vols.
(Norton, New York, 1955), p. 91.
35. M. Scriven, Prose and Cons About Goal-Free Evaluation,
'The Journal of Educational Evaluation', vol. 3 (1972),
pp. 1-4.
36. W.A. Reid, Making the Problem Fit the Method: A Review
of the 'Banbury Enquiry', 'Journal of Curriculum Studies',
vol. 11 (1979), p. 168.

37. L. Hudson, 'The Psychology of Human Experience' (Anchor Books, New York, 1975), p. 19.
38. C. Parsons, The New Evaluation: A Cautionary Note, 'Journal of Curriculum Studies', vol. 8 (1976), p. 134.
39. Hudson, 'The Psychology of Human Experience', p. 20.
40. F.M. DuMas, Science and the Single Case, 'Psychological Reports', vol. 1 (1955), p. 72.
41. D. Walker, A Barn-storming Tour of Writing on Curriculum in A.W. Foshay (ed.), 'Considered Action for Curriculum Improvement' (ASCD, Alexandria, Va.), p. 73.
42. Ibid., p. 73.
43. J.R. Searle, 'Speech Acts' (University Press, Cambridge, 1969).
44. W.A. Hall, 'Patterns Teachers' Handbook' (Longman, London, 1973), pp. 59-60.
45. Fenstermacher, 'A Philosophical Consideration of Recent Research on Teacher Effectiveness', p. 182.
46. Churchland, 'Scientific Realism and the Plasticity of Mind', pp. 54-63.
47. Ibid., p. 2. See also, C. Argyris and D. Schon, 'Theory in Practice: Increasing Professional Effectiveness' (Jossey-Bass, San Francisco, 1980), pp. 1-12.
48. Churchland, 'Scientific Realism and the Plasticity of Mind', p. 61.
49. Ibid., pp. 66-9.
50. Ibid., p. 68.

BIBLIOGRAPHY

Argyris, C. and Schon, D. 'Theory-in-Practice: Increasing Professional Effectiveness' (Jossey-Bass, San Francisco, 1980).
Barr, R. and Dreeben, R. Instruction in Classrrooms in L. Shulman (ed.), 'Review of Research in Education', vol. 5 (1977).
Berlak, H. and Berlak, A. Toward a Political and Social Psychological Theory of Schooling: An Analysis of English Informal Primary Schools, 'Interchange', vol. 6 (1975), pp. 11-22.
Carlson, R.O. 'Adoption of Educational Innovations' (Centre for the Advanced Study of Educational Administration, University of Oregon, 1965).
Churchland, G. 'Scientific Realism and the Plasticity of Mind' (University Press, Cambridge, 1979).
Connelly, F.M. The Functions of Curriculum Development, 'Interchange', vol. 3 (1972), pp. 161-77.
Delamont, S. 'Interaction in the Classroom' (Methuen, London, 1976).
Doyle, W. and Ponder, G.A. The Practicality Ethic in Teacher Decision-Making, 'Interchange', vol. 8 (1977), pp. 1-12.

Dreeben, R. 'The Nature of Teaching: Schools and the Work of Teachers' (Scott, Foresman, Glenview, 1970).

DuMas, F.M. Science and the Single Case, 'Psychological Reports', vol. 1 (1955), pp. 65-75.

Egan, K. Some Presuppositions That Determine Curriculum Decisions, 'Journal of Curriculum Studies', vol. 10 (1978), pp. 123-33.

Fenstermacher, G. A Philosophical Consideration of Recent Research on Teacher Effectiveness, 'Review of Research in Education', vol. 6 (1978), pp. 157-85.

Hall, W.A. 'Patterns Teachers' Handbook' (Longman, London, 1973).

Hanson, M. Beyond the Bureaucratic Model: A Study of Power and Autonomy in Educational Decision Making, 'Interchange', vol. 7 (1976), pp. 27-38.

Harré, R. and Secord, P.F. 'The Explanation of Social Behaviour' (Blackwell, Oxford, 1972).

Heron, M. On Teacher Perception and Curriculum Innovation in J. Weiss (ed.), 'Curriculum Theory Network Monograph Supplement' (Ontario Institute for Studies in Education, Toronto, 1971).

House, E.R. 'The Politics of Curriculum Innovation' (McCutchan, Berkeley, 1974).

Hudson, L. 'The Psychology of Human Experience' (Anchor Books, New York, 1975).

Kelly, G. 'The Psychology of Personal Constructs', 2 vols. (Norton, New York, 1955).

Lacey, C. 'The Socialization of Teachers' (Methuen, London, 1977).

Lortie, D. Observations on Teaching as Work in R.M. Travers (ed.), 'Second Handbook of Research on Teaching' (Rand McNally, Chicago, 1973), p. 478.

——. 'School Teacher' (University of Chicago Press, Chicago, 1975).

MacIntyre, A. The Idea of a Social Science in B. Wilson (ed.), 'Rationality' (Blackwell, Oxford, 1979).

Musgrove, F. Research on the Sociology of the School and Teaching in W. Taylor (ed.), 'Research Perspectives in Education' (Routledge & Kegan Paul, 1973).

National Science Foundation, 'Case Studies in Science Educarion' (Centre for Instructional Research and Curriculum Evaluation, University of Illinois at Urbana-Champaign, 1978).

Parsons, C. The New Evaluation: A Cautionary Note, 'Journal of Curriculum Studies', vol. 8 (1976), p. 125-38.

Perrow, C. 'Organizational Analysis: A Sociological View' (Wadsworth, Belmont, 1970).

Peters, R.S. and White, J.P. The Philosopher's Contribution to Educational Research in W. Taylor (ed.), 'Research Perspectives in Education' (Routeledge & Kegan Paul, London, 1973).

Reid, W.A. 'Thinking About the Curriculum' (Routledge & Kegan Paul, London, 1978).

—. Making the Problem Fit the Method: A Review of the 'Banbury Enquiry', 'Journal of Curriculum Studies', vol. 11 (1979), p. 167-73.

Sarason, S. 'The Culture of the School and the Problem of Change' (Allyn and Bacon, Boston, 1971).

Schwab, J.J. The Practical: A Language for Curriculum, 'School Review', vol. 78 (1969), pp. 1-24.

Scriven, M. Prose and Cons About Goal-Free Evaluation, 'The Journal of Educational Evaluation', vol. 3 (1972), pp. 1-4.

Searle, J. 'Speech Acts' (University Press, Cambridge, 1969).

Shipman, M. 'Inside a Curriculum Project' (Methuen, London, 1974).

Sieber, S.D. Images of the Practitioner and Strategies of Educational Change, 'Sociology of Education', vol. 45 (1972), pp. 358-62.

Taylor, P.H., Reid, W.A., Holley, B.J. and Exon, G. 'Purpose, Power and Constraint in the Primary School Curriculum' (Macmillan, London, 1974).

Walker, D. A Barn-storming Tour of Writing on Curriculum in A.W. Foshay (ed.), 'Considered Action for Curriculum Improvement' (ASCD, Alexandria, Va.).

Wilson, B. The Teacher's Role: A Sociological Analysis, 'British Journal of Sociology', vol. 13 (1962), p. 22.

Winch, Peter, 'The Idea of a Social Science and its Relation to Philosophy' (Routledge & Kegan Paul, London, 1958).

Wise, A. Why Educational Policies often Fail: The Hyper-rationalization Hypothesis, 'Journal of Curriculum Studies', vol. 9 (1977), pp. 43-58.

2 THE SCHOOL, THE COMMUNITY AND THE OUTSIDER: CASE STUDY OF A CASE STUDY

Rob Walker

INTRODUCTION

My purpose in writing this paper is to provide a methodological commentary on one of the two case studies I wrote
for the National Science Foundation 'Case Studies in Science
Education' Project during 1976-7. Within the constraints of the
study itself there were not many opportunities to discuss
methods in detail, though one of the volumes of the final
report does consider methodological issues for the project as
a whole, and a subsequent conference report has pursued
these issues further. [1]
I believe there is a need for case studies of case studies
because most case studies are completed by people doing
them for the first time (it is after all a relatively new field
of educational research). While much can be learnt from other
disciplines (from anthropology, history, psychiatry, literature
and journalism), we lack a variety of good accounts of the
particular circumstances encountered in schools, classrooms
and other educational settings. Ideally we need accounts of
problems reported as they emerge, for these are most useful
to the reader hoping to learn directly from the experience of
others. This account is, regrettably, an account given in
retrospect, with all the distortions, understandings and post
rationalisations to which such accounts are prone.
Although it looks at one study in detail, this chapter will
be self-contained and will include quotations from the original
study where these are necessary. It is important, however,
to remember that this case study was not intended to stand
as an independent 'ethnography', but was functionally related
to the other case studies commissioned by NSF and to the
overall programme. Nevertheless, the presentation of this
account of one element of the research programme in isolation
in what was clearly an ambitious and novel research design,
and by the strong differences of opinion that the study
prompted in its reviewers. [2]
The section which follows sets the scene, giving a little
more detail on the 'Case Studies in Science Education'
project, though I should stress that the view it gives is
mine as one of the site case study workers and not the
'official' view. This will be followed by a section which looks
at the problems of arrival and first contact with the people
and places who are to figure in the study, leading into the

problems of how and where to begin. I give some examples of
organising ideas that emerged from observation and interviews
and how these were gradually worked into the case study.
Finally, I consider some of the uncertainties I have about this
particular study and review some of the problems that emerged
in the process of doing it.

The knowledgeable reader will be aware that I have avoided
giving references to the standard texts on participant observation and fieldwork. It was difficult to decide whether or not to
do so, but in the end I chose to give a personal account,
assuming that the reader is likely to want to find out what this
approach might have to offer in the study of science curriculum,
rather than wanting to be led into the literature on techniques
and methods in the social sciences. Those who wish to follow
this course will no doubt find it easy enough to do so.

CONTEXT: THE CASE STUDIES IN SCIENCE EDUCATION
PROJECT

This chapter describes the conduct of a school case study made
in the course of a multi-site programme of research into pre-
college science education in the United States. Overall, the
intention of the programme was to provide the National Science
Foundation (who sponsored the studies) with a status report,
informing them of current issues in the areas of science, maths
and social studies teaching. The case studies and their analysis
constituted one element of a research strategy which also involved independent questionnaire surveys and a literature
search. (For further details on the total programme of research
the reader is advised to refer to Stake and Easley (1978), Weiss
(1978) and Hegelson (1977).

The case study element of this large and ambitious set of
studies involved eleven people producing case studies at eleven
sites in scattered and very different locations across the conti-
nent. On site for periods which varied from three to twelve
weeks, each case study worker was required to produce a
close-to-final draft of some 50 pages within a week or so of
leaving the site. This timing was critical in order to meet a
series of deadlines which linked the case studies to a set of
sample surveys, which in turn were derived from a commitment to complete the whole project within 18 months of starting
it.

The case studies were carried out in two batches. One set was
completed in autumn 1976; a second set in the early months
of 1977. The full set of studies was as follows:

Set One (September–December 1976)

Site	Author	Fieldwork Period
River Acres – a suburb of Houston	Terry Denny	6 weeks
Fall River – a small city in Colorado	Mary Lee Smith	12 weeks
BRT – a consolidated school district in rural Illinois	Alan Peshkin	6 weeks
Urbanville – metropolitan community in the Pacific NW	Wayne Welch	4 weeks
Pine City – a rural community in Alabama	Rob Walker	6 weeks

Set Two (January–April 1977)

Site	Author	Fieldwork Period
Alte – a suburb of a large mid-western city	Louis Smith	12 weeks
Western City – a small city in mid-California	Rudolfo Serrano	6 weeks
Columbus – Columbus, Ohio	James Sanders and Daniel Stufflebeam	4 weeks
Archipolis – an eastern seaboard city	Jaquetta Hill	4½ weeks
Vortes – a small city in Pennsylvania	Gordon Hoke	4 weeks
Greater Boston – urban section in Metropolitan Boston	Rob Walker	12 weeks

At each site, case study workers were expected to observe and to interview in one High School and its contributory Junior High and Elementary Schools. They were required to collect such other information as they needed to depict the school science curriculum in ways which emphasised those issues and conditions which people felt were most significant. Eventually, we were told, and told people at our sites, the information we collected would be used by the NSF in assessing national needs when they planned future efforts to support curriculum and teacher development.

Behind the project lay a story. In outline the story was that the NSF, having invested quite heavily in school curriculum development and teacher institutes since the 1950s, had run into Congressional criticism. Although this criticism drew on general concerns about the 'New Maths' and other innovations, the argument revolved around the issue of whether the prime responsibility for the curriculum should

rest with elected school boards and state agencies, or with
federally-funded, university-based curriculum development
groups. Traditionally, education has been valued as a local
activity in the United States, allowing each school board and
each state to devise a system and a curriculum best suited to
its own local circumstances. The effect of curriculum development projects like those funded by the NSF was, some argued,
to centralise decisions and to reduce local autonomy and local
choice. In particular, it was to give prestigious, private
universities a greater say in the school curriculum than had
previously been the case.

Pressure on the NSF had reached a point where Congress
was demanding a close scrutiny of its budget, and requiring
the Foundation to present new grants item by item for
approval. In the face of this threat to its autonomy the NSF
decided to fund a set of 'needs assessment' studies, in order
to get some information on what were seen as key issues at
school and community levels. It should be noted that this
marked a considerable shift in perspective for the NSF. Two
decades previously, when the first maths and science
curriculum development projects were funded, the assumption
was that if something was wrong with the school curriculum,
then the obvious place to turn was to high status university
academics, and to ask them to redesign the school curriculum.
The technical problem was then largely one of how to dis-
seminate this expertly produced package to the teachers and
the schools (see for instance Atkin's (1980) account). It is
also important to note that the NSF is primarily a body which
funds science research - science education is only one of its
many concerns.

The funding of these 'needs assessment' studies marked a
shift in thinking, for it indicated that the current state of
the school curriculum, and of the schools themselves, needed
at least to be taken into account in considering curriculum
renewal. Previously, the assumption had always been that the
academic community knew best what the schools should be
doing. Now, it seemed, the intention was that, following these
'baseline' studies, a further set of studies might be funded to
design an ideal state of affairs, and a third set to attempt to
close the gap between aspiration and practice. Overall
perhaps the model might be questioned, but the attempt to
inform policy with accounts of the actual state of affairs in
schools seemed long overdue.

Before going on to look at the case study in detail it is
important to note that, by the time the project started work,
the background scenery had already been changed. Those
Congressmen who had been pressing hardest on the NSF
suffered setbacks in elections. The NSF, once the immediate
pressure was removed, seemed to lose some of its interest in
the projects it had requested and then funded. Soon after,
the project officer left and another took over. As a project we

found ourselves with the feeling that we were all dressed up but with nowhere to go. Perhaps it is a feature of Western democracies that bureaucracies respond to pressures from organised groups and especially political groups rather than from the primary press of perceived 'real' issues. And we too found ourselves in an analagous position: the pressure was off and with it some of our sense of direction. This feeling was bound to be exacerbated in a study which involved the research team largely working in isolation and at a distance from its directors. The people carrying out the case studies had little contact with each other, except for a 4-5 day 'orientation' programme prior to immersion in the field. However, each did have contact with the central project team (the 'Kremlin' as it became known to some of the case study workers) via a 'site co-ordinator'. The site co-ordinator visited each site at least twice, kept in regular contact with the case study worker during the course of the study, and was responsible for organising a site visit towards the end of the fieldwork period. This site visit was primarily designed to provide some check on the case study, and people with expertise in relevant areas spent some three days at the site independently collecting information which might provide a basis for assessing the validity of the case study written by the resident fieldworker.

In practice the site co-ordinator was usually someone who filled multiple roles in the project. In the study described here, Gordon Hoke, the site co-ordinator, also later wrote one of the other case studies, was responsible for negotiating access to all the schools in the study, and wrote some of the overview sections in the final report. It should be mentioned too that the final report includes the full set of eleven case studies, as well as a number of booklets that consider substantive and methodological issues across the case studies.

ORIENTATION AND BRIEFING

During a one week 'orientation week' for the first group of fieldworkers held late in August 1976, the outline brief that emerged was clear. The aim was to report curriculum issues rather than to produce 'school case studies', length limits were severe on the grounds that the longer the studies were, the less likely they were to be read by busy administrators, and delivery dates were strict - first drafts of the case studies had to be available to the project team within two weeks of emerging from the field.

It may seem trivial to mention some of these things, but they were important. Those who make references across from studies like this to 'ethnography' should particularly note the difference. These studies were carried out in condensed periods of fieldwork time, were written fast and were intended to be short and issue focused. We adjusted to the demands in different ways - for instance, a 50 page report might be conceived as a summary of a much longer study which could have been written. But I know the 50 page length limit was a major consideration for me from the start. I planned out the study thinking in terms of how many pages could be given to each significant theme, and how these themes related to the task. Interviews and observations were often planned to fit this structure, and some lines of enquiry were dropped solely because it was difficult to justify the space they might occupy in the final report.

It is important to note that the project developed a remarkable record in completing its studies. Anyone who has worked on this kind of study will know that to engage eleven people to complete eleven studies in a short period of time, and with most of the people working at a distance from the project team, presents a major problem of management. While some of these studies arrived late, some missed the length demands by a factor of five and others met major problems in relation to fieldwork relationships, all eventually reached a state of completion in time for the project to meet its timetable. This necessarily required a considerable amount of time, energy and patience on the part of project staff, and seems to me a major, and perhaps neglected, accomplishment. Case study research is notorious for its record of delayed deliveries, the non-appearance of reports and failure to complete studies that have been started. For the most part, this record is understandable given the nature of the problems. Case studies frequently run into problems of clearing data with subjects, of the conduct of the fieldworker, and of the sheer difficulty of writing coherent reports on the basis of large amounts of collected material. Compared to other available research methods it is particularly difficult to predict where a case study will lead. The very openness of the approach means that, once in the field, there is a sense in which the subject imposes its own authority on the study, and it becomes difficult to impose pre-ordinate intentions without creating major problems.

A structure for the study which was strong on procedures and weak on content provided an interesting challenge to the fieldworker. The project team did not tell us what issues to report (though they gave us a number of ideas to follow). The line they took was that the fieldworker was in the best position to decide what should be said about each site, and how the necessary information might best be collected and reported.

So much for the official story. What was it actually like to do the case study?

Pine City: Arrival

Twenty-four hours after leaving London we saw our first
glimpse of the Deep South, flying in over Atlanta on a sunny
November morning just a few days after the United States
had elected its first Southern President in living memory. Even
from several thousand feet in the air the 'New South' was plain
to see: the glass towers of downtown developments and extensive suburbs. Beyond stretched the hills and forests of the
rural, and older (I thought) South.
   It was the rural South we were to see. A four-hour drive
along the inter-state highway took us to Pine City, a town with
one Public High School, two motels, one country club, one
medical practice and several churches. The old part of the
town was built alongside the railway, which now seemed little
used, and a newer part was being developed along an intersection on the highway.
   We were met in Pine City by Gordon Hoke, the site co-
ordinator, who had already negotiated access with the Superintendent and had booked us into a motel. One of the School
system staff had found us a mobile home on a trailer park
where we were to live for the next six or seven weeks, and the
secretaries from the School Board Office had been along and
cleaned it up and lent us some cutlery, plates and kitchen
utensils. Already we entered into a set of obligations, relationships and debts, not really knowing their significance in the
local context.
   What were our first thoughts?
   As strangers, and especially as foreigners, it is inevitable
that you adopt something of the tourist mentality. Every piece
of information gained, however trivial, comes to take on great
significance. Comparisons are difficult to resist; time stretches
and shrinks; you become highly dependent on a few understandings; a few relationships; a few truths.
   I am reminded of a story Alastair Cooke tells about the distinguished visitor to Rome, who in audience with the Pope asks
how much time is required to understand the Vatican. 'Two
days is good', was the reply, 'Two weeks is better; but two
years is not long enough.' The longer you stay the more
difficult it is to be sure of what you understand.
   The first stage of any case study is almost one of some confusion. Information comes at you from all directions, contact
has to be made with a number of people at different levels and
different locations, often before you really feel ready to take
in all that they tell you. The study has to be explained, you
have to establish a pattern of work, and in a case like this, a
pattern of social and family life. It is a period when, typically,
you are least clear about what you are going to do, about
what the problems and difficulties are likely to be, and about
what it will be important for you to say or include in the study
or report you will eventually write, but a period too when

people are most likely to want to ask you just such questions
and to expect convincing answers.

In Pine City I found myself explaining at some length why the
NSF had established the study, and how this was an opportunity
for people to use me to say to the NSF what they thought it was
important for them to know about conditions and issues in the
pre-college science curriculum. I said too that I would be showing people sections of the study as I wrote it, and that by the
time I left most of them would have the opportunity to see what
I intended to put into the case study. I said I would be sending
them copies of the draft and that I wanted to encourage them
to comment and to criticise the study so that it might be improved before it reached a final draft.

Most people listened patiently. The second day I spoke to the
High School Principal and then to the school faculty as they
assembled for morning coffee. I said that while the Principal
might be happy to give me free access to the school I would
quite understand if they would prefer me not to observe
particular classes. They seemed to respond well to the suggestion I made that they might invite me into their classes rather
than have me turn up unannounced at the classroom door.

They did invite me too, but not quite in the way I expected.
My instructions from the Kremlin were to remain unobtrusive;
to observe rather than to participate, but when the geography
teacher told me she was 'doing Europe', and would I mind
coming into class and answering students' questions, I did
not feel there was any way I could reasonably refuse. It seemed
quite a good idea in fact to appear to be useful and helpful.
Soon afterwards the business education teacher told me he
was doing some work on 'free enterprise' and asked me if I
would come into his class to talk about 'that socialist system
you have in England'. Word got round. I found that classes
I went into to talk often had three times the normal numbers
of students present, and often the teachers too were sitting
in class. I thought I was used to being checked out by a
school, but this was a whole new dimension to the process.

In a small country town, where very few people had
travelled overseas, there was something intriguing about
the idea of a foreigner, and there were certain questions
the students would come back to over and over again, often
apparently simple ideas like: the fact that you could have
money that was not dollars; that though I was English I had
never seen the Queen; that though England has an established church we seemed so non-religious; that in England
drug addicts could register with doctors and receive drugs
officially. . . Some students would hold me in conversation
in and out of school just to test out their sense of different-
ness between me and them.

Perhaps it was a minor contribution to Anglo-American
relations, but it made me worried when, three weeks into the
case study period, the interest showed no sign of waning. In

some ways it was escalating; one group of students took me
with them on a day trip to the State capitol, where I was
introduced to the State Governor and collected a personally
signed photograph as a memento of the visit. Word of this
got back to the project team, who I think began to worry about
my interpretation of the word 'unobtrusive'. It proved difficult
to be a fly on the wall and to be the town celebrity; every
visit we made was recorded in the town newspaper ('English
visitors Mr. and Mrs. Walker and their two children visited
the Smith family in Red Gulch where they were shown the
family's one hundred year old log cabin. The visitors much
enjoyed the banana bread and pecan pie Mrs. Smith had
prepared and presented Mrs. Smith with an African violet. . .').
While it was difficult to be unobtrusive (a mobile home is not
the most private place to live), we did find ourselves caught
up in some remarkable friendships, some of which have persisted through letters and telephone calls and the exchange
of family gossip.

There were times when I wondered if all this interest was
a subtle means of controlling the report and muting any
criticism that might have found its way into the case study.
Such a response would have been unusual on such an
orchestrated scale, and I really think that most people were
not too interested in the report, or worried what I might
write. The NSF were after all a distant agency, and one with
little opportunity to have an impact on life in Pine City.
Certainly the Superintendent was occasionally curious about
the case study, and wanted, I think, his schools to come out
of the study in a creditable light, and the schools too would
sometimes ask me what would appear in the study. Overall
there was a surprising lack of concern about the report, and
much more interest in us.

I did worry about the role I had taken; it was uncharacter-
istic of me, it seemed to break all the rules I had read about
in the textbooks, and it concerned me that I was flattered by
all the attention I received. But, whatever the costs, there
were some considerable gains; some of the students gave me
remarkable interviews, and a number of people went out of
their way to tell me about themselves and to explain to me
about life in their schools and in their community. It was
difficult to observe classrooms unobtrusively, but it proved
easy to ride a school bus, attend a High School football
game, a Veterans' Day Parade and to attend a Christmas
Nativity play.

From the start I chose to interpret the word 'context'
widely, partly out of personal preference, but also because
circumstances required me to do so. In a small town all
aspects of social life are interconnected. To understand what
is happening in a classroom requires that you know about the
circumstances of families, about church affiliations, about
community issues and local politics. Perhaps this is always

true, but in a small town you are constantly reminded of the context in which events need to be understood. It is impossible to treat the school as freestanding and autonomous and creating a world of its own; people's perspectives and horizons are not easily contained. As the outsider you need help to come to terms with this completely; ethnographers frequently write about the importance of locating 'reliable informants'. I am not sure I quite understood what this meant until I found one. One of the guidance counsellors in the school, who was also the wife of the Superintendent and mother of two High School students, proved an invaluable source of information and insight. I only had to express an interest in a student and she would arrange for me to visit the student's home or to talk to them at length somewhere out of class. It was her idea that I should talk to some past students of the school and she arranged the interviews during the Christmas holiday. An intelligent and able woman, who more than anyone else understood what I was trying to do, she would have been a key informant in any circumstances. What made her particularly valuable in this study was that, while she knew the students and the High School as well as anyone, and better than most, her position as the wife of the Suprintendent was a publicly sensitive one. She could not seem to be critical without seeming to be disloyal, so she tended to work in subtle and invisible ways, putting a lot of effort into counselling individual students.

I was never quite sure, but I sometimes had the feeling that she saw in the case study a means of expressing ideas she had developed over a number of years, but mostly kept to herself. I don't mean by this that she wanted to co-opt the study, but that she gave freely of her time, ideas and interest. Her position in the community gave her access to a number of sources of information and she was generally trusted more highly than one might expect. In part this was a personal accomplishment, but it was also due to a sense of marginality that came from her identity as an 'outsider', for though she had lived in the area for 30 years and her husband and children were considered 'local', she was originally from California and retained a rather different identity, accent and a measure of self-confidence that marked her off from other women in the community and the school. Although I had an aspiration to develop a 'contextual' understanding, without her help I would not have achieved it in so short a time.

I tried to present myself to the school as someone who would be unobtrusive, who would take great care with whatever information they provided, and who was primarily there to write a relatively technical report to the NSF. Well, that was the rhetoric, and it was important to say those things, but what really intrigued people - teachers and, even more, students - was that I was English and that with my family I

was to live for two months in their town. 'Why us?' was everyone's first question - not in a defensive manner but out of
curiosity and a sense of disbelief. Eleven school districts in the
US and they had been chosen. I explained that one of our
project team (Gordon Hoke) had worked with the Superintendent
on a Tri-State kindergarten project some years previously and
that was what had led us to them. They listened but the sense
of disbelief remained, and it never did dissolve completely. There
was always something of a feeling that they had won me in
some bizarre national lottery. Pine City was simply a town no-
one visited except on the way to somewhere else. To have come
from England, and to be 'writing a book' about them, generated
a fascination and an enthusiasm that simply overwhelmed any
of the ordinary facts of the story. And when they discovered
that we were going next to Boston these feelings were magnified
yet again. Boston was seen as the source of desegregation and
other liberal ideas which had been imposed on the South; but
when Boston itself had had to implement them it had, it seemed,
failed badly. That was the icing on the cake. Through me Pine
City was going to show Boston how it could be done. It was a
wonderful joke, shot through with all kinds of ironies, of which
my being English was a sub-theme. Somewhere in the NSF, or
in the University of Illinois, they figured there must be someone with a deep and magnificent sense of humour; to have
created this situation revealed a set of qualities they didn't
normally associate with the Yankee North.

Within days of our arrival we were known in the town. Once
during the first week the manager of the grocery store did not
want to take my cheque, because though it was drawn on the
Pine City Bank, 'he didn't know me'. One of the girls on the
check-out came to my rescue. ('I know him, He's OK. He's the
Englishman working at the school.') She'd even remembered my
name.

A lot of things we had to do the first week or so might be
thought peripheral to the case study. Finding our way round
the stores, opening a bank account, buying sleeping bags for
our two small children, enrolling our eldest child in kindergarten, buying a cheap radio (a source of entertainment in
the evenings), buying a second-hand car; they might all be
thought of as things that would get in the way of the study,
especially when we had only six or seven weeks in total to
complete it (and I decided early that I had to meet the dead-
line and complete writing this study well before I was due to
travel to Boston in early January to begin the next one). Yet
a lot of those early social and family tasks were very important. They introduced us to a range of people and they
established us as a family in the town. Access to a number of
networks and sets of relationships is important in a small town,
so is the fact that you are spending money in local stores and
businesses. If we had confined ourselves to the school we would
have come away with a very narrow view of the school and of

the issues and conditions affecting the curriculum. It was
often the outside contacts we made that allowed some insight
into the views of employers, of the private schools, of parents
and others. It was such contacts that allowed me to visit the
black Junior College, and Lynne, my wife, to observe white
upper class female society. We also got to visit factories, the
Lions Club and small farms. While the task was not to complete
a study of the community, there was no doubt that some access
to the community gave us a better understanding of what was
happening in the school.

Of course I made mistakes. The Lions Club asked me to talk
to them, then put me on the spot to offer judgements about
the effects of desegregation on the High School. Faced with a
challenge I defended the school, at the cost of losing some
valuable informants, including the newspaper editor.

Being socially visible had other effects I really only appreciated later. At the time we were so caught up in events it was
hard to realise what was happening. But I realise now how
difficult it would have been to be a single male of marriageable
age in such a community, and to be on my own. There were
some such outsiders in the community (some of whom who
were teachers) and social life was not made easy for them.
The visibility of the family was especially important given the
licence I expected. I crossed social lines that most inhabitants
of the town rarely even touched at the boundary. I could be
left alone to talk with black teenage girls because that was
'an interview'. I could ask naïve questions about race because
I was a foreigner. The combination of being foreign, of being
some kind of writer, of being part of a family that included
young children, opened doors in a quite remarkable way,
and, to be honest, none of it was really planned that way.
There are quite a lot of books you can read about fieldwork
methods (and I have probably read most of them at one time
or another, and certainly I have told students to read them),
but not many of them could have predicted the kind of complex
chemistry of factors we found in Pine City.

A Place to Begin

I usually find that in the early stages of a case study a lot of
my questions are questions about recent history. Whenever
I notice anything, or other people point things out to me, I
am curious to know why people think things are as they are.
'Why is it you have no physics classes?' 'Why is it that most
of the Science rooms have no water or electricity?' 'Why are
there more girls than boys in advanced math classes?' You
will notice from the questions that they are not historical
questions in the academic sense, but in the sense that people
will normally answer them with reasons that emphasise past
events. 'Well we did have physics a couple of years ago, but
at that time we had a teacher who made physics seem pretty

hard, and that has put a lot of students off.' 'The main reason
we have such poor resources is that this used to be the black
school, and that sort of money just was not spent here.'
'Well, I think it goes back to the boys choosing not to do math
rather than the girls choosing to do it.'

In the Pine City study I found myself asking these, and a
host of other questions, but some underlying questions kept
recurring. One of these was about the sequence of events in
the desegregation of the schools. It might be thought that this
was a somewhat peripheral question in the context of a study
of the science curriculum, yet it seemed that 'integration'
was a theme that teachers and administrators often returned
to in response to more narrowly focused questions. The story,
from the bits and pieces I picked up, seemed very complicated,
but it also seemed people either didn't know the whole story
themselves, or if they did know it they were not sure how much
they should tell me. Late in the second week I managed to get
a consistent account of events, and interestingly I got it from
one of those non-school events I have already mentioned. As a
family we had decided that we needed to buy a car. Life in the
country was difficult without one. Renting was very expensive,
and given that we had to travel from the South up to Illinois
for Christmas, and then across to Boston for the second case
study, it would probably pay us to buy a second-hand car. We
were given a lot of help by Chris Taylor one of the curriculum
supervisors in the School Committee Office who not only knew
everyone in town, but also it seems knew the history of every
car. With his help we bought exactly what we wanted and fixed
up the licence and insurance we needed. This involved the best
part of a day driving round town visiting various garages and
offices and in between we got to talk. Some time in the afternoon
Chris told me the story of how desegregation came about in the
schools. That night I wrote it down, and a few days later
typed it out and showed it to him. He made a few comments and
changes and later I added some further comments as I picked
them up from other people.

At first I did not intend using this account as part of the
study. I thought, early on, that most of the study would be
more specifically tied to science education issues. But when the
site visit team came to Pine City late in the study they asked a
lot of the same questions, and found the account helpful, and
so I decided it would probably be the case that many readers
would come to the study with the same, or similar, questions.
To emphasise more narrowly defined science education issues,
and to leave this account out would be in effort to distort
the study. If desegregation was the issue, it had to be given
prominence and that required some historical explanation. As
a necessary part of the context of the study I put the story
of the desegregation process in very near the beginning of the
case study. It read as follows:

The Desegregation of Pine City Schools

Through 1968 and 1969 Pine City Schools were voluntarily desegregated under the State policy of 'freedom of choice'. One or two white teachers taught in black schools and black teachers began to teach in the white schools. A few black students enrolled at what had previously been all-white schools, but overall the actual changes were small in proportion to the anxiety that was generated. Even these small concessions fired debate and controversy and many people, black and white, feared what the immediate future would hold. To many outsiders integration did not seem to have proceeded fast enough, and in 1968 the situation in the town precipitated a federal court hearing.

Mr. Collins, the superintendent at the time, had been in office for twelve years and in this time had established himself in a position of some power. Although the School Board was strongly against integration, Mr. Collins had foreseen the day when it would become mandatory. In consultation with his staff he had drawn up contingency plans for desegregating the city schools and awaited events before presenting them to the School Board. No-one knew what his chances of success were, but his personal position was a strong one and it seemed that he might be able to convince School Board members that it was better to implement the plan rather than face outside intervention under a Court Order. In the event he never did act to present his case for during 1968 he suffered a heart attack and died. One of his former colleagues pointed out that this was not an uncommon fate of school superintendents at the time, faced with both outside pressures and local hostility.

Mr. Allen took over as superintendent but being new to the job and lacking Mr. Collins' authority he was unable to get the plan that Mr. Collins had worked out accepted by the School Board. In his position he may well have been unwilling to confront the Board on fundamental issues, and have lacked the detailed knowledge necessary to persuade or out-manoeuvre them. Instead a scheme was evolved – under pressure from a federal court order and with professional advice from one of the new state universities. This plan, implemented in 1970, involved extensive bussing of students between the different school sites in Pine City (see Figure 2.1).

Though this plan was implemented in 1970 it was considered an administrative nightmare. It was expensive to operate. It alienated both students and teachers without resolving community concerns. Students were seen roaming the downtown area during school hours. Rumours of riots and sexual misbehaviour ran rife through the extensive social networks that characterise small towns. The Administration seems to have felt that the plan adopted by the School Board was impractical

and had been inadequately considered. Privately they sus-
pected certain School Board members of being near the centre
of the rumour mill. It was said that School Board members
were recruiting students for the private academies.

Figure 2.1: Changes in the Use of Buildings under Various
Integration Plans

Present name	In the 1960s	In 1970	Since 1971
Pine City Kindergarten	Black Elementary Grades 1-6	4th Grade	Kindergarten
Pine City Primary	White Elementary Grades 1-6	Grades 1-3	Grades 1-3
Pine City Elementary	White High School Grades 9-12	North Campus Grades 10-12	Grades 4-6
Pine City Junior High	White JHS Grades 7-8	Grades 8-9	Grades 7-8
Pine City High School	(a) Black Training School (b) Black Elementary 1-8 (c) Black HS	South Campus plus ROTC and vocational school	Grades 9-12

One private school opened in the late sixties (Fort Smith
Academy). The founders were mainly lawyers, doctors and
business people. One former High School student wryly
comments: 'They were people who wanted to keep their
children away from most other white children just as much
as they wanted to keep them away from blacks.' Mr
Collins, architect of the original desegregation plan, did
little to discourage the founding of this school and another
similar school elsewhere in the county, seeing them as a
means for containing the kind of dissatisfied parents who
might be difficult to contain in a fully desegregated public
school system. Like other private schools in the region,
Fort Smith Academy quickly filled its rolls. The events of
1970 increased further the demand for private schooling.
Next came the founding of Pine City Academy.

Perhaps more than any other single event the founding
of Pine City Academy hurt the pride of the public schools.
Not just because yet more students opted out of the public
school system, but because this time they tended to be from
middle-income white families, and in particular from parents
who were teachers in the public schools. Worse still, the
Academy was largely founded on the initiative of teachers,

and even two curriculum supervisors, dissatisfied with the
way the public schools were being run.
Although it was white families who actually put segre-
gationist pressure on the public school system, many black
families were as beset by anxiety. They after all had as much
to lose from a faltering education system. But, as one black
woman resignedly put it, 'No-one was listening to us.'
It may be hard to imagine what this loss of confidence meant
in a small rural town like Pine City. For some it was devas-
tating. The city had always felt great pride in its football
team and immediately prior to desegregation the community
had given it considerable support - 'We had a marching band
with 250 instrumentalists,' one contemporary remembered.
But after the events of 1970 there would only be 'about half
a dozen spectators at the game, and they would have come in
the buses with the team, and the band would be 10 kids, and
maybe 3 who could play'. In a small town in the rural South it
is difficult to imagine a greater catastrophe befalling the
community. 1970 is still remembered as the 'bad year', the year
when the system reached its nadir.
The following year membership of the School Board changed,
some of the old hardline conservatives were replaced by younger
members; they promptly appointed a new superintendent (Dr.
Williams). Faced by the failure of a court-directed desegregated
plan the new administration invited in consultants from another
state university.
The consultants agreed that the current plan was ill-
conceived and asked if anyone had any alternatives to suggest.
It was then that Chris Taylor, the vocational supervisor and
a long-standing member of the administration, who had worked
with Mr. Collins on the original scheme, suggested that it be
resurrected. Essentially that happened. In 1971 a new desegregation plan was implemented, the overall structure of
which remains unchanged in 1976.
In 1973, Mr. Tyson, the present superintendent was
appointed. Since then things seem to have run more smoothly
than anyone had expected. The last segregated Junior High
School class has now graduated from High School. The rumours
of breakdown in the schools appear to have stopped, or at
least to have lost their force. The growth of the private
academies has been checked, middle class white students seem
to be finding their way back into the public school system.
To the outside visitor it begins to look like a success story.
The schools seem to be working smoothly and integration
appears to be accepted. Even those who don't like it seem
prepared to accept that the process is irreversible and that
they will have to learn to live with it. It is still probably
true that 'given their druthers' 50-70% of blacks and 70-90%
of whites would still feel most secure if their children were in
'their own schools'. But more realize there is no going back
and are prepared to live with the system. As one black High

School senior put it: 'It doesn't matter much to me whether I
am being taught in a class with white kids, or whether I'm
being taught with black kids, just so long as I'm being
taught.'

This may seem to the staunch integrationist a poor epitaph
for the brave days of Civil Rights, but in the context of the
rural South it is a giant leap for mankind. And generally it
perhaps gives more hope for optimism about the human
condition than Neil Armstrong's perpetual footprint.

Deciding whether or not this kind of account should be included was not easy, and the dilemma is a frequent one in
studies of this type. I mentioned earlier that the stress in
this study was to be on curriculum issues and conditions,
not on the specific and particular features of Pine City
schools. Overall, the study was seen as an issue analysis,
not as a set of case studies of particular organisations. Now,
it seemed to me that the account of desegregation I have just
given includes elements of both approaches. There are some
things, for instance the influence of individual Superintendents
at critical points of the story, which seem to be mainly about
the particular case. Perhaps such a level of detail was not
strictly necessary in presenting the account. On the other
hand it did seem important not just to describe the sequence
of publicly visible events, but also to give some feel for the
process, and particularly to indicate the kind of role that the
Administration had taken. Without some information of that
kind I felt the reader would be left with a lot of unanswered
questions.

Sometimes people ask: 'But what has this got to do with
science education?' It's not a question science teachers in the
schools would ask. For them, the connections and the relevance were obvious. They were now teaching racially integrated classes, often in buildings that were outside their
own racial communities. In any discussions of curriculum or
of teaching this was the first thing on their minds.

Occasionally I have been asked, why did I make the value
judgement at the end - in particular, why that funny reference to the moon landings? The answer was - panic. I found
myself writing about the progress of desegregation, and
justifying doing so. Meanwhile I was nearly halfway through
the period I was allowed to complete the study, and, while I
had collected a good deal of information on science, maths
and social studies teaching, none of it yet cohered into a
story. The short piece on desegregation I felt said something
interesting and important, but how did I justify it? The
reference to the moon landings, while it was in some ways
oblique, was therefore directed at the NSF. Think of the
effort it took to place a footprint on the moon, I was saying,
and then think again about being impatient with schools if
social change seems to be a slow process. Having made the

point I felt I could get on with looking at what was happening
in the classroom. In the case study itself I made the point as
follows:

In the eyes of everyone in Pecan County integration is the
key issue, perhaps particularly in the schools, but anything
tied to education pervades the community as a whole. Sometimes it seems as though the schools, and the High School
especially, are a laboratory for the community, for it is there
that social problems are brought to scrutiny. Some people
feel that if integration fails in the schools few aspects of
people's lives would escape the impact of the failure.

One consequence of the mood of successful social experiment in the school is to make the schools look and feel
important. In other parts of the country people may question
the relevance of schools as institutions, and ask them to
justify themselves. In Pecan County there are people who may
question the relevance of some parts of the curriculum but
no-one seems to question the schools themselves.

It is not hard to detect this feeling of the schools running
ahead of the community in desegregation even though the
clues are often apparently trivial. They are seen more clearly
on social than academic occasions. For instance, a year ago
the High School scheduled the first dance to be open to
both black and white students. Although the principal had
been hesitant about allowing it to take place and ominous
rumours ran through the town prior to the event, it proved
to be an evening of innocent pleasure. Apparently stimulated
by the students' success, the faculty this year organized
their own party. It was a friendly if somewhat formal affair
but it developed into a square dance in the gym, perhaps a
third of the guests staying on. Next day various stories
circulated the town. There's no knowing for sure but it
seemed the white girls on the faculty quite enjoyed the
scandal of dancing with blacks. And some of the black
teachers were apparently amused at the incredulity of
soul brothers out of school ('Square dancin'!').

Another aspect spotlighted by the faculty party: some
of the women whose husbands were not in education were
being carried along by the process of integration ahead of
the 'head of the family'. This was especially true of those
whose children attended white academies. One such teacher
admitted to me that she had been surprised to see her
husband join a square dance set which included a black
couple.

Such detail may seem trivial to an outsider in the face of
the real inequities that exist in terms of income, employment,
health and housing. Yet despite the reality and permanence
of the inequities a trend in attitude is clearly apparent. The
school is running ahead of the community and, it seems, on
balance to be carrying people with it rather than leaving

leaving them behind. (I am reminded of Samuel Stouffer's classic study of desegregation in military combat units during World War II. He found that opposition to desegregation came mostly from people not directly affected by it. He wrote: 'The further they are from accomplished fact, the more they disliked it.' Pretty much the same seems true of life in Pine City.)

By all accounts those close to the fact have had to learn to live with drastic changes in the circumstances of their lives. One teacher, now in her thirties, told me how during her childhood on a cotton farm her father had made her shut herself up in the house when the workers went out to work in the fields each morning, and again when they returned. For her the blacks were a close yet strange society which she only saw in glimpses. Yet with desegregation she found herself teaching black students and working with black teachers. She confessed it took some time to learn to listen and to talk to the students, and like several other white teachers she confessed it was only the tolerance and patience of some of the black teachers that enabled her to adapt to the new circumstances.

The process of adaptation may still be active. The gaps in communication are less marked than they once were, but spaces still exist between words. One teacher articulated the point clearly when she said, 'You know I talk to Miss Hall (a black teacher) every day. We work together. But I never really know what she is thinking.' The cordiality and hospitality that remain characteristic of social behaviour in the rural South retain a degree of ambiguity that allows people to retreat behind custom and habit.

For those pressing more directly for integration there are still significant barriers. Banking, medicine, pharmacy and the law are still exclusively white - as are most public offices. Yet there is a feeling amongst those in leadership positions in the school system that these are protected more by the expense and exclusivity of higher education than by the local custom.

A mood of optimism, almost of crusade, seems to be what holds the school system together and sets its tempo. Paradoxically even those teachers who do not share the conviction of the integrationists seem carried along by it, almost despite themselves. I found it quite common for white teachers, who seemed to give no hint of prejudice in school, to return to conventional racial prejudices and stereotypes out of school, albeit in muted and oblique form. It seemed to me at times that those who were making integration work in school, out of school found themselves puzzled by their own motives. Many of the teachers ran small farms in their spare time, an occupation which provided little financial reward, but which, like hunting and fishing, provided an opportunity for solitude and escape.

It would be stretching the point to explain this entirely in
terms of a search for a return to older values and a previous
way of life, but at times there did seem to be an element
of this about it.
I confessed to one black girl that I didn't know how to
react when teachers, who in school seemed intent on making
integration work, out of school expressed prejudice. Should
I admire their professionalism or condemn their hypocrisy?
She admitted it was often confusing for black students:

'There are teachers who will be real nice to you in school,
but then you'll meet them in town walking along the
street, and because they have their wives or their husbands with them, they'll just act like they don't know you.'

The superintendent is seen by most people as being in a key
position on the integration issue. He is generally regarded,
by opponents and supporters alike, as the person who is
making integration work in the schools. His refusal to provide private schooling for his own sons, and his determination to approach integration positively have made a big
impact. 'Since he came', one teacher said to me on a number
of occasions, 'the situation has turned round and things have
just got better and better.' However the Superintendent
cannot be seen to let the schools run too far ahead of the
community; as he repeated to me several times, 'Integration
is the dominant issue here - I can truthfully say that I never
take a decision of any consequence without considering its
effect on integration.' His own success is bound up with the
commitment to make the system work. In steering a way
through public concern and established attitudes he has had
to develop a sensitivity for situations not unlike that previously cultivated by blacks. The anecdote that best captures
this concerns the mural painted in the Primary School under
the direction of an artist-in-residence. It just happened, she
explained, that the black children wanted to paint people,
while the white children wanted to paint houses, buses,
trees and flowers. The result was a colourful landscape
peopled by black figures. The mural is in a prominent
position readily visible to visitors to the school and the
school board office, and as it neared completion the superintendent walked across from his office to take a look.
'Very colourful,' was his pointed comment. Shortly there-
after there were some white faces too, roughly in the proportion they are in the schools (but still with brown bodies).
His sensitivity may not be infallible, but it is ever active.

Again, I sometimes have to justify the relevance of this
statement to curriculum issues, though not to those in Pine
City. Because education in the US is valued as a local concern, educational and community issues connect closely; it is

difficult to consider one without considering the other. To
understand what was happening in the classroom and the
school required an understanding of the role the school played
in the community.

I have quoted this section at some length because it brings to
light another issue. The first quote from the study - the condensed oral history - while it might be improved by the collection of further evidence, cross-checking with the written
record (court transcripts, the local newspaper), does I think
make reasonably efficient use of the data I had at the time.
Given that I had not time to pursue the story further I think
the accounts stands up fairly well with the passing of time.
The second passage I have quoted though is of a different
character. It is more interpretative, both in the sense that it
uses interpretations collected from people in Pine City, and in
the sense that this is presented through a meta-interpretation
of my own. It now seems rather inadequate. It is not too well
constructed as a piece of writing and it lacks much depth or
edge to it. As a section from an evaluation report, intended
to be immediate and ephemeral, I feel happy enough with it.
It was written fast and it looks like it; it almost has a Sunday
supplement style. But as a piece of considered writing - the
kind of thing you might expect to find in a book or a professional journal it seems slight and inadequate.

The point I want to make is that in applied research and
evaluation this dilemma is almost always present. The aspiration
is to report quickly, to present the record before the situation
has changed too much. This tends to push the case study
worker to description rather than explanation; portrayal
rather than analysis. Explanation and analysis take more time
(perhaps more thought). They require the writer to write
and rewrite, and to discuss ideas with others away from the
scene of action. The production of a classical ethnography
typically takes years rather than weeks or months. There may
well be other reasons for wanting to write portrayals rather
than analyses (to 'tell people like it is', to avoid an explicitly
judgemental stance, to allow the reader to construct his or her
own interpretation), but the sheer mechanics of short term case
studies makes the decision for you, on technical rather than on
any other grounds.

STORIES IN SEARCH OF AN AUTHOR

I mentioned earlier that the putting together of this 'context'
story took me two to three weeks into the case study. It is
true that I had also collected some data on classrooms and
teachers by this time, but none that seemed to cohere into a
story in quite the same way. This again marks something of a
dilemma in the study. Collecting data is easy enough; given a
tape recorder or a notebook most people with a minimal training

can generate at least 30 or 40 pages of single space typescript in a day. But given a 50 page limit for the final study ways have to be found of making some sort of compression, condensation or selection. There are a number of ways this might be done. The classic research technique is to turn from words to numbers, or to turn to general theories of one kind or another. My preference is to look for stories. That is to say to look for interesting discrepancies, coincidences or paradoxes that allow you to bring together diverse sources in a way that is readable. I thought the story of the desegregation process was quite an interesting one, though not a story in the literary sense (at least not a 'good one'), it does carry the reader through quite a rich area of information with a degree of economy and efficiency. Finding comparable stories in the classroom seems to take more time, and in the end what the study included was a couple of emerging stories set in a selection of related documentary records.

Looking back I can see the stories more clearly ('Hindsight is always 20-20') and perhaps here the simplest thing is to tell the outline of the stories first, though the reader should be warned that at the time of the events they were not so clear in my mind, and, though they began to emerge more clearly as I wrote, it was by then too late to engage in the kind of major rewriting that would have made it possible to allow the stories to take on a more clearly defined structure. The key 'story' that emerged from observing science classes and talking to teachers and students concerned 'interest in science'. The story begins with a general statement about discipline in the High School and the problem presented to me was the key teaching problem by a number of faculty – the problem of motivating the interest of students.

A Key Issue: How to Motivate the Students

Motivation and Discipline

Discipline is not a major issue for teachers in the High School. The school shows none of the marks of a faculty under siege from the students. The teachers come into the teachers' lounge at break relaxed and talkative. The corridors and classrooms seem free of the usual signs of vandalism. Between classes students move in groups rather than as masses. The police rarely visit the school, and then only on invitation.

If you ask the teachers about discipline what they tell you about is the problem of getting students interested in the subject, rather than how to handle confrontation. Those incidents that do arise seem mainly to involve students talking in class, or at worst, talking back to teachers. The worst discipline incident that occurred while I was at the school concerned a boy who let off a firecracker outside school – an action that cost him five days suspension from school.

As you walk down the corridors during lessons you don't hear teachers shouting or students clamouring for attention. It is not a common occurrence for students to be paddled. The general atmosphere is one of an efficient, perhaps unquestioning institution, where most people (administrators, faculty and students) seem mostly concerned with getting on with their work.

Most teachers agree that the key problem is motivation. 'In every class there are one or two, perhaps sometimes it's more, who just sit there, and whatever you do, however hard you try, it's just really difficult to reach them.'

One of the Guidance Counsellors sees the problem as being a general one:

'Motivation really is the big problem here. I don't understand why it is, but looking at it rationally, students in the NE of the United States consistently score higher on tests of academic motivation than students in the South. Yet I am sure our students are just as able.'

Motivation is an issue at the Junior High School too, though here it is more often expressed as a discipline or behaviour problem. Where the Assistant Principal of the Senior High School despairs of students' (black and white) failing to capitalise on their abilities and opting for courses below their capabilities, the Principal of the Junior High School worried more about disorder and changing moral values.

I followed up this statement by including accounts of lessons which showed different ways teachers coped with the perceived problem of motivating the students. These included a biology teacher who taught a fast-paced lesson, used a lot of tests, and kept up a series of running jokes with students, a math teacher who involved students in publicly working through examples on the board, and a general science teacher who was trying in a crowded ill-equipped classroom to introduce more demonstrations of experiments into her classes. The general science lesson caused me to consider the importance of distinguishing between 'motivation' as something primarily the concern of the teacher, and 'interest' as something primarily the concern of the student:

Why does Patricia like Science?

Observing Mr. Griffin's and Miss Green's General Science classes led me to feel that I should try and distinguish between motivation and interest. Motivation seemed to be something the teacher could create, or at least inspire, by skilful teaching. Interest, seemed a more permanent and elusive factor, coming from the student rather than the teacher.

Patricia is the quiet girl in Miss Green's 9th grade General
Science class who held the glass tube during the making of
the barometer. It was also Patricia who asked Miss Green
what if you put more mercury in the beaker at the bottom of
the barometer then wouldn't the weight of mercury press the
column further up the tube?

The records show she has done well in General Science,
having virtually straight A's this semester. She'd started
the year in Biology but had missed some classes while out of
school following an accident. On her return she had worried
about the work she had missed (though she'd been a good
student in Biology getting A's there too). Eventually her
mother came up to the school and it had been agreed that
Patricia should transfer to General Science. She didn't
regret the decision; Biology had seemed to be mostly learning
words and some of them were long and difficult to remember;
'Several of my friends who are still in Biology wish now
they'd done what I'd done. General Science is more interesting
and you get to do different things. The other thing is there
is less homework to do.'

When did she first get interested in science?

She says she's been interested in science as long as she can
remember, certainly since third grade, but what really
spurred her on was being in Mrs. Clark's class in seventh
grade. Mrs. Clark had clearly made a big impact on her.
Patricia described her as 'fussy', but she made science
interesting; there had been no experiments and mostly it
was about planets and atoms. She liked experiments and
found it was much easier to remember things when you had
seen them instead of just reading about them.

I asked if she read science out of school but except for
sometimes looking things up in the encyclopedia she didn't,
mainly because 'homework takes up all your time. There
isn't much time for anything else.' She wasn't interested in
science fiction or science magazines. She enjoyed the science
she did at school and had always been quite good at it, but
she really didn't know if she'd take it any further.

Talking to Patricia led me to the Junior High School, and particularly to Mrs Clark's science class:

Words and Things

After talking to Patricia I talked to other students who
confirmed that Mrs. Clark had been an early influence on
their liking for science. I found Mrs. Clark in the Junior
High School and asked her if I could observe in her seventh
grade General Science class.

Mrs. Clark is one of the most experienced teachers in the
city and, as one of the first black teachers to work in the
previously all-white Junior High School during the voluntary

desegregation of the late 60's, she has an identity in the system outside the subjects she teaches.

The class I observed had spent the previous lesson in study hall working on a test that Mrs. Clark duplicated from the Teachers' Handbook (accompanying the textbook). The text chapter is called 'The Diversity of Life', and the section covered by the test is mainly about plants, fungi, algae and bacteria. There are twenty-seven students in the class.

'How many have completed the test?' Mrs. Clark asks the class. Most raise their hands. 'How many have mastered it so that they can talk about it?' A smaller number raise their hands. 'It isn't enough just to be able to give the answer to the questions. You've got to know the words and be able to use them in sentences. How are you going to be scientific if you can't do that?'

Mrs. Clark stands at the front of the class and asks Shirley to tell the class what she has on her paper. Shirley is a tall white girl sitting in the middle of the class; she stands and reads the questions and her answers. After the first question she pauses but Mrs. Clark asks her to go on until she reaches the bottom of the first page. Some of the words are long and difficult to pronounce. Shirley stumbles over 'saprophyte' and ends up spelling out the letters rather than saying the word. 'I have the answers', she explains to Mrs. Clark, 'I just can't pronounce them.'

Next Mrs. Clark asks a black boy sitting up near the front to 'stand up and expostulate'. He has real difficulties and is unable to get past the first question. 'I don't mean to pick on you', Mrs. Clark explains to him, 'but I think we have what we want.'

A girl stands and reads her answers to the first page of questions, perhaps not quite so fluently as Shirley but with not too much difficulty. All this time Mrs. Clark gives no indication as to which answers are correct. Her main concern seems to be to listen to the students using the words. She reminds the class again, 'You have to be able to master the words and put them in sentences.'

Finally, Mrs. Clark selects one of the boys - 'Give me the answers to the first three questions, and I think we'll have what we need.' Then she asks the class to turn to page 239, to the phonetic spelling of three bacteria types. In turn she asks a number of students to read:

coccus (KAH-kuhs)
bacillus (buy-SIHL-uhs)
spirillum (spye-rihl-uhm)

Then a sudden change of tone. 'Right', she challenges the class. 'Right, all bacteria are harmful, Right?' There are some murmurs of disagreement. 'You mean they're not?' Mrs. Clark asks the class. When it is clear everyone has grasped the question, she collects some answers, again without commenting on them. The students suggest that bacteria can take nitrogen from the air and make nitrate, that they can make organic matter decay, and some other things that are useful rather than harmful.

'We know that all bacteria are not harmful', Mrs. Clark exlaims, 'but it isn't enough just to say it. You've got to be able to convince me that you know what you are talking about. When I asked you the question some of you said, 'No-oh'. I know from how uncertain you sounded that you didn't know what you are talking about.'

'Now some bacteria are harmful. Can you tell me about some of those?' The students make several suggestions including scarlet fever. Mrs. Clark comments, 'I don't just need the answer. I want to know the source of your information.' Someone says p. 240 and reads out the relevant section. Mrs. Clark says to the student who first answered: 'You know the answer, but you didn't know the page number. This is what we refer to as being scientific. You must know the source of the information.'

The next problem Mrs. Clark raises concerns the growth of bacteria colonies. 'Every twenty minutes we have new cells. How many do we have after four hours?' '128', someone answers. 'Look at it seriously', Mrs. Clark urges. 'Read that paragraph again carefully and as you do so I want you to become fully conscious of its true meaning.' There's a pause. One of the students says, 'After two hours there's 64 cells.' Mrs. Clark says, 'But I believe the author asks you to go on – if there are 64 cells after two hours, how many will there be after four hours?' '128', someone says. 'Let's look at it seriously', Mrs. Clark urges again, 'You've only scanned this paragraph. Would you read it with concern and then give an answer.' There's another pause. 'Yes, sir', she says to a student with his hand raised. 'Multiply by two and you get 128.' Mrs. Clark turns again to the text, 'It says one cell gives you eight cells in one hour, and 64 cells in two hours. So how many do you get in four hours?' One of the girls begins thinking out loud, 'In the first hour you get eight, and in the second hour you get 64, so you get more in the second hour than you do in the first hour.' Mrs. Clark encourages her to continue this line of reasoning, 'Right, so. . .?'

'I have 256', someone offers.
'4026', someone adds.
'456', another.

Mrs. Clark tries to help out. 'It's more than 2000. 64 times 64 gives you what? The main issue is, you can see why the doctor quarantines you when you have a disease.'

'3056'.
'Four thousand and. . .'

Four thousand and something', agrees Mrs. Clark while
several students hurriedly try and work it out. 'It's more
than 4,000 - close to 5,000. We can see how bacteria multiply
all right. We can make use of them, or they can be harmful
to us. We can make cottage cheese out of milk if we are
thinking about our waistline. Milk is a liquid. If you let it
stand the cream comes to the top, and the milk is a liquid
that will congeal like jelly congeals when you let it stand.
The cream can be churned to make butter, and the milk
congeals and can be cut into layers.' Seeing the expressions
of some of the students' faces she adds, 'You don't like
cottage cheese, right? Mother gets it because she is watching
her waistline. Milk comes from what animal?'

'Cow'.
'And cheese comes from?'
'Goat,' someone suggests.

Mrs. Clark changes the topic: 'Let's talk about something
else - parasites, saprophytes. What does a parasite do to a
non-parasite, the animal or plant it is living off? How does
the parasite make its living?'
Chris says: 'It lives off another plant or a rotten tree or
something.'
Mrs. Clark repeats the question emphasising she is asking
about parasites rather than saprophytes.
James suggests: 'A parasite lives off another living
organism's life substance.'
At this point the text says merely that fungi are parasites
or saprophytes (though the previous chapter included a
paragraph elaborating the distinction between them). Mrs.
Clark however chooses to extend the point further.
'Parasites are sucking the blood out of another plant or
animal, right?' She pauses. 'Look in our community at
persons who aren't doing what they should be. If we are
doing all we can to beautify the neighbourhood by cleaning
up the yard and planting shrubs and someone comes along
and leaves litter, are they parasites?'

'Yes ma'am', someone replies.
'If people are living on welfare and are not fully partici-
pating citizens, are they parasites?'
'In a way', a student replies.
'Explain that', Mrs. Clark asks.
'It may be all they can do', the student says.
'They may be old', someone adds.
'They may have been in an accident', someone else says.

Mrs. Clark accepts all these qualifications: 'This is not a
parasite, OK? If they are doing all they can and have
paid their social security it is all right.'

One of the white girls asks a thoughtful question: 'We're living off our parents, so you could say we are parasites.' Mrs. Clark replies:

'I don't want to make you parasites. Society owes you something, your parents owe you something. You have a right to education. But if you don't use your education and come to school and fool around, then you're a parasite. You are helping this community grow, but the person who sits around and doesn't work when there is work available, that's a parasite. As long as you are in school your parents owe it to you to keep you, just like the Federal Government owes you social security. But over and above that we know there are people in school, in the church, and in the community who do not take a full part. In school there are those who fail to enrich the school programme – at this point they become parasites.'

An important feature of Mrs. Clark's lesson to this point is that she has made very few comments on the answers students give to the test questions. In her class this is done by students challenging the answers given.
One of the boys says: 'I'd like to challenge number 3 on page 241':

'What did the person say?' Mrs. Clark asks.
'It was Shirley, she said roots and stems and the text says bacteria lack chlorophyll.'

Mrs. Clark replies: 'OK, let's look at the higher plants. What are the structures?'

'Stems, roots and leaves.'
'OK so what is the challenge?'
'It says "true tissue",' someone suggests.
'Root is a true tissue. It's a structure and an example, OK? What is your challenge?'
'It says bacteria belong to a group of plants that lack true tissue like roots and stems.' Shirley reads from the text.
'And you challenge. . .'
'Chlorophyll. It says on p. 241 that bacteria lack chlorophyll.'
'Stems, roots and leaves is the right answer. Give yourself credit for true tissue. Are there any other challenges?' Mrs. Clark asks.

Two more challenges in the nature of competing definitions are offered before the end of the lesson. No points are awarded for success. In one case Mrs. Clark offers someone a choice, 'Do you still want to challenge, or are you asking a question?'

Comments

Mrs. Clark is a charismatic figure in class; the students
watch her as she teaches, and she uses her voice to considerable effect, altering its tone, intonation and pitch. She
is the kind of teacher who would hold the students' interest
whatever topic or subject she was teaching.
    In this lesson we can see her using the device we have
seen before in Mrs. Griffin's class of elaborating the parts
of the text that have some interest value outside science
(here it is such things as the cheese making process and an
excursion into the topic of social parasites).
    Perhaps most striking is the way she stresses the students'
oral expression. When they read she listens, not just for the
correct answer, but for the fluency and facility with which
students use scientific terminology. This combination of
teaching from the text, and stressing oral expression con-
centrates attention on the task of defining and labelling
terms. It is a well-tried teaching technique, particularly
developed in religious communities. Much Jewish and Moslem
teaching has traditionally been of this kind. It is perhaps
not surprising that respect for the text and an emphasis on
oral expression should remain at the centre of educational
values in the Bible belt of the United States.
    It is important to point out that Mrs. Clark does not use
the text as an instrument of propaganda, for students are
able to 'challenge' answers, and the fact that the teacher often
refrains from giving clear indications of correct answers means
that this is a lesson where students are encouraged to think
and to reason for themselves. The example of the student
raising the question of students being parasites is a case
in point.
    The link between the culture of the classroom and the
culture of the church seems, in this case, to be one of style
rather than of ideology. Mrs. Clark is teaching science as
though it were a language and using the book as a text, in
a style which has its parallels in the Sunday School. Formally
church and school are separate (though three flags fly outside the High School; the United States flag, the State flag,
and a Christian flag). Though in a community where social
life is largely dominated by the churches, and where the life
of the churches retain a strong educational element, such
continuity may be a key feature in the culture. Similarities
and continuities between the cadences and tempo of classroom and Sunday school may connect to an oral tradition that
is deeply incised in the imagination of children. The curriculum analyst may seek the replacement of existing styles of
science teaching by a 'discovery' or 'enquiry' approach, and
the related changes in the performance of the teaching role
that follow. The effect of success in this enterprise may be
to cause a disjunction between school and community, the

detail of which must remain highly speculative.

I have quoted this section at some length in part to give
some idea of the kind of record an observer can produce from
one visit to a single lesson armed only with a notebook and a
pencil. I don't mean by this to claim that it is an exemplary
account, but it does give some idea of what it is realistic to
expect from one-off classroom visits, and the constraints and
demands of this project were such that it was not very often
that the observer could afford to go back to classrooms for
more than one visit without seriously reducing the coverage of
the range of classrooms it was required we should observe.
   The 'Comments' section illustrates further the dilemma I mentioned earlier. The theme that emerged, of a possible continuity between the kind of talk to be observed in the classroom
and the talk to be found in church, was one later picked up by
a number of sociologists as being of some interest. Of course
they would have liked more data to take the theme much further,
but not only would this have been time-consuming to collect
(though I did learn later that Mrs Clark was a leading figure
in her church, which she invited me to visit), the problem was
also that at the time this theme was really only half-formed in
my mind: it clarified a little as I wrote, and became clearer as I
talked to others about the study. If I had worked on it no doubt
it would have been an interesting problem to research further,
but in evaluation it is rare to have the luxury of pursuing such
themes. The interests and priorities of the researcher have to
some degree to be shelved in the face of the pressing responsibility to report accurately, and with some degree of balance
on the concerns of the people and institutions in front of you.
Perhaps as a note of frustration I presented the idea in the
study in a somewhat bold and unjustified manner, knowing I
had not the opportunity to take it further I made the most of the
tiny evidence I had. In this sense the style of the report is
often very different from the style of research; the traditional
research values of circumspection, careful scholarship and
understatement were somewhat thrown aside for a single brash
and largely unfounded claim.
   Instead of following up the theme that had emerged I felt I
had to return to the theme of motivation and interest, which was
the one the teachers had indicated was most pressing for them.
This time I returned to student interviews:

The Voices of Students

Visiting Mrs Clark's science lesson left me feeling that I
had not adequately touched on what made students <u>interested</u>
in science, as opposed to just liking science lessons. In order
to pursue this point further I talked at some length with a
small number of students in both Junior and Senior High School.
Accounts of a number of these conversations follow.

Tony (7th grade)

Tony lives out in the country with his mother (who is
divorced). He loves the outdoors and spends much of his
time fishing and hunting. While he sees school as important,
he sometimes talks as though coming to school was a tire-
some chore between fishing trips, a price to be paid rather
than a positive attraction. His mother explains that there
was a time he lived in town, but that 'No-one was ever more
pleased to move back to the country. He often says to me,
"I never want to think of going back".'
Tony is very enthusiastic about science. He is a bright
student who consistently gets good grades and he feels
science is his best subject. He likes science because it is
close to his interests and what he knows; because 'there is
more to do in science than in other subjects', and because
'you learn about different things'. Tony says, 'Science is
not easy, there's a lot of studying, but it is interesting.'
He is an avid viewer of Cousteau films and Wild Kingdom,
and thinks perhaps he would like to be a marine biologist.
He told me about a sea fishing vacation in Florida including
detailed descriptions of the habits of sharks, sailfish and
dolphins. He is very observant, and an eager collector of
information. He likes to read the encyclopedia entries on
the different fish and animals he encounters, and at home
he has built up a small collection of books on animals and
fish.
Part of the fascination of the outdoor life for Tony is,
'just the different things you see. When you go out in the
woods you never quite know what you will find.' It might
be a raccoon eating freshwater mussels, a deer, or a beaver
building a dam. Fishing especially is almost a science to
Tony. He's noticed that catfish and bream take different
kinds of bait according to the time of the year, the weather,
the time of day, and a host of other things, including the
phases of the moon. He seems to store each of these facts
away in his mind as he encounters them, and enjoys the
opportunity of talking to knowledgeable adults about them
whenever he gets the chance.
The world of science has a tangible quality for Tony not
dissimilar to the world of the woods and creeks he knows
best. It is a sense of reality few people possess and it
carries with it a slight feeling of isolation. The world of
hunters and fisherman is a world of the adult male, and is
often alluring to teenage boys; Tony's grasp of a deeper
quality that carries over into the world of science is more
rare however. He seems well on the way to appreciating
some of the abstract qualities of the world of science,
whether he continues with his formal education or not. It
may be important to note that his science teacher is a woman,
but she shares and understands his background. She

explained to me, 'I was an only child and had to be a daughter to my mother and a son to my daddy.'
I asked Tony if he felt he could learn more about science by staying at home and exploring the woods and creeks. His answer, surprisingly, was no, a lot of science you couldn't learn from experience, at least in this part of the country. He felt science was not just about the immediate environment, but provided a window on a wider world. One of the things he liked about science was that it did provide some escape from the constraints of his limited world. He summed up his feelings saying: 'Maths is just a bunch of numbers, English a bunch of words, but science is different. Science changes, you move on, you don't stay on one thing.'

Bill (8th grade)

Bill is a student of few words, and he doesn't use these to say good things about school. It's not that he doesn't like school, his feelings are less active than that. School is just time that has to be served when he could be doing more interesting or more useful things. When asked to describe his ideal school he said, 'It wouldn't be worth coming. There'd be no Math, no Science, no English, no Social Studies, well Social Studies maybe.'
Out of school he works on a farm and most enjoys driving the tractor, but overall, farming offers little more attraction than school. 'Working in the garden don't seem worth it. It's a lot of trouble and you don't seem to get out as much as you put in.'
The oldest of three children his ambition is to be a truck driver. Four years seems a lot more school to wait out till graduation but he has no plans for dropping out because his parents would be disappointed in him. A more immediate ambition is to own a car.
The one bit of the academic curriculum that seems to have reached him is Social Studies, but in the end it is still school. 'It's all right to hear about the constitution and history and all that, but then you get a test and it's dull. You can often remember things when you want to but then you go into a test and get some dumb questions you can't answer.' Although Social Studies was his worst subject last year, this year it's his best.
On reflection his ideal school would have less tests and it would be all computers: 'You'd come into school, mash them buttons and away you go.' 'That's right', said his science teacher, 'just like driving a tractor.'

Steve (11th grade)

When I asked people if there were any students who studied science out of school, kids who had chemistry sets at home and that sort of thing, everyone said I should talk to Steve. From the way students talked about him it was obvious they felt he was a little different from them. He actually lived in a world of science and liked to speculate and talk about those things.

On first meeting he explodes some of the stereotypes. Yes he does feel a bit isolated in his interests, but he is also a 180 pound football player and champion weightlifter, activities that have won him a position of some respect in his peer group.

He lives out in the country and is an avid collector. He collects coins, old bottles and books. He has a library of science books, reference books and science fiction (Asimov and Tolkien are his favourite authors) but he talks too about H.G. Wells and Thor Heyerdahl, whom he admires considerably. He reads <u>Popular Science</u> and <u>Popular Mechanics</u> regularly and also subscribes to a science book club. He has a chemistry set and a geology set and analyzes rocks for fun. At Christmas he plans to get an optics kit. He builds and flies model rockets and model airplanes in a scheme organised by the Civil Air Patrol.

His interests are wide but he most likes chemistry and math. 'I've grown up around numbers', he explains. 'Daddy is a clerk and I've always watched him work with figures. It always puzzled me how he could keep track of a sheet of numbers that was longer than I was. I couldn't see how he did it. So I sat there and watched him work with a sheet of numbers and a slide rule until I had it figured out.' He adds with a smile, 'Now in algebra I'm working with letters instead of numbers and my Dad is working with a calculator.'

Janice (12th grade)

Janice is one of a family of six children. She has two older brothers who are both in College, a younger brother and a twin brother both in school, and a sister who died suddenly just before leaving home to go to College. Janice also has a baby boy born last summer. The family lives in a small wooden house in one of the two main black areas of town.

Janice is taking elective courses in advanced math, chemistry and home economics. She says:

'I chose home economics because I want to learn to cook and sew and look after myself. I chose math because I liked it. And I chose chemistry because I thought I needed it.'

She has always liked math ('to tell you the truth it's the only thing I ever have liked'). She has never had to work too hard at it ('my mother thinks I don't study for it because I don't bring no books home!'). Even when she has missed lessons she hasn't had too much trouble making up classes.

She prefers to do math problems in school rather than at

home, 'Because there are always people around you if you
get stuck.' But she is not too keen on working problems at
the board ('I don't mind too much but when you are up
there in front of all those students you get scared you
might get things wrong').
Although she has not had any trouble learning math,
Janice never thought of herself as an outstanding student.
('I never wanted to compete with all those 'A' students'),
in fact she planned on giving up after Algebra 2, but a
guidance teacher persuaded her to continue.
Chemistry was a bit different. Janice had really wanted
to take physics but too few students signed up for it.
Her brother told her she should try and take science and
the guidance counsellor encouraged her. After the first
few weeks she tried to get out - 'I was scared I couldn't
do it' she said, but the counsellor persuaded her to stay
and she now feels that was a good decision. ('Now I'm
doing pretty good and I like it.')
A lot of students are scared of math and science courses,
she feels, because everyone thinks they are so hard.
'Students think if you are taking chemistry and advanced
math and geometry, you're taking the hardest courses and
you must be really smart.' Janice says she once felt the
same but now she doesn't feel it holds much truth - 'a lot
more students could do math and science if they wanted to.'

I was at this stage still attempting to pursue what the
teachers had identified as the key issue in curriculum and
teaching - the problem of motivation. From these interviews
another theme emerged: it seemed that there was some
association between students who had a high interest in
science and a certain life style; in particular, boys who lived
'out in the woods', who by family circumstance or personal
preference lived lives of some social isolation, who spent much
of their time hunting and fishing, and who often had close
friendships with older men; this kind of pattern seemed in
some way associated with a quite intense interest in science.
I knew there was some research evidence that lay behind
this theme, enough perhaps that I recognised the theme when
it emerged, but again it would have been inappropriate to
impose this too heavily on the data, or to make too much of
what was an interesting, but admittedly flimsy theme. Again
I had to face the evaluator's dilemma of discovering a theme
of considerable research interest, but having to leave it to
one side in order to cover the ground because it was more
important to remain close to participants' interests and concerns than to pursue my own.
The end result is inevitably a study that lacks coherence
or logical clarity, and a story that lacks tension and economy.
Descriptive evaluation reports tend to be long, and often
become tedious in their attention to detail and their failure

to exercise a strong editorial hand. The difference is in part
that the researcher and the story-teller both know what it is
they want to tell, they share a desire to work certain effects
in the minds of the reader. They have a message and often
a point of view to establish. The evaluator or applied researcher however, is more hesitant; always looking to multiple
audiences and knowing that different people are likely to
look for, and take away, different things from the report. The
lack of structure and clarity that are frequently characteristic
of the reports is partly a result of hesitancy in knowing or
deciding what to tell and to whom. The desire is to write
studies or reports that are open to multiple interpretations and
to several levels of concern, not to produce convincing argument, for that is seen as the responsibility of others. Tech-
nically, the difficulty comes in trying to include enough detail
to maintain a high level of redundancy while not losing the
reader in a mass of material, a lack of tension in the story
or a lack of clarity in the logic.

REFLECTIONS

One of the points that has recurred in this account of the Pine
City case study is, that although the case study was intended
to be primarily concerned with curriculum and teaching issues,
I kept finding myself returning to community issues, and
particularly to the desegregation issue. One line of justification
I give is that this reflects not just my own interest and bias,
but that people would keep returning to the theme without
prompting on my part. At the time I was there the issue was
something of an obsession for the community. Of course it
could be that people were simply telling me what it was they
thought I wanted to hear, and I can't discount that my training
in sociology and anthropology might have led me and them in
that direction, nor can I discount my preconceptions about the
Deep South, stemming from 'Gone with the Wind', 'Caste and
Class in a Southern Town' and a long time addiction to country
blues.
　　Some check was afforded on these biases when the site visit
team came to town. One person in particular, Charlie Weller,
a physics education professor from Illinois was able to get
closer to more detailed science education issues than I had.
Partly this was simply that he knew what questions to ask.
Most of my knowledge of science education comes from being
a spectator rather than a player and that inevitably limited
my effectiveness as an interviewer of science teachers. But
then again, I wonder if in part people were able to talk to
Charlie about these things just because he was a science
teacher; again they were (with the best of intentions) telling
him what they thought he wanted to know.
　　One use of multiple observers is to get some grip on this

problem, though I suspect that one person who stays around
long enough, asks enough questions, penetrates enough
different situations, eventually comes up with a picture that
is reasonably balanced, even if it lacks depth on some issues.
My aim was to give some sense of what it was like to be a
teacher, a student or an administrator in Pine City. I wanted
to report what they felt the key issues to be, not to impose
on them my own. If the technicalities of science teaching
seemed relatively insignificant set against other issues, then
that is what I would report. My concern was with the general
picture. I wanted to convey a sense of urgency and emphasis
given to a range of possible concerns: to set the specific
issues concerning science teaching in a context of more
general concerns. In retrospect I did not perhaps get close
enough to the particularities of science teaching, but I am
less worried about that than I would be if I had covered them
in detail but neglected the dominant concerns felt at the time.

It is attention to context that the case study handles best.
As a research method its strength is not so much its capacity
for analysis, but in its ability to synthesise. The case study
reassembles ideas, information, insights and understandings
into a human and institutional whole; it provides a sense of
reality; it constrains the imagination and the planner.

In attempting to 'case study the case study' I have tried to
reassemble the experience by putting back together accounts
of what I did and what I wrote.

The points I have drawn attention to are probably endemic
in the writing of any educational case study. In this project,
however, they were exaggerated by the fact that this was a
multiple-site study in which people took quite specialised roles
and tasks. The case study workers for instance handed over
their studies to others who wrote 'assimilation' and 'summary'
sections of the report. The case studies were seen as an
important part of the project, but the project's final report
contained considerably more than the case studies alone. It
is important to remember this because I have presented the
Pine City study a little as though it was an isolated ethnography. The other case study workers in the project have
other stories to tell, often very different from the story I
have told here. There are though, I am sure, some points of
similarity. One is that when we began each study we could
not be exactly sure what would happen and how things would
work out. Even though we may approach such studies with
well worked out methods, plans, time lines and task analyses,
there are always surprises.

One of my best ideas in planning this study was that I
persuaded one of the science teachers, who was enrolled in
a part-time Masters course at a nearby university, to get a
course credit for writing an 'insider's critique' of the case
study. One reason for wanting to include such a statement
was that an important consequence of 'condensed fieldwork' is

that you run the risk of misjudging events, situations and people more seriously than you do when the fieldwork extends over a long period of time. The short period of study results in a lack of redundancy in the information that you collect. It gives you little opportunity to cross-check, to accumulate instances over time, to search out and to follow apparently deviant cases. This is evident even in the kind of thing I have written here. I have, for instance, said that I thought the fact of my 'foreignness' overwhelmed the formal statement of my intentions, and I have claimed too that the final case study was generally accepted by people with little critical comment. But I am not very confident about these statements. I was not in Pine City long enough to really feel I understood people's responses, nor did I get the opportunity to return in order to gauge the impact and effect of the study. I really have very little idea how the study was received, whether it led to any discussion or argument, or whether I should have defended it better.

Asking a teacher to collect comments and write me a critique from the inside, which I intended to append to the final draft as a kind of built-in book review, would, I hoped, overcome some of these problems. Though I wrote to the teacher concerned several times after the draft was completed I never heard from her. Perhaps she was too busy, perhaps she did not like the case study when she saw it, perhaps I did not give or offer enough help or guidance. I sometimes wonder if the celebrity status I enjoyed, even though I tried to scale it down, had its costs. Maybe some people resented me, or found me intimidating, or felt I misused my position in some way. I have no way of knowing. On the other hand, what happened was largely a result of circumstance, and not something I planned or expected; the only criticism I feel appropriate to my own conduct is to ask if I acted intelligently in the circum- stances. I know I made some mistakes and some errors of judgement, but then everyone always does. I think in this case I mostly overcame them, but the doubt still remains, perhaps I totally misjudged the whole situation.

Where I find 'case study methods' and 'ethnography' have something in common is mostly in this respect. They are human and social research processes carried out in human and social contexts. The most you can do is to hope to act intelligently and reflectively in the situations in which you find yourself and to trust not to offend people inadvertently. Inevitably you do make mistakes; it is difficult even to talk to a teacher or administrator for twenty minutes without regretting something you said, an unfortunate phrasing, an inappropriate joke, or just a feeling that you misjudged the conversation in some way. The best you can hope to do is to create situations and relationships that maximise the chance of such information finding its way back to you. When you are on your own it is very difficult.

In the context of this book, it is perhaps important to
emphasise that what I have written is not specific to science:
a case study of a school is likely to run into some of the same
issues even if the problem is different and the situation dissimilar. As I wrote at the outset, there is an increasing
interest in the use of case studies in research and evaluation,
and there is also a shortage of experience. Most people learn
from making their own mistakes, or from those of others.
The literature may be of some use, but it tends to focus,
naturally enough, on big issues rather than practicalities.
On the whole we lack many diaries of case studies, or even
hindsight accounts like the one given here. There are many
reasons why this should be so, but perhaps we should make
a greater effort to tell stories about the stories we tell, for
only in that way can we begin to accumulate experience as a
profession rather than merely as individuals.

NOTES

1. For methodological details see Stake & Easley (1978),
   vol. 2, pp. C1-C56.
2. Some account of this interest is given in the report of a
   follow-up conference to the project (Stake, 1980).

BIBLIOGRAPHY

Atkin, M. 'The Government in the Classroom' (John Adams
   lecture, Institute of Education, University of London,
   1980).
Hegelson, S.L. et al. 'Status of Pre-College Science, Mathe-
   matics and Social Science Education 1955-1975', 3 vols.
   (Ohio State University, Centre for Science and Mathematics
   Education, 1977).
Stake, R.E. 'Report of the Pere Marquette Conference'
   (CIRCE, University of Illinois at Urbana-Champaign, 1980).
Stake, R.E. and Easley, J.A. 'Case Studies in Science
   Education', 15 vols. (CIRCE, University of Illinois at
   Urbana-Champaign, 1978).
Weiss, Iris S. 'Report of the 1977 National Survey of Science,
   Mathematics and Social Studies Education' Centre for Educa-
   tional Research and Evaluation, Research Triangle Park,
   North Carolina, 1978).

3 THE PROGRAMME, THE PLANS AND THE ACTIVITIES OF THE CLASSROOM: THE DEMANDS OF ACTIVITY-BASED SCIENCE

Edward L. Smith and Neil B. Sendelbach

INTRODUCTION TO THE STUDY

The Design

Many science educators have advocated the use of hands-on activities, involving materials and phenomena, for teaching abstract science concepts and related science processes at the upper elementary and middle school levels. The major effort to implement these prescriptions has been through the development and dissemination of instructional programmes. Although most comparative studies have shown such activity-based programmes to be equal or superior to text-based instruction on the variables measured, [1] several problems have emerged. Superiority in outcomes are not consistently found and the improvement in learning is frequently not as great as anticipated. The activity-based programmes have not been as widely adopted and actually implemented in classrooms as had been expected. [2]

Several reasons for this have been identified including the lack of in-service training, money for equipment kits and materials and logistical support systems to provide needed materials and equipment to avoid unreasonable demands on already overburdened elementary teachers. These problems are primarily at the school building or system level. Let us suppose, however, that these problems were overcome and teachers attempted to implement the programmes - would they experience success and satisfaction and continue to teach them?

What about the classroom level? To what extent is the limited actual use and persistance of innovative programmes a result of problems encountered in the classroom when teachers attempt to use them? What problems are encountered in the classroom and how do teachers cope with them? Available research does not provide many answers; yet considering answers to such questions would seem to be a crucial part of deciding how to improve science curricula at the system level. They are also crucial if we are better to prepare teachers effectively to use science programme materials. The case study reported here is part of a research project designed to answer these kinds of questions.

We believe that understanding of classroom teaching requires going beyond the description of observable behaviour to the investigation of the meanings and antecedents of that behaviour; much of a teacher's use of materials, such as teacher's guides, takes place prior to instruction, i.e. during planning and preparation.[3]

In order to better understand science teaching and the role played by programme materials and teacher intentions, we developed a research strategy, related to an instructional unit of several weeks duration, in which we analyse the materials, teacher planning and classroom instruction. Our analyses are conducted in a manner which enables us to compare directly the suggestions in the programme materials and the teacher's intentions for instruction with actual instruc- tion and each with the other. The patterns of similarities and differences thus identified then become the focus for further inquiry. Our goal is to make some sense of these patterns in terms of the teacher's perspective and the social system of the classroom.

This research strategy is reflected in the following major objectives for the study reported here; a case study of a sixth-grade teacher teaching a five-week segment from the Science Curriculum Improvement Study (SCIS) programme.[4] The major objectives were to:

(1) Determine the extent to which the teacher's intentions and the actual instruction reflect the materials;
(2) account for the differences between the materials and the teacher's intentions; and
(3) attempt to account for the nature of actual instruction in terms of the materials and the teacher's intentions.

As reflected in Figure 3.1, each of the research foci - pro- gramme materials, teacher planning and actual instruction - requires its own method of analysis. The analysis of the materials was done to determine what instruction would be like if the programme were taught as described in available sources (the literal programme). The unit of analysis was the instructional activity; with a new activity being indicated by a major change in the student task (e.g. change from setting up an experiment to recording observation). The analysis of individual activities employed a set of activity features: the task; the materials; the teacher's role and planned behaviour; the student's role and anticipated behaviour; the knowledge addressed; the instructional strategy; and its management and organisation. Such a small unit of analysis provided a means for comparing both the teacher's intentions and actual instruc- tion with the literal programme to determine similarities, modifications and exclusions.

The primary method utilised for determining the teacher's intentions was the analysis of the teacher's planning. This involved video-taping the teacher while she was engaged in planning for instruction. After each planning session, the teacher reviewed the video-tape with the researcher to

Figure 3.1: Overview of Research Approach

Research Focus	Characteristics of Methods	Analyses
Programme materials (literal programme approach)	Activity as unit of analysis Activity feature scheme, e.g. student task, teacher role, knowledge addressed Propositional knowledge mapped	Literal programme (activities and their features)
Teacher plans and planning (teacher's intended approach)	Video-recording of naturalistic planning Stimulated recall with video-tape	Intended instruction (activities and their features) Comparison with literal programme planning process
Classroom instruction (actual classroom approach)	Classroom observation and audio-recording Selected video-taping Interviews Field notes documentation	Actual instruction (activities and their features) Comparison with literal programme Ethnographic analysis

stimulate recall of thoughts during the planning process. [5] This was done in order to understand what the brief and often cryptic written lesson plan notes produced during planning meant to the teacher and to obtain additional information about the activities the teacher intended to use. This procedure also provided information about the nature of the teacher's planning process and especially the use made of the 'Teacher's Guide'.

The methods of ethnographic fieldwork were used to determine the activities of <u>actual classroom instruction</u> and to address our goal of making sense of what was happening. Ethnographic research is methodologically pragmatic, making use of any number of research procedures, strategies and operations. [6] Primary procedures included classroom observation, interviews, and audio- and video-taping of classroom instruction.

One characteristic of ethnographic procedures is that the researcher is not confined to collection of particular kinds of data determined in advance. This does not mean, however, that the researcher has no initial perspective. Typically, the perspective is based on the researcher's purposes, background and experience. For this study the perspective obtained from the literal programme analysis and ongoing teacher intention analysis provided many of the initial questions about the classroom instruction. There was a critical balance between prior knowledge as a useful tool and prior knowledge obscuring the observation of actual interactions. Initial analysis and explanation of the interactions that constituted the teaching-learning process for this instruction were carried out as data gathering continued.

Our research strategy involved studying an instructional unit of several weeks duration. We selected a unit from the life science sequence of the Science Curriculum Improvement Study (SCIS) programme. The unit 'The Oxygen-Carbon Dioxide Cycle' is the third of five 'parts' in the sixth-grade life science unit entitled 'Ecosystems'. The SCIS programme was selected because of its relatively wide usage, both nationally and locally, and our preference for the conceptual approach to science teaching reflected in it. The 'Ecosystems' unit was selected because of the importance of that concept from the perspective of both the elementary science curriculum and societal relevance. 'The Oxygen-Carbon Dioxide Cycle' was selected because it dealt with a basic relationship among important components of ecosystems (gas exchange among plants and animals) and was of the appropriate scope. It had its own distinct content, but also provided opportunities for relating back to major concepts introduced earlier in the unit including 'ecosystems' and 'cycle'.

As implied in this description, the SCIS programme is organised around the development of scientific concepts. However, this should not be taken simply as being 'fact oriented'; the programme emphasises science as a process of organising facts; process-oriented concepts such as 'property', 'system'

and 'model' are developed in the programme. These are viewed
as being 'at the heart of the processes of observing, describing,
comparing, classifying, measuring, interpreting evidence,
and experimenting'. Student inquiry activity with natural
phenomena is a basic feature of SCIS.

'The Oxygen-Carbon Dioxide Cycle', hereafter referred to
as 'Part Three', consists of six chapters (10-15). [7] In these
chapters, the students do a series of investigations using the
acid-base indicator bromothymol blue (BTB) to detect the
production or use of carbon dioxide by plants and animals.
These investigations lead up to the 'invention' by the students
of a simplified model of the oxygen-carbon dioxide cycle.

We observed students working through chapters 10 to 15
in that unit. In chapter 10, they study the effects of carbon
dioxide on the indicator BTB (a blue to yellow colour shift).
In chapter 11, they attempt to explain why, upon standing,
the solution returns to the original blue colour. In chapter 12,
a carbon dioxide generator which uses Alka Seltzer tablets is
demonstrated. Chapter 13, which is optional, involves testing
the hypothesis that oxygen causes BTB to change from yellow
to blue. In chapters 14 and 15, the students use the BTB
indicator to study gas exchange in plants and animals.

The Setting

Our goal was to make sense of a particular instance of activity-
based science teaching. This section describes the general
context in which the selected unit was taught. This perspective
is important in understanding the more detailed results and
descriptions to be presented later.

The school is in an urban community with a public school
enrolment of 30,675 students in the northern Midwest of the
United States. It is located at the edge of the city and the
student body is of mixed racial origin and socio-economic
background. Grades from kindergarten to sixth are included
in the school. The teacher, Ms Ross, [8] is an experienced
elementary teacher using SCIS for the second year. She has
a split fifth- and sixth-grade class. By choice, she co-
operates with another teacher in the school with a similar
class. Ms Ross teaches all the science and social studies while
the other teacher handles all of the mathematics. The teachers
said that split classes and student rotation were established
in order that they could supplement each other's strengths
and provide better instruction by not having to teach all
subjects to their students. The teachers also said that rotary
classes during the fifth and sixth grades helps to prepare
students for life in the junior high schools.

Science and social studies are taught by Ms Ross in the
afternoons; from 12.30-1.00 she teaches science or social
studies to the fifth graders (18 students); from 1.00-1.30,
the sixth-grade students from the other class (14 students)

come in for science or social studies and from 1.30-2.00 her
own sixth graders (16 students) come back for science or
social studies instruction. Science is taught on Monday,
Tuesday and Wednesday and social studies on Thursday and
Friday. The timing for subjects is not rigid; on some days,
for example, science was taught for twenty of the thirty
minutes and social studies for the other ten. The split class
rotation procedure has been used for several years by these
two teachers. This year, however, is the first year they have
split the sixth-grade class into two sections for science and
social studies.

Last year was the first year Ms Ross used SCIS as the
science programme, and all the sixth graders were taught at
one time for a fifty minute period. Ms Ross reported that this
procedure had been unsuccessful and she attributed many of
the problems to the size of the group, about 35 students, which
resulted in material shortage and student confusion in doing
the investigations. This year she split the sixth graders into
two groups, with a resulting reduction in the time period for
each group.

What were Ms Ross's science lessons like? We observed her
teaching on numerous occasions and from those observations
we have constructed a portrait of the 'routines' of activity-
based science teaching. This portrait will serve as a backdrop
to the more detailed analysis of the planning that lay behind
what we observed.

Our observations of Ms Ross's instruction yielded patterns
of activity which were not those suggested by the 'Teacher's
Guide', but which were important features of her classroom
organisation. These patterns, or routines, are the fundamental components which provide much of the structure and
organisation for classroom operation.

Eight routines commonly occurred in her science lessons.
In sequential order they were: entering; introduction; beginning transition; instructions; material distribution; working;
clean up; and ending transition. These eight routines
structured the students' and teacher's procedures and
behaviours throughout the science period. A description of
each routine and its function in classroom operation follows.

Entering. Routines start as soon as the students enter the
classroom (see Figure 3.2). The students always enter the
room through the east door and go to their assigned desks.
During this entering routine, the students may be talking
to each other but are supposed to be moving towards their
desks. The teacher was always either watching the students
in the hall as they changed classes or was behind her desk. A
variety of student behaviours was observed during this time.
Some students would move immediately to their desks and
either read a book or magazine; others would work on an
assignment for the class; and others would just sit and talk.

Figure 3.2 Physical Arrangement of the Classrooms

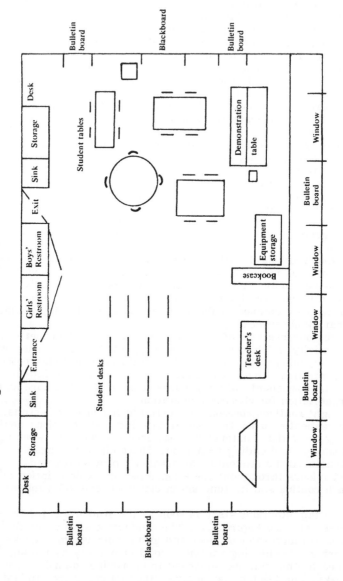

Unacceptable student behaviour, as inferred from critical intervention by the teacher, was movement in the room to an area other than their assigned seat or being 'too loud'. The end of this routine was when all the students were sitting and the teacher said 'Okay' loud enough for the students to hear. This entering routine appeared to serve the function of orderly student classroom rotation. The events identified as a part of the routine occurred on a regular basis whenever students changed classrooms.

Introduction. The 'Okay' statement signalled the end of the entering routine and also signalled the start of the introduction routine. The statement 'Okay' by the teacher always resulted in the students stopping all other activity and listening to the teacher, a fundamental transition. In the introduction routine the teacher outlined what was to be done during the period. During this time she announced if any assignments were to be handed in and whether they would be doing science or social studies. In either case, the teacher briefly stated what the students would actually be doing. After the announcement portion of the introduction routine, assignments were collected or other such administrative tasks were completed. The completion of such tasks ended the introduction routine.

Transition. The teacher signalled the start of the next routine - the beginning transition routine - by stating: 'All right, move to the science tables.' This routine consisted of the students moving from their desks to their assigned seats at the science tables. The teacher also moved from behind her desk, where she had given the introduction, to the demonstration table. Students could talk during this transition, but were expected to be moving to their seat. The teacher signalled the end of this routine by standing behind the demonstration table and looking at the students. This appeared to signal another behavioural and role transition. The students were to be attentive, as they were during the introduction routine. At times this signal was further clarified by the teacher saying 'All right'.

Instruction. The end of the beginning transition routine was immediately followed by the start of the instructions routine. The function of this routine was to provide the students with additional detail about what they were going to be doing and how they were going to do it. This was almost totally teacher-centred with the students listening. During this routine, the students would be sitting in groups of four at their tables. Each student at each table had been assigned an identification number of one, two, three or four at the beginning of the term. As the teacher provided instructions for obtaining and assembling or using materials, she used the identification numbers to assign

each student a task. With each task she called a number. This
procedure eliminated the need to specifically assign tasks to
individual students from each group.

Distribution. The distribution routine varied depending on
the behaviour of the students up to this point in the science
period. Noise level appeared to be the determining factor,
because the teacher's behaviour related to the student talking.
If the students had been quiet during the entering, introduction, beginning transition and instruction routines, the teacher
simply stated they should obtain their materials. Then each
student moved through the room according to the task assigned
in the instruction routine. If, however, the students had been
noisy and the teacher had continually directed them to be quiet
in the distribution routine, the teacher called only one of the
identification numbers. Those identified students accomplished
their task (such as obtaining vials), while the rest of the
students sat at the tables. After one task was completed, she
designated another number, then another. While this study did
not investigate the establishment of routines, it appeared that
such variations relating to structure illustrated the process of
how the routines were established in an evolutionary manner.
After successful negotiation of acceptable behaviour, the
distribution routine became less and less structured. If problems occurred, however, the teacher resorted to previous and
more structured variations of the routine. Similar forms of
variation were also observed in the clean up and ending transition routines.
    Each of the above five routines had to be successfully
accomplished before the students began the investigations.
The establishment and accomplishment of these routines was
a considerable task for the teacher and students. The teacher
constantly monitored student behaviour to ensure the amount
of structure for each routine was appropriate. Likewise, there
were many requirements for the students in each of the
routines, including a monitoring of the teacher to assess the
appropriateness of their own behaviour.

Working. Having successfully completed each of the above
five routines, the class engaged in the actual investigation.
The procedure for this segment of the period was less
routinised since the specific behaviours required for actually
doing the investigations are much more variable than for
entering the classroom, or obtaining materials, for example.
Some patterns were observed to occur during this segment,
however, and have been labelled the working routine. As
with the other routines, the working routine is very teacher-
centred. The teacher assigns the tasks that the students are
to do and then monitors their progress. The specific content
within the routine varies according to the activities designated
by the programme. The procedure and behaviour of the

students for doing the activities were, however, established
by the working routine.

Clean Up. Once the particular activities for the period were
completed in the working routine, a reverse process was
initiated. This reverse process started with the clean up
routine. The clean up proceeded the same as in the distribution routine. The same procedure of assigning tasks according
to student number was used. As in the distribution routine,
there were several structural levels of the clean up routine
observed. As before, student behaviour - primarily level of
noise - determined the structural level of the routine implemented by the teacher.

Ending. The last routine of the science period, the ending
transition, moved the students from the science tables back
to their desks. Typically, this transition immediately followed
the clean up. As students finished their assigned task they
moved from the science table area back to their seats. Once at
their desks, their behaviour was very similar to that during
the entering routine - reading, working on another assignment
or talking quietly. At this point, the science lesson was completed. No science was ever discussed when they were back at
their desks (a point we shall refer to later). As with other
routines, there were more or less structured versions of the
ending transition routine. If during the working and clean up
routines the teacher indicated there was too much noise, or
if it had not gone as directed in previous periods, she would
direct them to go to their clean up task and then return to
their science tables. The teacher would direct the students
to move back to their desks either as a whole group or table-
by-table. When this form of the routine was implemented, the
students were much quieter and more orderly.
    The eight routines described provided the structure for
the students and teacher to actually do the activities and
investigations. They are an important factor in the establishment of the classroom milieu - a milieu which is quite structured
and teacher-centred. The routines are processes for accomplishing many of the required classroom functions. The result is
that the students were able to manipulate the materials as
advocated in the literal programme. Very few discipline problems occurred, since the routines were structured in a
fashion to allow the teacher to monitor and adjust procedures
in order to control student behaviour.
    The establishment, implementation and maintenance of these
classroom routines is an extensive and important task. Without routines it is unlikely the class would be able successfully
even to try the manipulations. The described routines not only
provided the opportunity for all students to attempt the manipulations, they resulted in their being done according to provided directions.

We were, of course, interested in probing the nature of
Ms Ross's planning, particulary how she made use of the
'Teacher's Guide' to 'Ecosystems' and how those plans were
translated into action in the classroom. Within the routines
established by the teacher, what were students learning about
the nature of gas exchange in plants and animals?

THE PROGRAMME, THE PLAN AND THE CLASSROOM

Ms Ross's Planning

A significant amount of effort was devoted by the teacher to
planning for instruction. Four basic levels of planning can be
identified logically; yearly planning; term planning; weekly
planning; and daily planning. The planning practices described
by Ms Ross, however, led us to consolidate the four into two
types, each fundamentally different from the other and suited
to different purposes. Yearly and term planning attend to such
long-range issues such as: when will science be scheduled in
the daily routine? where physically in the classroom will
science be taught? which of the two science units will be
taught first? what size groups will the students typically work
in? and so forth. Weekly and daily planning were said to attend
to the micro-concerns of instruction, such as: how often will
science be taught this week? which activities will be done which
days? what specific materials are required for each activity? and
so forth. We focused primarily on weekly and daily planning.
The teacher had a consistent approach to planning. Late in
the week, either Thursday or Friday after school, Ms Ross
would sit at her desk with the 'Teacher's Guide' and her weekly
lesson plan book and plan the next week's lessons. These planning sessions, as they naturally occurred, were video-taped.
In her first weekly planning session, Ms Ross planned activities
from Chapter 10, 'Breath and BTB', and Chapter 11, 'Where did
the Yellow Go?'
Ms Ross's planning process typically resulted in several
directly observable outcomes. First, the 1.00 to 2.00 square
in the plan book was designated as either science or social
studies for sixth grade and notes were prepared relating to the
intended lesson. These notes are shown in Figure 3.3 as they
appeared in the plan book for Part Three. The nature of these
notes from lesson planning is consistent with the results from
previous studies. [9, 10] The notes are very cryptic and specific
with the primary components being (1) specific chapter and
title; (2) materials; and (3) a phrase identifying the major
activity. Other observable products of the planning sessions
were written notes and underlinings by the teacher in the
'Teacher's Guide'. These referred to materials, timing and
procedural points for the activity. The 'Teacher's Guide' was
the only reference the teacher used while lesson planning.
The last observable outcome of the weekly planning process

Figure 3.3: Documentation of items ...

Week Beginning November 13	Week Beginning November 20	Week Beginning November 27
1 hour for entire 6th pre-test for whole group	#11 in science text to do rest of page 16 except last one	Do #12 science-seltzer gas and BTB - vial with hole in cap, tubing, seltzer tablet. Discuss
Begin new unit	Finish science investigation from yesterday	Do #13 - Demonstration of soda and BTB. Discuss Monday expt. and today's
Neil - video tape #10-Breath and BTB, vinegar, ammonia, BTB, straws		Discuss briefly about science
#11 - Where did the yellow go? BTB vials with caps, straws, labels, dots. Observe yesterday's		

Week Beginning December 4	Week Beginning December 11
#14 - Invention of O_2 and CO_2 cycle. Terms - 4 vials, labels, dots, straws, BTB-green and blue. p. 18 and 19. Record	Do #15 with plant and BTB-in light and in dark Discuss CO_2-O_2 cycle
hypothesis Record data on p. 18 and 19 after observation of data from yesterday. Record class on board	Discuss science results from yesterday Be sure to clarify reactions to green solution: CO_2 to O_2
Discuss if light or dark would effect the above. Place 1/2 of each of items in dark (some). Do p. 20 hypothesis	
Check the above in light or dark. Record p. 21. Discuss their results	

was the accumulation of materials for the intended activities. These materials were obtained from a variety of storage locations in the room and were consolidated in the science teaching area near the teacher's reference table.

The Influence of the Teacher's Guide

We wanted to compare Ms Ross's planning with the suggestions in the 'Teacher's Guide' and with her instructional activity. One approach we used involved the identification of activities from the literal programme which were reflected in Ms Ross's intentions as noted in her planning documents, and in actual instruction. Also noted were any major differences in those activities as intended, or actually taught, compared to those in the literal programme.

From this analysis it was apparent that the literal programme had clearly influenced Ms Ross's planning and, ultimately, the activities which her students experienced. Evidence from her planning indicated that, at a minimum, she intended to use over half (53 per cent) of the 51 activities identified in the unit. Almost all of these were reflected in actual instruction. In addition, about half of the remaining activities were also reflected in actual instruction. However, while it was clear that the literal programme had influenced what was presented to the class, it was also clear that Ms Ross was making significant modifications in the programme, primarily through deletions and modifications of activities. Further, we perceived a pattern in the nature of the activities which were deleted and modified; discussion activities were deleted most frequently

To characterise this pattern of modification, activities in the text were classified into four categories: activities associated with the problem or topic of an investigation (what activities); how the investigations were going to be carried out (how activities); the manipulation of materials and observations (doing activities); and interpretation or elaboration of the results (why activities).

The results of the comparisons among the literal programme, the teacher's planning and actual instruction are summarised in Table 3.1 in terms of the four types of activities. An analysis of the literal programme shows that it follows a cyclical pattern of what-how-doing-why activities, yet the actual instruction reflects a curtailment of this pattern with how and doing activities often stripped of context through omission or curtailment of what and why activities.

This orientation of the teacher towards emphasis on the how and doing activities appeared to have important consequences for students who had many opportunities for hands-on experiences with science materials, and opportunity to observe a number of phenomena, several of which they seemed to find quite interesting. These opportunities

Table 3.1: Comparison of Literal Programme, Teacher's
Planning and Actual Instruction

	Type of Activities			
Source of Analysis	What	How	Doing	Why
Literal programme	9*	10	22	19
Planned activities	4	6	15	5
Actual instruction	6	9	18	10

*Number of activities identified in each type of analysis.

reflect goals expressed in the 'Teacher's Guide' and are
advocated by many science educators. However, it was also
evident that the apparent potential of the programme to
address important conceptual learning goals was not being
fully realised since several major concepts are addressed
primarily in the why activities.

The discovery of the teacher's orientation towards how and
doing activities was considered an important finding. However,
this finding itself became something better to be understood.
As data collection and analysis continued, attention was focused
on trying to understand both the cases and consequences of
this orientation.

Ms Ross's Perspectives on Planning

Why did Ms Ross approach her planning in the way she did?
To understand her approach we asked her to comment on her
planning activities. We did this by recording her comments
about planning using a stimulated recall method. This further
analysis was accomplished by reviewing the video-tape
recording with her to stimulate her recall of her thoughts,
feelings and actions during the planning. These are recorded
below.

Video-taped actual planning events	Teacher's stimulated recall comments
The planning process begins with the teacher obtaining the 'Teacher's Guide' (TG), taking it to her desk, and opening	I was mainly thinking of the (overall) schedule and what I would have time for be- cause on Monday you will

the plan book to the following week.

Very brief look at TG, p. 58, the general introduction to 'Part Three' and then turns to chapter 10 and looks at pages 62 and 63. Writes chapter number and name into plan book and then adds a list of required materials: '#10 - Breath and BTB, vinegar, ammonia, BTB.'

Looks ahead to ch. 11, back to 10.

Gets out her schedule book. Goes back to TG and circles the suggested time required ('less than one class period').

Goes back to p. 58 (the introduction to Part Three in TG) and says: 'Trying to find the instructions for mixing the BTB solution is somewhat of a problem in this book.' Finds something at the bottom of page (58) and makes a note on the page.

doing testing. Conference time (is) Monday morning so there will be no school then so I will have to work around that.

I think at that point I was writing down some of the things, supplies, that I will need as another reminder because it is a little easier to glance in my plan book and look - Do I have these out? Need to check these out at the kit at this point, because I find it a little more awkward looking here (TG). Because here (TG) I have to look at what each child needs and what the class needs, but here (plan book) I can see what I need to have read.

I was looking at the next page that follows (Ch. 10) to see if this is something that continued on or such. Some of the thoughts were that this went well last year. . . . Since it went well last year what I have done is to go over the material a couple of times and have it in my mind. What I haven't done is . . . read the white page. I will do this Tuesday before class.

(Then) I was looking for how long the experiment takes. I circled the time (in the TG) as another reminder of the time the chapter will take.

I was thinking there were no more straws left in the kit and I would have to remember to get some.

Turns to ch. 11, adds 'straws' to the materials list in the plan book under ch. 10.

As I looked at ch. 11 I didn't remember doing it the previous year. This whole chapter seemed sort of vague to me.

In Wed. block of plan book writes number and title of chapter: '#11 - Where did the yellow go?'

A list of materials required for ch. 11 is written in the plan book below the chapter title: 'BTB vials with caps, straws, labels, dots.'

There is a brief look at the text of ch. 11 on page 65, a look at p. 66, a check of the plan book, and then back to p. 64 and the description of ch. 11. The note 'Observe yesterday's' is added to the plan book below the materials list.

She leaves her desk, goes to the science equipment storage area and starts gathering materials. The required quantities are placed in trays and stored on top of the equipment box.

I wanted to start getting out materials so I don't have to bother getting materials ready for the next week. I only focus on the materials now.

She returns to her desk and says she has finished planning.

I did plan for two science lessons (for) next week. But I have no way of knowing if I can cover both of them or not because of conferences (as shown in her schedule book). At least I have a general outline of what I'm going to do for the week. I do have Tuesday and Wednesday but it's possible I might shift Wednesday to the following Monday because we might not have a chance to discuss any of number (chapter) 10. I'm not sure whether the BTB has to sit for a period of time and I have to be sure to have enough cups for each student.

Weekly Planning. As can be seen from the transcript, weekly planning invariably began with the determination of the major activity(ies) to be done on a particular day. This involved identifying an activity, finding out how long it would take and fitting it into the weekly schedule. The 'Teacher's Guide' is organised by chapters with a synopsis at the beginning of each chapter which usually specifies the number of class periods or weeks required. This first step was very simple when a chapter required only one class period, but, if more than one period was involved, it is clear that further perusal or recollection was required to identify where the breaking point(s) would come. These are indicated only in the text of the 'Teacher's Guide', when made explicit at all.

Once the activity(ies) for a particular lesson had been scheduled, the transcript shows that the teacher identified the materials required. For each chapter, the 'Teacher's Guide' provides a list of materials required for each team of students. The teacher had to determine the total requirements by taking into account her organisation of teams (groups of four); chapters involving more than one class period added to the task by requiring the teacher to decide which materials would be required for each class period. This could be determined only by recollection or searching through the text of the 'Teacher's Guide'.

The 'Teacher's Guide' included a section at the beginning of the unit labelled 'Background Information'. This contained a variety of information including statements about what sixth-grade students might already know about the content of the unit and a brief explanation of the natural processes to be studied in the unit. However, there was no indication as to whether this was intended as background for the teacher, or as a specification of the level of understanding which students might be expected to achieve. Also included, but not clearly distinguished from the explanatory material, was information about procedures for preparing the acid-base indicator (BTB) used in many of the activities. As can be seen from the transcript, locating such needed information often occupied significant portions of Ms Ross's planning time and resulted in her feelings of frustration.

Daily Planning. The other level of planning investigated was daily planning, which occurred during the whole-school silent reading period from 12.15 to 12.30 and just prior to the science period. While the students sat at their desks and read, Ms Ross reviewed the 'Teacher's Guide' and the notes she made from the weekly planning sessions, and gathered or arranged specific materials for the day's lesson. For example, during a post-instructional interview (17 November 1978) she commented about the daily lesson planning to be done for the next class period:

I will read this (the 'Teacher's Guide') again Monday morning or Monday afternoon before class to have it fresh in my mind as to what they (the students) are going to do. Also, I will review the notes I've made reminding me of the various things I should bring up in class – such as fill to capacity with no air space and placing it in a place of their choice in light and the temperature.

Daily lesson planning, therefore, was primarily a review and preparation process done in blocks of 'spare' time and with students present. The multiple demands made on the teacher can be seen in the following description of planning taken from the field notes:

> Today is the first day for starting Part Three and chapter 10. The students enter the classroom from lunch and begin to start their silent reading. Ms Ross is sitting at her desk and has the 'Teacher's Guide'. There is some talking by three of the students. Ms Ross tells them to stop talking and do their reading. Some students are not reading but are quiet; that seems to be acceptable. Ms Ross starts again to look at the 'Teacher's Guide'. She underlines something on the top of the second page (carbon dioxide and CO_2). She suddenly gets up from her desk and walks over to the science supply area. She says to me that she forgot she had to make the BTB solution. She proceeds to make this solution but appears to be very rushed. Silent reading ends and the students get ready to change class. Ms Ross has just finished making the BTB solution, walks back to the student desk area and dismisses the sixth graders. The fifth-grade students begin to enter the room.

This description of daily lesson planning is typical. In contrast to other planning, daily lesson planning occurs while the students are present, and requires the teacher to divide her attention between planning and the monitoring of student behaviour.

The effect of lack of time can be seen in this excerpt. While Ms Ross might have been able to address some of the content background for the chapter, the need to prepare the BTB solution was an immediate priority. After the BTB was prepared, the available time for planning was over, and even if the teacher had wanted to continue planning and to attend to more of the why related content and activities, time became a limiting factor. Once the silent reading segment of the afternoon was over, no additional time was available for the teacher to review or plan beyond the preparation of materials. The how and doing competed with what and why.

The following describes the daily planning session for the next lesson, the beginning of chapter 11:

> During silent reading Ms Ross sits down at her desk. She

gets out the 'Teacher's Guide' and looks at her lesson plan book. She looks at the bottom of the page (64) of the 'Teacher's Guide' (where the associated page from the student manual is reproduced). The student manuals for the sixth grade are behind Ms Ross on the book shelves. (She had collected them after the last exercise from Part Two, chapter 8.) Ms Ross gets up from her desk and moves the student manuals over to the demonstration table. She comments to me that all they have to do today is look at the results from yesterday and write it down. 'I think I will have them go back to this page 14 (from chapter 9) and have them do that. Some didn't finish.'

The daily lesson planning again primarily consisted of identification of activities to be done and preparing materials for the actual instruction.

Daily lesson planning for the teacher is intended to be the time during which she can attend to some of the other instructional concerns that she did not address during weekly planning. In actuality, however, the process is dominated by final material preparations. Furthermore, the daily planning process has to occur while the teacher must monitor another student activity and is defined within a limited time span. This is the only block of 'free time' the teacher has.

Synopsis. Several important features of Ms Ross's planning and orientation emerged from these analyses. First, the 'Teacher's Guide' was the only reference used in planning; and in referring to the 'Teacher's Guide', the teacher was usually looking for a specific kind of information. Secondly, the teacher typically sought the same kinds of information in the same order and the organisation and sequence of information in the 'Teacher's Guide' often did not correspond with that order. Thirdly, the teacher often experienced difficulties in finding information she sought, and planning was frequently sustained by means of recollections of having done the activities last year.

Ms Ross had, by necessity, to focus on preparing for activities, and the time required to do this used up her 'budget' of time. The management concerns which emerged from the activity basis of the course dominated her planning activity at the expense of other elements of the planning cycle implied by the 'Teacher's Guide'.

The Plan in Action

What did Ms Ross's plans look like in action? Having gone over the plans with her, we observed her teaching. In the following discussion we pursue our interest in the teacher's interpretation of the SCIS literal programme and particularly the teacher's orientation to only some elements of the cycle of instruction of the SCIS materials.

As we have seen, Ms Ross had identified activities, determined all material needs and completed preparations for chapter
10 ('Breath and BTB'). How was the lesson taught? The
following field notes describe the classroom activity for which
Ms Ross had prepared (See Figure 3.2 for a plan of her classroom.):

The first sixth-grade class begins to enter the classroom
while some of the fifth graders are cleaning up. Ms Ross is
still over in the table side of the room also putting materials
away. She still seems upset with the fifth graders not
having listened to her instructions and therefore not having
finished on time. (The major problem seemed to be too many
students trying to get materials from the same area – the
sink.)

Ms Ross moves to her desk. She seems to be looking for the
TG and can't find it. She goes back to the demonstration
table where she had made the BTB solution earlier and finds
it. She moves back to her desk and stands. The students
see her and become fairly quiet. She tells them they are
going to be starting a new part and will not be using their
terrariums but will be doing some experiments and using
some chemicals. The students seem very excited about this
and talk to each other. This excitement seems to make Ms
Ross happy and she tells them to move to the science tables.

The students move from their desks to their place at the
science tables – Ms Ross moves to the demonstration table.
She tells the students they are going to be doing an experiment with a chemical called BTB and they will be breathing
through it with straws. Again, the students seem excited
and start talking to each other.

Ms Ross calls the 'ones' to the demonstration table to get
the cups and the 'threes' to get the straws. After these
are distributed, Ms Ross tells them she will be coming
around to put the BTB solution into their cups. They should
then breathe through the straw to make bubbles in the BTB
and watch what happens.

Ms Ross then moves from table to table and fills each
student's cup about half full of BTB. The students then
begin to exhale through the straws and make bubbles. When
Ms Ross gets to the third table (out of four), the BTB starts
to change colour from some of the first students. There is a
lot of loud talking as the students call each other to see what
their BTB is changing to. Some students start trying to get
attention from others by humming through their straws as
they blow. Ms Ross tells them to stop and just watch and see
what happens. They do so.

Everyone's BTB has changed from blue to yellow. Ms Ross
then says: 'So, what happens? The BTB changes from blue
to yellow?' Some students say yes and a couple are describing

the change in more detail in terms of the colour change. Everyone is talking at the same time. Ms Ross says: 'All right. Now I am going to give you some tape to put your name on the cup and then we are going to put them over by the sink and look at them tomorrow.' She then passes out the tape and calls the tables one at a time to put their cups by the sink. She tells the 'twos' to use the sponge and make sure the tables are clear. When they are done they should move back to their desks.

This clean up is completed and the students move back to their desks.

The nature of her accomplishment deserves comment. The spectre of straws flying about the room and BTB spilling and staining clothes is very real for anyone who has experienced groups of students of this age. Yet none of this happened. Ms Ross accomplished what she had intended. The students had experienced and enjoyed 'hands-on' science. The students were business-like and on-task most of the time and the manipulations of materials and movements around the room were accomplished efficiently.

If we examine this portion of chapter 10 from the perspective of the literal programme, however, we note that while the first four activities were done, one activity was modified in a significant way. The 'Teacher's Guide' suggested an introduction in which some reference would be made to how to study the gases organisms give off and take in. In the lesson we observed, neither organisms nor gases were referred to. The introduction simply informed the students they would be 'breathing through' a 'chemical called BTB'. Here we see a what activity curtailed; an activity designed to give the students a clue to what the investigation is about.

In a subsequent presentation, the teacher explained that it was the carbon dioxide in the students' breath that had caused the change. However, all but one of the five remaining follow-up activities were omitted, including one that provides feedback on students' understanding by having them predict what would happen if they breathed through water first and then added the BTB. Also omitted were opportunities for students to make predictions and suggest controlled experiments for testing effects of variables.

As we observed Ms Ross's lessons, it became clear that the pattern of curtailing follow-up why activities and further what and doing activities continued into chapter 11 ('Where Did the Yellow Go?'). Actual instruction for the first half of the chapter followed the literal programme in many respects. The students observed that their BTB returned to a bluish colour overnight. Many of the students hypothesised that the carbon dioxide 'went out'. Several thought that temperature might have been involved. A few speculated that oxygen or air getting in might have caused the change. The students carried out experiments providing some evidence relevant to their hypotheses, but the discussion and interpretation of results was omitted. A few students recorded interpretation along with their results, but most did not. The student manuals did not ask for interpretation.

The curtailment of the activities in chapter 11 had important consequences, from a logical point of view, for student learning. The change back to blue (of BTB that has been made yellow by adding carbon dioxide) is an important observation that will be made on several occasions in later chapters. If students have an unclear interpretation of this change (that CO_2 has left the solution, they will be unable to properly interpret results of investigations of gas exchange in plants and animals.

Ms Ross's stress on procedural instructions at the expense of the development of ideas can also be seen in the transcript of a lesson in which she demonstrates the operation of a gas generator; the introductory activity in chapter 12. The relevant portion taken from the 'Teacher's Guide' precedes the transcript. [11]

Teaching Suggestions

Demonstrating the gas generator. To introduce this activity, set up a gas generator as follows:

(1)   Fill a plastic cup about half full of water and a vial one-quarter full of water.

(2)   Insert a plastic tube into the hole in the vial cap to a depth of about $1/4$ inch.

(3)   Drop one seltzer tablet into the vial of water and snap the cap on the vial (the open end of the tube should not touch the water).

Ask your students what is happening to the tablet. They should be aware that the tablet is bubbling as it dissolves. Now place the other end of the plastic tube into the cup of water. When the children see the gas bubbling through the water in the cup, ask them how they might test whether this gas contains carbon dioxide. They will probably suggest using BTB.

Children's experiments. Have the children pick up the materials they will need and begin the experiment.

Ms Ross: All right. I'm going to be showing you what we're going to be setting-up so you follow along (directions to put away social studies because of water, etc. . . .).

All right, I'm going to give you the instructions as to how you're going to do it. Then I expect you to follow . . . are you ready to listen? . . .

you can't follow very well if you are talking (two
students are talking). . . All right, you're
going to be given one of these cups, a vial that
has a hole in the cap, and a piece of tubing and
a couple of other items that you're going to be
using.

What you're going to do, first of all, is put the
tubing through this (she demonstrates putting
tube through cap hole). Now it's going to seem
like it doesn't fit at first, but just sort of squeeze
it through a little and then put it (the tube) down
so it's pretty close to the line on your vial; it
shouldn't go down below that. The other end will
go in here (the cup). This (the cup) is going to
be filled half full, about half way. The other (the
vial) will be filled about a quarter of the way.
This is the way it's going to be set up. Then
you're going to put this (the hose) down into it
(the cup) after you do another step. You will be
given one Alka Seltzer tablet (student giggles
and statements of 'plop-plop, fizz-fizz') and BTB
solution.

I'm sure you all know what we're going to be
testing for. . . . What are we going to be testing
for?

Students: . . . the blue in the vial, carbon dioxide. . .
             (inaudible)

Ms Ross: OK. Where are we going to put this BTB?

Students: In the big cup.

Ms Ross: In the big cup. What are we going to test for
             then?

Student: If the . . . . transferred. . . .Blue. . .

Ms Ross: Uh, there are too many people talking, I can
             only hear one or listen to one. Yes, David.

David: [12]   Carbon dioxide will come from the vial.

Ms Ross: OK, to see if there is carbon dioxide in here.
             Yeh, right, that is what you're going to be
             testing for. So, while one person is setting this
             up - getting the tube in here, getting the cup
             on - the other person is going to put twelve drops
             of this. Think you will remember that? (Wants to
             write 12 drops on the board, but doesn't have any
             chalk) Twelve drops. And this is really rather
             quick to do because you uncap this (the BTB
             bottle) - Mike, would you listen - then you are
             going to squeeze this carefully and count out -
             don't squeeze it too hard, you're going to get
             drops out of there, if you squeeze it too hard it's
             going to squirt out and you will have a mess on it
             and probably stain your clothes - so, I put two
             drops in there, but you will count up to twelve.

> Sometimes it takes a little while because air gets
> in there (she tries squeezing to get more drops
> and has some trouble). (Finishes adding the 12
> drops) OK, you can then mix it up (the solution)
> with the end of the hose. OK, I will bring around
> the Alka Seltzer tablet when you are ready for it.
> I will bring the water around to you too. Now,
> I am going to ask . . . (passes out cups to each
> pair of students and must relocate two students
> to have pairs). 'Twos' come up and get the vials
> (student movement and talking). 'Fours' come up
> and get the caps and the BTB. Do not open the
> BTB until I tell you.
> (from field notes 2-6, 27 November 1978)

The manner of actual instruction of chapter 12 is understandable when considered in the light of the conditions in which
Ms Ross plans. Her main concern appeared to be the students'
successful use of the materials and this required the teacher
and students to distribute the materials and assemble them
properly. Accomplishing these requirements was in itself quite
demanding! No directions regarding the assembly of the gas
generator are available in the student manual; this is all part
of the teacher's task. The directions provided by the teacher
included far more information about the assembly than was
indicated in the 'Teacher's Guide'.

The comments of the teacher in the post-instructional review
suggest why she chose to give such detail and emphasis:

> I did it intentionally (omitting demonstration of the Alka
> Seltzer). I guess I didn't want to get them involved in what
> they were going to do. I thought that I wanted them to know
> what process - what they had to do in getting the set up -
> that they would maybe get the instructions better if they're
> not distracted by this other stuff - what we're going to be
> using - because that was taking their minds off of maybe
> listening to the different parts and what they're going to do.
>   It seems very simple, but for kids, this is not simple. I
> think if I had brought in the fact that, okay, you're going
> to put some water into this vial and then you're going to
> put the cap on it too, they would have lost a lot of informa-
> tion along the way, because they would be so involved in
> getting that water in there and sort of forget what they
> have to do - Well, what do I (the students) do now? That
> was my attempt - (it) was to get that thing set up so they
> knew the parts and set it up.
> (Post-instructional review 27 November 1978)

The lesson which formed the conclusion of chapter 12 also
reflected the pattern of curtailment of follow-up we have
identified. Here again, the modification was one of orientation

and emphasis. The literal programme indicated discussion in which the students are to identify the bubbles and support their answers with evidence from the results of the gas generator demonstration. Furthermore, the discussion is to involve a comparison of the results from the demonstration with those from blowing breath through blue BTB solution. The discussion as it happened consisted of the following:

Ms Ross: OK. If you've had yours work now, your solution has turned yellow. You know there is the presence of what?

Several
students: Carbon dioxide.

(Students then clean up)

Ms Ross did not pursue the evidence that would support the claim made by the students. Her focus was on a successful completion of the experiment - doing it properly.

UNDERSTANDING MS ROSS'S PLANNING ORIENTATION

Conceptualising the Activities in Science

Ecological factors are not the only ones which appear to have influenced Ms Ross's planning and instructional activities. The following extract from her introduction to chapter 13 suggests that she did not understand the logical relationships amongst the experiments involving BTB. Her failure to attend to the logic of the experimental design (the 'why') left her apparently confused about the purpose of one of the experiments. The following excerpt, transcribed from her lesson, illustrates this problem. In this experiment, students watch what happens when carbon dioxide in soda-water passes into BTB and subsequently comes out of solution. Ms Ross seems to think that the set-up is simply another demonstration that BTB turns yellow in the presence of carbon dioxide:

Ms Ross: OK. Just to review a bit some of the things we have done over the past few days. You have been using the solution BTB and you have been trying all sorts of different things with it. What are some of the things we've been doing with it? Sue?

Sue: We put it in the vials and breathed through it. Then we did it again and put it in different places - some of us put it back there, some over there - (inaudible). Then we used it with Alka Seltzer and it turned another colour. . .

Ms Ross: Did it turn different kinds of colours or did it turn kind of the same reaction each time?

Tony: Yesterday it turned kind of an orange.

Ms Ross: (inaudible) . . . how did it change before?
Students: Turned green first.
Ms Ross: OK. Um, so those were the experiments. What were we trying to find out? What was the purpose of this? Erika?
Erika: To find out if there was carbon dioxide in the air.
Ms Ross;   In which air? In the room air or. . .
Erika: In the air we blew into it. In the air we exhale.
Ms Ross: The air exhaled. That's the air blowing in there. All right. Sue said you put the things away for a day and some changed and others did not. How did that happen?
Student: One was covered and one was not.
Ms Ross: That's a very important point to make isn't it. Whether it is covered or not covered. OK, today I'm going to see if I can try another experiment with BTB solution and uh, we will try it with this (holds up ginger ale bottle). (Long pause while the teacher arranges materials - the students talk about the ginger ale - and then the assembly of the materials begins)
(from field notes 28 November 1978)

This discussion explicitly illustrates an important point about understanding the logic of the subject matter to be instructed. Her questions focus student attention only on the colour change of BTB solution in the presence of carbon dioxide and on the fact that various reactions were consistent in changing from blue to green to yellow. The implication of her final comment was that this change was also what the new investigation was about, which it was not. Chapter 13, 'Soda Water and BTB', is an optional set of activities to be used with chapter 11 if students insist that the uncapped yellow BTB solution had changed back to blue because of some factor other than the release of carbon dioxide from solution.

However, Ms Ross had not dealt with the significance of the reverse colour change; hence the activity of chapter 13, a way of controlling for the possibility that oxygen in the air caused the yellow to blue change, was not relevant. Not having explored the meaning - the 'why' - of the observation herself, Ms Ross did not seem to appreciate the logic of the soda-water experiment, and why the system was isolated from the atmosphere.

The problem of communicating to teachers the logic of the experimental procedure can be seen in the way subsequent experiments involving the use of BTB were conducted. In chapter 14, the students are to use their knowledge of the interactions between BTB and carbon dioxide to conduct experiments on the production and use of gases by plants and animals. These investigations lead up to the 'invention' of the oxygen-carbon dioxide cycle. From the first investigation in chapter 14 students collect data which suggest that snails produce and plants (Anarchis) use carbon dioxide. The classroom events we observed reflected the pattern of planning for how and doing activities, but omitting or curtailing what and why discussion. The difficulties for students which resulted from this planning pattern can be seen in the way the second investigation in chapter 14 was conducted. In this investigation students collect data on the effect of light on the gas exchange of plants and animals. When this investigation was carried out, the results for gas exchange in the water plant (Anarchis) in the dark were ambiguous. The teacher encouraged the students to observe that BTB changed from green towards blue. The significance of the results was not discussed, and the results, as recorded, implied that plants always use carbon dioxide rather than this use being dependent on light. In other words, the ambiguous results were left as they were, suggesting, erroneously, that plants were capable of using carbon dioxide in the absence of light. The 'why' of the experiment was ignored here, leaving open the possibility of misconception.

The after school discussion with Ms Ross of the day's activity revealed that her conception differed from that addressed by the activities. In fact, she did not realise light was a significant variable for oxygen production and carbon dioxide uptake in plants. As a result she accepted as unproblematic experimental results which appeared to indicate that plants produce oxygen and use carbon dioxide in both light and dark conditions. This misconception resulted, in part, from poor printing in the 'Teacher's Guide'. Page 74 of the 'Teacher's Guide' contained an illustration of the oxygen-carbon dioxide cycle including reference to light and dark conditions. An arrow appears to indicate that plants release oxygen in the dark. This unclear printing, the teacher's lack of subject matter knowledge relating to this topic and her planning priorities contributed to her having an erroneous conception of the factual basis of this experiment.

The climax of the unit, the invention of the full oxygen-carbon dioxide cycle, including a discussion of gas exchange in the light and dark, was not included in her planning. However, a 'brain teaser' was assigned which assumed that students understood the differences between gas exchange in the light and in the dark. The students found this exercise confusing since they did not understand the differences.

A post-instructional interview during planning for chapter 15 dealt with the oxygen-carbon dioxide cycle as presented by the literal programme. Ms Ross said that she realised she ought to have covered more subject matter content than she had to that point, but that she had not been able to determine what it was from the 'Teacher's Guide'. She brought up this point; clearly it concerned her. The discussion about the subject matter had not been a comfortable session for the teacher.

As a consequence of her concern for covering additional subject matter content, the invention of the oxygen-carbon dioxide cycle through class discussion was done prior to starting on chapter 15. This went very poorly, with very little student contribution, as the transcript indicates:

Ms Ross: OK, we've been doing the experiment with the BTB - are you ready to listen now? - with the BTB solution with a snail and with a plant in the BTB solution and a control each time - to see what colour it changes and also we put some in the light and some in the dark. We did not have very dramatic changes in the - almost no change - with those in the light and those in the dark, but we put them - a few people put them - by the light - and we had more of a change. I asked my class (the second class) to put their Thursday's investigation, um, by the light, and they looked at them Friday and they had a change much like what Tony and Peter had with theirs. What happened with your Anarchis?

Peter: When it was by the light, turned back to blue.

Ms Ross: It turned blue when it was right close to the light. So it's possible that the ones we did the other day and put on the table here did not have as much light as that one had because we do not leave these lights on overnight. The others did not have as much light over there (on the table) so we did see a lot more change than the others and my class overnight noticed the same kind of results - that the Anarchis turned blue, so, in other words, what is this telling us? (eight-second pause) If the plant changes from green to blue in the light - what is there the presence of?

Peter: Takes in carbon dioxide and gives off oxygen.

Ms Ross: All right. Did anyone have their plant turn blue when it was in the dark? (pause) Did it change? Did it remain green in other words? Like you put it in?

Peter: Got lighter?

Ms Ross: Did it give off carbon dioxide then? (long pause, teacher moves back to demonstration table and looks at the 'Teacher's Guide') Or, excuse me, yeh, right, I'm getting myself turned around. Um, it's um, then it gives off, uh, then it gave off carbon dioxide - or take in carbon dioxide is what I'm trying to say. . . that's what we're working on. (uneasy, nervous laughter by students)

Peter: Problem with the fifth graders (the class previous to this one)? Were they bad again?

Ms Ross: Yes, they were a little restless again - some of
them. OK, so that changed? You said the ones
that were in the, uh, dark stayed green. And
the Anarchis in the light we had more of the blue
here in my class then. So we did have more of
a change after we tried the difference. So, are
the plants doing the same thing in the light as
they do in the dark? (very low voice, almost
inaudible) Yes, they are.
(from field notes 11 December 1978)

This discussion illustrates the teacher's continued confusion
about the subject matter content. The confusion at this point
resulted in the teacher actually presenting incorrect content.
The problem here was not that the teacher had not planned to
look at the 'why' of the activities but that she was confused
about what was to be understood. Facts, not lack of time, were
the problem here.

The next day, prior to engaging in the start of chapter 15,
the first science class reviewed the previous activities, their
results and conclusion. Chapter 15 is the last chapter in Part
Three and is a set of activities designed for the students to
'discover' that the oxygen-carbon dioxide cycle applies to
terrestrial plants as well as to aquatic plants. The investigation
activities, therefore, are almost identical to the ones from
chapter 14. The students place blue BTB solution in an enclosed
environment with a terrestrial plant. Some of the set-ups are
to be placed in the dark and some in light.

As the students in the first class were preparing the materials
for the investigation, one of the students asked the teacher
why the BTB solution they were to use was blue instead of
green. No response was given to the student as the teacher was
busy directing students using materials. The teacher indicated
during the post-instructional interview that she had heard the
student, between classes had reread the 'Teacher's Guide', and
then had realised that the reaction of plants relating to the
oxygen-carbon dioxide cycle is different, depending on whether
they are in light or dark. The discussion in the second class
also reviewed the previous activities prior to starting chapter
15, and included the idea that plants produce oxygen in the
light and carbon dioxide in the dark. The purpose of chapter
15's investigation was also made clearer.

During the final part of Part Three students were asked to
observe the results of the previous day's investigation and to
see that terrestrial plants also produce carbon dioxide in the
dark. The teacher realised the previous day's discussion in
the first class did not address the dependence of the gas
production of plants on whether light is present or not. Therefore, the invention and discussion of the oxygen-carbon dioxide
cycle was repeated. Again the discussion was awkward, the
teacher having difficulty forming questions, and the students

contributing little to it. The bulk of the discussion involved a review of previous investigation results and the development of the idea that plants produce oxygen in the light.

Patterns of Modification

Many of the teacher's modifications of Part Three concerned the subject matter. Two forms of modification were observed. First, there was a lack of attention to facts other than that blue BTB solution changes to yellow in the presence of carbon dioxide. The investigations which were done in chapters 10 to 13 produced results from which additional ideas could have been developed, but were not. Secondly, instruction involved very little consideration of any systems other than the interaction between blue BTB solution and carbon dioxide. In the work of chapters 14 and 15, when new ideas were developed, their relationship to the results of previous investigations was not developed. Thus the result of the teacher's modifications of the literal programme was a lack of provision for student understanding of the subject matter content, as indicated by the nature of student participation in discussions and the difficulty they had subsequently in answering student manual questions, predictions and problems.

At this point we should take stock of where our analysis had led. The comparative analysis suggested that Ms Ross's orientation was towards planning manipulative (doing) and procedural (how) activities, and away from introductory (what) and follow-up (why) discussion activities. In the last section we saw how this orientation to planning affected classroom events. There we saw that limited time and problems of understanding the conceptual basis of the experiments led to the potential for student misunderstanding. However, there is another side to the teacher's planning orientation, namely, the attention she gave to student success in accomplishing the manipulative activities themselves. It is to an appreciation of the sources of success in this dimension and problems in the conceptual dimension that we now turn.

Planning Frames

Our interpretation of Ms Ross's planning activity and instruction is based on the idea that it was guided by the sequential application of a series of mental structures or 'frames', a construct used by Minsky and others [13, 14] in explaining comprehension of text and discourse (see Figure 3.4). Each frame constitutes a functional unit of the teacher's basic knowledge which has certain 'slots' for information to be filled in during the planning process. The 'activity' frame Ms Ross used for SCIS, as far as we can tell, held that the science programme consists of sequences of student activities organised into chapters in the 'Teacher's Guide', and that each chapter has

Figure 3.4.   Postulated Frames Underlying Ms Ross's Planning

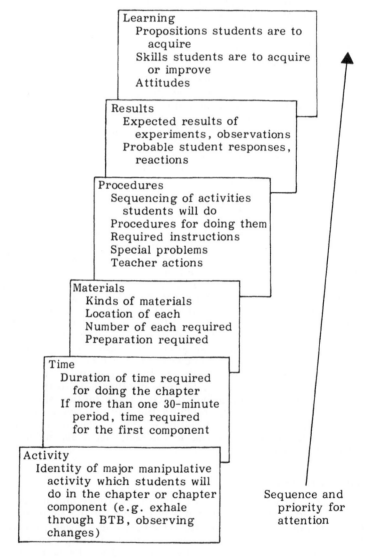

Learning
   Propositions students are to
      acquire
   Skills students are to acquire
      or improve
   Attitudes

Results
   Expected results of
      experiments, observations
   Probable student responses,
      reactions

Procedures
   Sequencing of activities
      students will do
   Procedures for doing them
   Required instructions
   Special problems
   Teacher actions

Materials
   Kinds of materials
   Location of each
   Number of each required
   Preparation required

Time
   Duration of time required
      for doing the chapter
   If more than one 30-minute
      period, time required
      for the first component

Activity
   Identity of major manipulative
      activity which students will
      do in the chapter or chapter
      component (e.g. exhale
      through BTB, observing
      changes)

Sequence and
priority for
attention

one or more major manipulative activities which constitute what
the chapter is about. In planning, this activity frame guided
Ms Ross's selective use of the information in the 'Teacher's
Guide', and she remembered what were the classroom features
of the next - major - manipulative activity. Using this model
we hypothesise that teacher planning can be viewed, in part,
as a form of text comprehension; what the teacher gets out of
the 'text' ('Teacher's Guide') is highly dependent on the
quality and nature of the frames applied.

The orientation of Ms Ross towards emphasis on how and
doing activities can be explained, in part, by the nature of
her planning frames. The low priority given the results and
learning frames is reflected in their position in the sequence
and the fact that her planning never got that far in the time
she had available. The what and why activities are much more
dependent on the 'results' and 'learning' frames, that is, on
an understanding of the logic of the activities, than are the
how and doing activities. Given Ms Ross's reluctance to use
the 'results' and 'learning' frames in her planning, possibly
because of her limited knowledge of the subject, we can understand the attention given to other, more functional, planning
frames. However, these planning priorities are themselves
something to be explained.

Part of the explanation for Ms Ross's preference for 'reliable'
frames may be in the nature of the 'Teacher's Guide' itself,
considered as a form of communication between innovator and
teacher. It is not clear to what extent the nature of the
'Teacher's Guide' influenced the frames Ms Ross used in
planning. However, it is clear that the organisation and
content of the 'Teacher's Guide' was not well matched to her
planning, which focused on steps to be taken to get ready
for the activities which she had decided would be completed
in the next one or two lessons. Information useful in developing
'activity', 'time', 'materials' and 'procedures' frames was
available in the 'Teacher's Guide' in an intelligible form. The
guide spoke about things Ms Ross was concerned about in an
organised manner useful to her. The same could not be said
about the 'results' and 'learning' frames.

Information about time and materials was usually easy for Ms
Ross to obtain since it was provided in special locations.
Information about the procedures was also relatively easy for
her to obtain since these were described sequentially in the
text. However, neither the expected results of activities nor
the learning students might be expected to achieve were consistently presented along with the corresponding procedures,
nor were they to be consistently found in any other particular
location. Information presented as 'objectives' was typically
too general or incomplete.

Critical information about student learning was located in
various places, including 'background' sections of the chapters
of Part Three. The location and organisation of the information

about student learning made it necessary for Ms Ross on her own to try to correlate activities with statements about learning outcomes. This difficulty was compounded, in her case, because her understanding of the subject matter was limited. Given the added constraint of time on the planning for science, it is perhaps not surprising that the 'results' and 'learning' frames were not developed by Ms Ross, who would have had to track down relevant information in the 'Teacher's Guide' and then have attempted to make sense of it.

Planning Frames and Curricular Guides

While the pattern of her planning, and its consequences in the classroom, were problematical for us, and to some extent at least for Ms Ross, the reasonableness of her practice became clearer to us as we better understood her situation. She had found from previous experience that managing manipulative materials with small groups was a complicated matter, and that failure to attend adequately to a variety of management concerns resulted in an intolerable situation in which behaviour problems abounded and little learning could take place. In response to this challenge we think she used management procedures – routines, which enabled her classes to carry out small group manipulative activities in an efficient, businesslike manner in the time available and with the materials she had. The students as a consequence experienced and enjoyed hands-on science.

Information about the routines of classroom organisation and management is absent from the 'Teacher's Guide'. As we began to appreciate functions of Ms Ross's classroom system, with its attention to time, materials and procedures, her planning priorities became much more understandable.

With our appreciation of the management skill of this experienced elementary school teacher, we were left with a strong desire to find a way to help Ms Ross improve the effectiveness of her science teaching. Much of what she was doing seemed successful; so the answers we might propose did not seem to involve throwing out the whole programme and starting again. Rather, we felt quite sure that some adjustments in her use of this programme could lead to major improvement. In particular, we felt that much could be done to improve the usefulness of the 'Teacher's Guide' and the effectiveness of her planning from it.[15] The direction for such improvement derived from our understanding of the use of the guide in planning. We tried to construct such an improved guide. Our first informal attempt to test this idea met with mixed results. In a revised guide for Part Three, prepared for Ms Ross, we attempted to include explicit information for all her planning frames, organised in a manner we hoped would help her to integrate the information relevant to each lesson. While some ambiguities were immediately resolved, in many cases our efforts to help simply added too much information to be useful. A revision which preserved the organisational scheme while being more selective and parsimonious seemed to help. Given the importance of a guide capable of communicating effectively with teachers, we would urge further research into how elementary teachers use science programme materials, and consideration of the feasibility of improvement of elementary science teaching through improvement of the teachers' guides and their use in planning.

NOTES

1. T. Bredderman, Process Curricula in Elementary School Science, 'Evaluation in Education', vol. 4 (1980), pp. 43-4.
2. H. Pratt, Science Education in the Elementary School in N.C. Harms and R.E. Yager (eds.), 'What Research Says to the Science Teacher' (National Science Teachers Association, Washington, DC 1981), pp. 73-93.
3. C.M. Clark and R.Y. Yinger, Teachers' Thinking in P.L. Peterson and H.J. Walberg (eds.), 'Research on Thinking' (McCutchan, Berkeley, Calif., 1979), pp. 321-63.
4. SCIS, 'Ecosystems - Teachers' Guide' (Rand McNally and Company, Berkeley, Calif., 1971).
5. L.S. Shulman and A.S. Elstein, Studies of Problem Solving, Judgment, and Decision-making: Implications for Educational Research, 'Review of Research in Education', vol. 3 (1975), pp. 3-43.
6. L. Schatzman, A.L. Strauss and L. Anselm, 'Field Research; Strategies for a Natural Sociology' (Prentice-Hall, Engelwood Cliffs, NJ, 1973).
7. SCIS, 'Ecosystems - Teachers' Guide', p. 61.
8. Ms Ross is a pseudonym to preserve the anonymity of the co-operating teacher.
9. C. Morin, 'Special Study C, A Study of Teacher Planning' (BTES Technical Report 76-31-1) Far West Laboratory for Educational Research and Development, San Francisco, 1976).
10. E.L. Smith and N.B. Sendelbach, 'Teacher Intentions for Science Instruction and their Antecedents in Program Materials' (paper presented at the annual meeting of the American Educational Research Association, San Francisco, April 1979).
11. SCIS, 'Ecosystems - Teachers' Guide', p. 66.
12. All names of students are pseudonyms to preserve their anonymity.
13. M. Minsky, A Framework for Representing Knowledge in P.H. Winston (ed.), 'The Psychology of Computer Vision' (McGraw-Hill, New York, 1975).
14. T. van Dijk, Semantic Macro-Structures and Knowledge Frames in Discourse Comprehension in M. Just and P. Carpenter (eds.), 'Cognitive Processes in Comprehension'

(Wiley, New York, 1977).
15. For other work in this area see, for example, I.B. Harris, Effective Communication for Guiding Practitioners (paper presented at the annual meeting of the American Educational Research Association, Los Angeles, April, 1981). See also, D.C. Anderson, Systematic and Modest Schemes for Health Education in Schools in D.C. Anderson (ed.), 'The Ignorance of Social Intervention' (Croom Helm, London, 1980).

BIBLIOGRAPHY

Anderson, D.C. (ed.), 'The Ignorance of Social Intervention' (Croom Helm, London, 1980).
Bredderman, T. Process Curricula in Elementary School Science, 'Evaluation in Education', vol. 4 (1980), pp. 43-4.
Clark, C.M. and Yinger, R.J. Teachers' Thinking in P.L. Peterson and H.J. Walberg (eds.), 'Research on Thinking' (McCutchan, Berkeley, Calif., 1979).
Harris, I.B. Effective Communication for Guiding Practitioners (paper presented at the annual meeting of the American Educational Research Association, Los Angeles, April 1981).
Minsky, M. A Framework for Representing Knowledge in P.H. Winston (ed.), 'The Psychology of Computer Vision' (McGraw-Hill, New York, 1975).
Morin, C. 'Special Study C, A Study of Teacher Planning' (BTES Technical Report 76-31-1) Far West Laboratory for Educational Research and Development, San Francisco, 1976).
Schatzman, L., Strauss, A.L. and Anselm, L. 'Field Research; Strategies for a Natural Sociology' (Prentice-Hall, Engelwood Cliffs, NJ, 1973).
SCIS, 'Ecostystems - Teachers' Guide' (Rand McNally and Company, Berkeley, Calif., 1971).
Shulman, L.S. and Elstein, A.S. Studies of Problem Solving, Judgment, and Decision-making: Implications for Educational Research, 'Review of Research in Education', vol. 3 (1975), pp. 3-43.
Smith, E.L. Assessing Propositional Knowledge: Children's Conceptions of the Oxygen-Carbon Dioxide Cycle (paper presented at the annual meeting of the American Educational Research Association, Boston, 1980).
Smith, E.L. and Sendelbach, N.B. 'Development and Tryout of the Science Teacher Planning Simulation System' (Michigan State University, All University Research Initiation Grant, Final Report, December 1977).
——. 'Teacher Intentions for Science Instruction and Their Antecedents in Program Materials' (paper presented at the annual meeting of the American Educational Research Association, San Francisco, April 1979).

4 COSTS AND REWARDS OF INNOVATION: TAKING ACCOUNT OF THE TEACHERS' VIEWPOINT

Sally Brown and Donald McIntyre

REFORMING SCOTTISH EDUCATION: THE CASE OF INTEGRATED SCIENCE

The research on which this chapter is based[1] was initially concerned with factors that influence the way curriculum innovations are implemented. The research questions were asked from the perspective of policy makers and curriculum planners, not from that of teachers. During the course of our research on innovations in schools, however, we found that what we were studying led us not only to try to understand the ways in which teachers responded to the proposed innovations, but also to use our understanding of teachers' perspectives as a standpoint from which to criticise assumptions underlying curriculum planning and implementation strategies. There was thus a tension within our research. On the one hand, it was sponsored by those who wanted to know how to be more effective in leading teachers to implement the innovations they proposed, and it was planned in order to answer such questions. On the other hand, instead of taking proposed innovations for granted and questioning the ways in which these were handled in the schools, it came increasingly to be grounded on teachers' ways of thinking and working, and to question innovative procedures and proposals. The tension is apparent in this chapter.

The framework for the chapter is provided by an account of a set of innovations which Scottish science teachers were asked to implement, and by a consideration of the various factors which have influenced the extent and manner of their use in schools. Within that framework, however, we will use our understanding of how teachers' think about their work to develop a critique of rational curriculum planning and to make proposals for improving the process of curriculum change.

The chapter begins with a general outline of the nature and context of the Scottish Integrated Science scheme and its innovative characteristics. We then describe how the teachers reacted to the innovative proposals. The differences in teachers' and planners' priorities lead us to consider relationships between the nature of proposals for change, science teachers' problems and aspirations, and the nature of support for innovation. In the final section we summarise our findings, using a framework of 'costs' and 'rewards' to the teacher, and contrast the goal of leading teachers to implement specific innovations with that of helping teachers to become self-critical decision makers about their own teaching.

The theory necessary in order to explain what happens when a particular innovation is attempted in a specific context must, we believe, be both eclectic and also adapted to the unique configuration of distinctive individuals, social setting and proposed innovation. Thus there is no tidy theoretical structure which pervades our discussion. Our thinking has, however, been helped especially by Schwab's 'The Practical: A Language for Curriculum'[2] and Doyle and Ponder's 'The Practicality Ethic in Teacher Decision Making'.[3] We see considerable relevance to our discussion in Schwab's thesis of the need to divert attention in the field of curriculum from narrowly 'theoretic' pursuits to those of the 'practical', the 'quasi-practical' and the 'eclectic'; and also in the analytic framework of Doyle and Ponder that proposes the perceived 'practicality' of a change as the crucial element in a teacher's decision to adopt and implement that change. 'Practicality' depends on instrumentality (realistic, clear, relevant procedural guidance), congruence (with existing practices, classroom conditions and the teacher's self-image) and costs (the ratio of investment to return for the teacher).

In one sense, Scottish Integrated Science has been a remarkable example of success in curriculum development. It has been adopted by 80 per cent of secondary schools in Scotland[4] and has been adapted for use in the Caribbean, Asia and Africa.[5] However, the extent to which the intended classroom innovations have been <u>implemented</u> is, as we shall see, rather more modest.

Scottish Integrated Science was not a product of a curriculum project but developed within the continuous process of curriculum reform that characterises the relatively centralised education system in Scotland. In 1964 the Secretary of State for Scotland set up a Working Party that met over a period of five years and devised a common course in science for all pupils in the first two years of secondary school (12 to 14 years of age). This was published as 'Curriculum Paper 7'[6] by the Scottish Education Department.

The Scottish educational system is relatively small; there are fewer than 450 secondary schools with less than half a million pupils. Although the curriculum is not legally controlled, the development, dissemination and evaluation of courses, the organisation of in-service work and the training of teachers is in the hands of a limited group of influential people. This has the advantages that committees can be set up with ease in response to perceived problems, that national educational policies and the suggestions made for change by these committees are almost always mutually supportive, and that communication and continuity among the various parts of the system are ensured. These are advantages, of course, only if it is seen as desirable to have a school system which

reflects the concerns and values of an elite group. Even if
this is seen as desirable, problems remain; curriculum development is carried out by people who have: other full-time jobs;
a vested interest in retaining the status quo of other aspects
of the system; pressures upon them to 'get into print' quickly;
and little opportunity for reading specialised literature. These
characteristics of the system are not conducive to the development on the part of curriculum planners of sensitivity to the
factors which make change in classrooms difficult. While adoption of educational reforms may be achieved quickly through a
centre-periphery mechanism, they are likely, in practice, to
be superficially implemented in schools. This is one of the
points that will be developed in this chapter.

   With these introductory comments about the developmental
background of Integrated Science in mind, we can now turn to
the nature of the innovative ideas the scheme urged upon
teachers.

   The Working Party which produced 'Curriculum Paper 7'
recommended innovations in four broad areas of science
teaching:

(1) a common course in science with mixed ability classes;
(2) the presentation of science in an integrated form;
(3) the use of guided-discovery teaching methods; and
(4) the planning of teaching and learning in terms of
     pupils' achievement of specified objectives.

   The introduction of a common course for mixed ability groups
reflects political pressure of the late 1960s to end the divisive
system of selection of pupils for academic and non-academic
schools or streams. 'Curriculum Paper 7' did not attempt to
justify this change, but assumed that mixed ability teaching
in comprehensive schools was a reality that must be taken
account of. A set of worksheets was prepared to cope with
the realities of mixed ability teaching. The worksheets were
extensively used but their adequacy for the task of individualisation, and appropriateness for the least able pupils,
were doubted by many teachers. This led to schools attempting
to modify the published sheets and later to the establishment
of a new Working Party whose task it was to reformulate groups
of objectives for each section of the course and to produce new
worksheets in order to take account of different levels of pupil
ability. The new materials were published in 1977. [7]

   The integrated subject matter appears to have been largely
determined by two practical constraints: first, that a minimum
of new equipment for the schools be demanded and, secondly,
that the content should be an acceptable base for later certificate work in the separate sciences. In fact, the integrated
science syllabus corresponds very closely indeed to an aggregate of the alternative biology, chemistry and physics schemes
for the first two years of certificate work in those subjects.

The promotion of guided-discovery methods reflected an awareness of competing theories of learning, and 'Curriculum Paper 7' reflects a compromise between arguments for discovery learning and programmed learning, both of which found support in the Working Party. However, in the absence of a clear conceptualisation of the nature of guided-discovery or general directions on how it should be used, it was not easy, as we shall see, for science teachers to implement these methods.

The introduction of broad aims, general objectives (for knowledge and understanding, attitudes and practical skills) and specific objectives for each unit of content, implies a commitment to a rational model of curriculum planning where the objectives for pupils' learning form the bedrock upon which the course content, practical work and assessment are founded. However, the nature of the linkages between these various aspects of the course were not made explicit in 'Curriculum Paper 7' and Jeffrey,[8] a member of the Working Party, reports that the general objectives were developed after the content was selected. Since the content was the familiar material of the separate science courses, it is not clear why the Working Party expected that teachers would abandon their accustomed practices of covering the content and constructing their tests in relation to it but, instead, start to think about their teaching in terms of pupils' attainment of specified objectives.

INTEGRATED SCIENCE IN PRACTICE: PRIORITIES AND CONFUSIONS

Conflict over Priorities

An attempt was made to ensure the involvement of science teachers in the planning of the Integrated Science scheme through representation on the Working Party. School science teachers formed the largest group (seven) among all those who served, although they were never in a majority. Of the others (five science inspectors, two College of Education lecturers and two science advisers), the inspectors traditionally exerted the strongest influence on the curriculum, particularly through their former control of the national certificate examinations. It appears that the presence of the teachers was expected to ensure that the deliberations of the Working Party would reflect the practical concerns of those who would have to implement the innovations in the classroom. In this respect the strategy seems to have had very limited success, judging from what teachers said to us during a series of group interviews conducted with the science staffs of 50 secondary schools. In fact, we identified a sharp division between the concerns of the Working Party as presented in 'Curriculum Paper 7' and those expressed by the science teachers.

The Working Party gave substantial attention to the demands that society makes of education for the provision of trained

scientists, a political leadership that appreciates the capabilities
and limitations of science and a scientifically informed lay population. 'Curriculum Paper 7' presented the course as a way of
developing 'awareness of the culture which is science' and 'an
ability to solve problems and think scientifically', and as a means
of providing pupils with exposure to 'many aspects of the work
of the scientist' and with 'many opportunities for discussing such
cultural implications'. [10]

A second focus of attention was on the nature of science.
'Curriculum Paper 7' argued that 'science must somewhere be
seen as a whole', and that presenting it in an integrated form
would help make clear the 'unity of science', the general
methodology of the scientist and the 'fundamental concepts
and ways of scientific thought'. In a similar way, guided-
discovery was suggested as an appropriate teaching strategy
because 'science is a subject admirably suited to discovery
methods'. [11]

For their part, the science teachers we interviewed scarcely
mentioned either society's concerns or the nature of science
(although a minority did argue that guided-discovery methods
were not appropriate exemplars of the scientific method). Their
attention was given primarily to questions of whether or not the
innovations provided the opportunity and conditions for the
teacher to do an effective and satisfying job. Would their training and competence be adequate? Would the substance of the
innovation reflect their own specialisms, skills and interests
and so be rewarding to teach? To what extent were they being
asked to put considerable effort into changing their familiar
and preferred ways of teaching in order to achieve something
they did not regard as valuable?

The majority of arguments of this type suggested that the
teachers took a sceptical view of the new scheme. For example:
they were hesitant about their ability to teach an integrated
course that took them outside the specialist areas in which
they had been trained; they considered it unlikely that they
could present the whole range of the material in an interesting
form; they doubted their ability to teach using guided-discovery;
they were concerned about the discipline problems that they
saw accompanying such methods and about the implications of
the wide range of ability and pace of working among pupils in
mixed ability classes. However, there were also some favourable
reactions to the innovations: teachers appreciated the opportunity to broaden their own knowledge and to have the increased
contact with pupils afforded by the integrated scheme (they
emphasised the greater interest for the teacher in taking a few
groups of pupils through the whole course rather than repeating
the same specialist lesson again and again); and considerable
advantages were seen in mixed ability grouping as providing
opportunities to diagnose pupils' relative abilities and to avoid
teaching all those with learning and/or behaviour problems in
the same class.

In contrast with the teachers we interviewed, the Working Party put little emphasis on the conditions that are required for effective teaching. They commented on the increased number of periods of contact that the teacher would have with any group of pupils (in comparison with science organised as single subjects), and suggested that this would reduce the time needed for revision and would facilitate valid assessments of pupils. They also argued that the worksheets developed in association with the course would provide a resource that would enable teachers to deal more effectively with mixed ability groups.

However, they did not examine in any detail the issue of the limitations that the subject specialisms of the teachers' training were likely to impose on their teaching of integrated science. They restricted themselves to stating that:

As teachers therefore we still, too often, see ourselves as chemists or physicists or biologists first and scientists second. The Working Party has felt, nevertheless, that the curriculum should be framed for the pupils' benefit rather than the teacher's convenience and that somewhere the unity of science should be made clear. [12]

Besides their concern about teaching the scheme, teachers were also worried about the extent to which their attempts to innovate would be constrained by the resources available to them. The Working Party's comments about resources were limited to the justifications for the course in terms of its more effective use of time and its provision of worksheets to encourage individualisation of work for pupils in mixed ability classes. The comments made by the teachers tended to reflect the particular resource constraints experienced in their own schools. Teachers in schools with problems of staff shortage and low time allocations for science viewed integration with favour; teachers beset with difficulties of dispersed science accommodation or of inadequate systems of equipment distribution favoured single subject teaching and storage systems that clearly identified apparatus as the property of biology, chemistry or physics.

A considerable amount of the general hostility towards guided-discovery was expressed in terms of the limited amount of time available, lack of materials, inadequate accommodation or equipment and staff shortages which, when compounded together, ruled out serious consideration of the methods for most people. In contrast with the negative attitudes towards guided-discovery methods there was general support for the Working Party's enthusiasm for individualisation of tasks. However, the suggestion that the worksheets provided an adequate resource that would free the teacher from the need to deal with the whole class at once, so that he could give his attention to individuals or small groups, make provision for different rates of working and different levels of understanding and make available additional exercises for the more able to try out their developing creativity, was denied by the teachers. They saw them as an insufficient basis for programmes of individual work.

Why should it be that a Working Party with a substantial block of science teachers involved in the planning exercise should have produced a document whose priorities so little reflected those of the great majority of teachers? Several factors are likely to have contributed to this. First, the Working Party was not simply a group of representative individuals who came together to discuss their diverse ideas of what a science curriculum for the early years of secondary school should be like. On the contrary, its members were recruited according to criteria which would tend to ensure their acceptability to the Scottish Education Department in general, and to the science inspectorate in particular. Thus the teacher members were likely to be people who had already attracted the approval of the science inspectors, and would, therefore, tend to be people showing a sympathy for the ideas which the inspectors wanted at that time to promote; but they would not necessarily express views that were representative of those of the majority of science teachers.

Recruitment of a teacher to the Working Party depends on his or her visibility, which means either occupying a senior teaching position or manifesting those publicly impressive qualities likely to lead to promotion to such a position. Those recruited were ambitious and professionally upwardly mobile people; by the end of the life of the Working Party, five of the seven 'teacher' members occupied senior administrative positions, e.g. headteacher, within the school system. On the one hand, the priorities of people in such positions, or hoping soon to be in such positions, would be likely to emphasise political and administrative issues rather than the practicalities of classroom teaching. On the other hand, membership clearly contributes substantially to teachers' chances of promotion, so that in nominating a teacher for membership the inspectorate is exercising powerful patronage; and, if this is so, it would be unreasonable to expect teacher members to adopt positions markedly different from those of their patrons.

An important factor likely to influence the pattern of working of the Working Party was the differences in other commitments among the members. Whereas the teacher members could only give time to the issues under consideration when not engaged in their full-time jobs, the working conditions of inspectors, advisers and lecturers would enable them to devote a considerable amount of their time to the Working Party's business. The non-teacher members would, therefore, tend to control agendas and to be able to produce well-prepared ideas and arguments, and thereby tend to place teachers at the margin of the Working Party's proceedings.

Finally, given that the Working Party's deliberations started
from new ideas for the structuring and teaching of science
courses, the teacher members would be unlikely to have had
any experience of the practical problems involved in implementing
such ideas; so that even if they were concerned about such
problems, they would not be able to speak with any authority
about them. Only by trying out the ideas in practice could there
be a basis for such authoritative expression of concerns. Yet
the theory-into-practice approach which was adopted was not
conducive to such practical trial of the Working Party's ideas.
By the time materials had been developed for trial in the
schools, after several years, the members of the Working Party
had invested so much of themselves in the project that they
were understandably interested only in perfecting these
materials, not in questioning the ideas underlying them.

For these various reasons, it is not surprising that the
deliberations of the Working Party were dominated by the
concerns of non-teacher members and especially by those of
the science inspectors. That they should have been so apparently unconcerned with the practicalities of teaching may
perhaps be understood, at least in part, in terms of their
institutional position. On the one hand, they are recruited to
the inspectorate partly because they are seen to be outstandingly
able and articulate science teachers; they are in regular contact with science teachers in Scottish schools, with academics
and teacher educators, and with science educationists from
other countries; thus they are exceptionally well suited to
provide leadership in the development of science curricula
and teaching. On the other hand, they are officials of the
Scottish Education Department, a branch of central government which, through its close collaboration with such other
bodies as the Consultative Committee on the Curriculum and
the Scottish Certificate of Education Examination Board, exercises an inevitably conservative hegemony over the Scottish
school system.

Accordingly, science inspectors in Scotland have displayed
an exciting radicalism in relation to ideas about their subject
specialisms combined with extreme conservatism with regard to
the institutional frameworks of the education system. In
particular, they are not prepared to challenge the universities
or the Scottish Certificate of Education Examination Board in
the furtherance of educational ideas that they believe in. In
this case, it can be argued that the success of the proposed
innovations was dependent on undermining the Examination
Board's control (through their separate biology, chemistry
and physics courses) of the first two years of secondary
science. But that was out of the question and the most obvious
constraint on the whole exercise was the requirement that the
content of the new course be equivalent to that of the three
separate subjects. So, despite the creative statements about
presenting science in a unified form, the course emerged as an

aggregate of the three familiar elements. The certificate
courses are, in turn, subjected to considerable control from
the Scottish Universities Council on Entrance and the inspectorate makes a substantial effort to avoid confrontation with
this academic body. Since innovations that relate to radical
new educational ideas have to give priority to considerations
of how to interlock with these existing administrative and
institutional frameworks, it is not surprising that scant
attention is paid to teachers' classroom problems (many of
which are associated with those pupils who will never be given
the chance to sit a Certificate examination, let alone enter
university).

It may be the case that substantial, coherent curriculum
innovations of the sort that have been attempted in this context cannot be formulated from the starting point of teachers'
classroom problems. The resolution of practical difficulties is
a purposeful activity but unless it is carried out within a
general strategy for achieving some well articulated educational goal, it will probably consist of a series of tactical man-
oeuvres, largely unrelated to each other and without a distinctly
innovative theme. Certainly, our evidence on teachers' concerns
in evaluating proposed innovations suggests that, as yet,
Scottish science teachers are too concerned with their own and
their pupils' immediate problems and satisfactions to attend to
the 'big ideas' of science or to relationships between scientific
education and political, economic and cultural issues facing
society. At least so long as that continues to be the case, it is
surely appropriate that innovations relating to such matters
should originate outside the school. To be effective, however,
any innovation strategy would then have to move quickly to a
dialogue with teachers that focuses on their concerns; and
it appears that the inclusion of teachers as members of a
Working Party will not necessarily ensure that this dialogue
takes place.

Rather than leaving this matter on a negative conclusion,
we should ask briefly whether our case study throws any
light on the conditions which would be necessary for such
fruitful dialogue. There are three debilitating circumstances
which we have noted in the Working Party arrangement which
might well be reversed:

(a) Marginality. It was postulated that teachers' concerns
    would not adequately be represented in Working Party
    discussions because of their marginal position, and also
    because of the dependent status of teacher members. A
    necessary condition for effective account to be taken of
    teachers' concerns is that teachers should be core
    members of a planning group and that there should be
    recognition of their expert status as curriculum planners
    because of their teaching experience.
(b) Lack of Practical Experience. It was also postulated that

teachers would not be able to express their concerns with any authority if they did not have practical experience in working in accordance with the new proposed ideas. If this is so, a second necessary condition would be that teachers should have had, or should be given, the opportunity to try out new proposals at an early stage in their development, and before decisions are made to adopt these ideas.

(c)   Orthodoxy. Thirdly, it was postulated that commitment to a generalised orthodoxy was not conducive to the expression of teachers' concerns. Although some such commitment to the predetermined purposes of the innovation would be necessary, a clear distinction would be possible and necessary between these purposes and the means by which they could be realised, with no prior commitments being expected in relation to the latter. In the Working Party arrangement, the commitment to orthodoxy extended to an assumption that agreement could and should be reached on a single course plan and a uniform set of recommended innovations. The opportunity for, and welcoming of, diversity might be a third condition which would facilitate the incorporation of teachers' concerns into curriculum planning.

The provision of such conditions may be exemplified by a report of teacher-centred curriculum planning in an Israeli project. [13] In this project, the status and centrality of teachers was assured by the fact that the non-teacher 'experts' associated with it were not members of the planning groups, but acted rather as external advisers, and by the fact that teachers received official recognition of the importance of their contribution in the tangible form of extra payment for this work. Practical experience in relation to the innovation was possible since it involved modification of an existing unit of the school curriculum within a framework which was already approved by the Ministry of Education. Finally, the remit of the project was for the teachers to develop different packages, all directed towards specified common purposes, but varying according to the teachers' own orientations, environments and preferred practices.

A further characteristic of this Israeli project, in striking contrast to the Scottish Integrated Science scheme, was the clarity with which its scope and concerns were specified. Such clarity would, on the one hand, no doubt help the teachers involved in the planning to think about its implications, and to experiment with its use, with greater confidence; on the other hand, it would be especially important for teachers who were asked to choose, from among the alternative forms produced, those which were most appropriate for their circumstances. It is to the issue of the clarity of intended innovations that we turn in the next section.

Confusions About Practice

Planners with creative ideas do not always have the time or
the inclination to work out the details or practical implications
of those ideas; they tend to hope that if teachers are given a
vague outline of what is wanted they will be able to develop
and tidy up the conceptual framework for themselves. There
are a number of different ways, however, in which teachers
might be expected to respond to such vague ideas.

If the concept has not been clarified, the teachers may
simply ignore it and make no attempt to implement the new
ideas. Alternatively, they may decide to try them out in the
classroom in the hope that 'doing' will lead to 'understanding'.
There are likely to be problems with this sort of strategy: if
teachers are not clear about what it is they are trying to
implement then their classroom activities will probably still
be directed towards those things that they <u>are</u> clear about
(e.g. maintaining discipline and getting through the work).
While such activities may or may not be appropriate to the new
ideas it is unlikely that they will match perfectly what was
intended by the planners. In those cases where teachers do
try to clarify the concept for themselves before implementation,
their chosen interpretation may or may not correspond to
that intended, they may or may not view the innovation with
favour and, consequently, may or may not attempt to implement
it. In this way, potentially valuable new ideas may be lost in
practice for want of understanding. Those who wish to introduce new ideas thus have a responsibility to communicate them
clearly.

Scottish Integrated Science provides us with several examples
of innovative ideas that have not been adequately clarified. The
most obvious new feature of the scheme when it was introduced
in 1969 was its <u>integrated</u> nature. An examination of 'Curriculum
Paper 7' suggests that several interpretations of integrated
science were in the minds of the members of the Working Party.
The first of these simply reflects an organisational facet of the
teaching and sees integration as an arrangement in which any
given group of pupils receives all its science from one teacher
rather than three (as is the case for the alternative separate
biology, chemistry and physics courses). There is no problem
with the conceptualisation of integration in this sense; teachers
may not favour such an arrangement, but they can understand
what it means.

Such clarity was not, however, a characteristic of the other
interpretations. Although it was suggested that integration
reflects the unified nature of science, and reference was made
to a structure of fundamental concepts of science and to a
process of scientific enquiry, there was no discussion of this
unity beyond a direction to teachers that it 'should be made clear'. [14]

Another interpretation of integration (interdisciplinary study, in which issues or topics are approached from a number of different subject perspectives) was implied by the structure of the syllabus as 15 different themes. However, these themes turn out, upon examination, to be blocks of subject matter taken from existing separate science syllabuses. No organising 'theme' is present.

The most ambitious conception of integration reflected in the document involves a holistic view of all knowledge as a unity. Science was seen as providing an explanation of 'ourselves and the natural phenomena with which we are surrounded', as a control of 'our morals, our ethics and our whole cultural environment' and as facilitating a general training in 'thinking'. But again there was no development or clarification of this very complex way of looking at integration. [15]

An examination of the interpretations of integration given by the teachers showed that, apart from the 'science organised as one subject with one teacher' meaning, their statements provided only vague references to other interpretations ('the oneness of science', 'breaking down the subject boundaries', 'it's all of life'). It may be that the Working Party believed either that the unifying features of science were self evident, or that they were implicit in the content and objectives of the courses and could readily be drawn out by the teachers. Our evidence suggests that neither of these assumptions was justified.

The failure of the curriculum planners to communicate about the nature of the ideas they were proposing can be seen in the discussion of mixed ability teaching. The guidance given in 'Curriculum Paper 7' about how teachers might take account of differences among their pupils was sparse, but the New Working Party addressed itself directly to that issue. [16] Teachers had suggested that the less-able pupils were 'finding difficulty with parts of the syllabus and were unable to follow many of the instructions on the worksheets', while the more-able were 'finding the course insufficiently demanding and the instructions in the worksheets too brief for them to work with some independence for more than a short time'. [17]

The New Working Party set about its task by formulating a programme of work of 'core plus extension' worksheets. This scheme consisted of core sheets to be attempted by everyone and extension sheets appropriate for the 'less-able', the 'average and more-able' and the 'most-able'. (The extension work was, however, provided for only a minority of the core sheets.) Different, but overlapping, objectives were also laid down for the different ability groups. The plan was to use diagnostic assessment after completion of the core work to determine how pupils would be allocated to the extension materials. The New Working Party suggested that an individual pupil:

'should be presented with extension 'a' or 'b' material according to his/her interest and success with the 'core'. [18]

The teachers were left, however, to conceptualise the criteria
of 'interest' and 'success' for themselves. In so far as any
guidance was given about difference among pupils, it related
to two quite different sorts of theoretical frameworks: Piagetian
developmental stages [19] and general intelligence operationalised
through test scores. [20] Such guidance was confusing since the
two suggested ways of construing differences among pupils,
each radically different from the other, were both fundamentally
inconsistent with the proposed teaching strategy. While this
strategy depended upon viewing the relevant differences among
pupils as temporary and related to the specific content of units,
the suggested ways of viewing differences among pupils involved
treating the differences as relatively stable and independent of
specific content.
    Similar inconsistencies are apparent in the conceptualisation
of other elements of the scheme. The different extension worksheets appropriate for different pupils were described in terms
of the relatively 'abstract' or 'concrete' thinking which each of
them was seen to involve, descriptions which might loosely be
related to the Piagetian framework for categorising pupils. The
expected outcomes of the activities specified on these worksheets were, however, described in terms of behavioural
objectives which were not explicitly related to, and could not
easily be understood in terms of, any such framework. Nor was
it explained how the described differences among either the
worksheets or their expected outcomes were related to the
differentiated course and section objectives specified for more-
and less-able pupils, and formulated in terms of a modified
version of Bloom's taxonomy categories. [21] Thus, in order to try
to understand the programme, teachers would have to articulate
for themselves the connections between five or six different
conceptual schemes for describing differences among pupils
and among the programmes seen to be appropriate for them.
    'Curriculum Paper 7' encouraged the use of guided-discovery
methods but the meaning it ascribed to the term is not alto-
gether clear. At different points in the document 'discovery'
was related to scientific discovery, pupils' abilities to discover,
the process of learning by discovery and discovery teaching
methods. It was the last of these with which the paper was
primarily concerned, but it is difficult to know what those
methods were intended to be. We distinguished several different meanings of discovery teaching which are consistent with
what is said in the document, including an 'inductive', as
opposed to 'deductive', way of teaching concepts and principles,
and teaching of a kind which seeks to simulate the ways in which
scientific discoveries are made; for present purposes, however,
we shall focus on what is perhaps the most emphasised meaning
in the document, the recommendation that the 'pupil is allowed

to exercise selection of approach and method'. [22]

Two interpretations of the meaning of 'guidance' seem to be endorsed by 'Curriculum Paper 7'. On the one hand, in the contrast it draws between programmed learning enthusiasts who try 'to shape behaviour' and the proponents of discovery methods who attempt to 'create situations in which it is hoped the desirable behaviour can develop successfully', the paper appears to see guidance as opposed to or as a limitation on discovery. On the other hand, the Working Party prepared worksheets 'to support these discovery methods', which implies a view of guidance as supportive of, rather than as a limitation on discovery. [23]

The suggestions in the paper about how one might go about providing guidance that would be conducive to learning by discovery neither clarified the concepts nor shed much light on how the teacher might manage the classroom activities. It was recommended that the pupil 'should never be in possession of the final and correct answer before he begins his investigation', and asserted that pupils 'have neither the skill nor experience to work on their own without support'. But just how the teacher might go about providing such support was not discussed. The only advice that was offered concerns the establishment of control by the teacher of what will be learnt by the pupils:

The introduction of work on the worksheets, the discussion afterwards, all of the demonstration work and the actual teaching which will establish the concepts under investigation, are still completely in the teacher's hands. [24]

To investigate teachers' use of guided-discovery methods, we explored teachers' perceptions of what they were doing by analysing their commentaries on specific classroom events. [25] The procedure consisted of replaying sections of an audiorecording of a lesson back to the teacher immediately after the teaching finished. The teacher was asked to stop the tape at any point where he or she was conscious of having decided either to give pupils some specific guidance or to allow them to find out or do something for themselves, and to explain what was done and why. In 45 such interviews the teachers identified a total of 225 events where they were conscious of having taken or refrained from such action. None of these provided examples of guided-discovery teaching used to aid pupils' independent reasoning; the authority of the teacher or an indication that there was a 'correct' answer or way of doing things was always imposed as a constraint on pupils' thinking and activities. A dominant pattern of teaching involved pupils being guided through the 'right' method for the task to the 'correct' results or conclusions, and there was little sign that teachers followed 'Curriculum Paper 7's suggestion that negative results were as likely to occur as positive ones, and were equally acceptable. The teachers, it seemed to us, apart from those in one exceptional school, were interpreting guided-discovery in such a way as to alter minimally their conventional ways of teaching. In seven of the eight schools, the materials provided for teachers gave very little scope for pupils to choose the tasks they would undertake or the methods they would use. In the remaining school, a teacher with special responsibility for integrated science had developed a course structure that attempted to operationalise the ideas for discovery learning in ways suited to the local context. The influence of this support on the classroom behaviour of the other teachers was quite striking: they gave much more encouragement to pupils to develop their own methods of approaching problems (in one case, even deciding for themselves what tasks should be carried out), they were much more likely deliberately to withhold information and they were more reluctant to indulge in 'corrective' sessions at the end of practical work than were other teachers.

An investigation of the innovation of 'teaching towards specified objectives' has produced similar findings. In 'Curriculum Paper 7' objectives for the course at various levels were identified, but no clarification was provided on how the recommended classroom activities, specific objectives and general objectives were related to each other, and, in most cases, the specific objectives were not stated with sufficient precision for their attainment by pupils to be tested. We found no evidence of schools taking on the task of interpreting the relationship among the different facets of the course nor of formulating ways in which teachers could plan and evaluate their lessons in these terms. It was not, therefore, surprising to find that the teachers paid little more than lip-service to the rational 'objective-lesson plan-evaluation' model that 'Curriculum Paper 7' prescribed.

The circumstances that lead, for example, to a set of ill-defined meanings of integration and a variety of inconsistent ways of conceptualising differences among pupils and the tasks appropriate for them are matters for speculation. One contributory factor may be that the rigorous reflection necessary to attain conceptual clarity is unlikely to occur in such part-time working parties, which are inevitably characterised by a good deal of 'thinking on the spot'. Another may be that the composition of such working parties tends not to include people who have distinctive expertise for such work, and that there is a need to recruit more people with philosophical training to these bodies. A third factor, of particular relevance to the present discussion, may be that the neglect of conceptual issues arises from working parties' awareness that their proposals are unlikely to be questioned at this level by teachers.

In all the various contexts in which we have discussed the proposed innovations with science teachers, and observed the ways in which they have dealt with them in their own teaching, we have rarely encountered any concern to seek clarification of the complex and frequently confused ideas underlying the materials presented and the procedural suggestions made. As we have hypothesised, it seems more plausible to understand this lack of concern as a contributory cause of the curriculum planners' failure to present clear conceptual frameworks than as a consequence of it. Evidence from other contexts indicates that even when planners do take care to clarify the ideas underlying their proposals, teachers tend to pay little attention to these ideas. Shipman (1974), for example, reports that in the Keele Integrated Studies Project the planners defined integration as 'a method of using subjects with distinctive procedures, concepts and methods of verification . . . a planned exercise involving different ways of finding out' (p. 45), but that the teachers 'were proud of their success in breaking down the boundaries between subjects . . . [and] producing general teachers'.[26] He suggests that, despite the provision of a clear and consistent definition, the teachers involved either did not understand or more generally did not bother to read the relevant sections of the document.

How should we understand this lack of concern of teachers with conceptual clarity? Is it not surprising that so many people of proven academic competence should show so little concern for the quality of the ideas which inform their work? One simple answer is that, in the context of science teaching in Scottish schools (and in many other contexts), teachers do not regard the making of decisions about the structure of the courses they teach, about the content included in these courses, or about the educational aims of these courses as being any part of their job. Such decisions are made by others and imposed on teachers, and even a teacher who wished to engage in such decision making would be prevented by powerful institutional constraints from doing so. Given such lack of opportunity to make decisions of these kinds, and a corresponding lack of accountability for the decisions made, it would be a fruitless and frustrating waste of energy for the ordinary teacher to spend time attempting to clarify his thinking on such issues. There is plenty to occupy a teacher's energies in getting on with the practical job. (Those who cannot reconcile themselves to operating at this level and persist in seeking theoretical clarity and coherence tend to give up teaching as an occupation.)[27]

If this simple explanation has any validity, then we would not expect that the majority of teachers would develop a concern for clarifying the concepts implicit in proposed innovations unless and until they were given the power, the obligation and the time to act as 'extended professionals' responsible for a wider range of decisions.

This cannot, however, be presented as a sufficient explanation on its own, because teachers clearly do make sense of what

they do in classrooms everyday, and of the innovations which
they are asked to implement. One must ask how they can do
this without attending to the central ideas which inform such
proposed innovations? This is possible because teachers do
not make sense of their activities at a level which involves
such matters as the nature of the differences among pupils,
the nature of scientific knowledge or the educational goals of
the curriculum, but rather at a level involving much more
immediate problems and satisfactions. Certainly, teachers rely
on taken for granted ideas at the former level: there are more-
and less-able pupils; there are differences between physics
chemistry and biology, though these differences are minor
compared with differences between science and other kinds of
knowledge; and it is important that pupils should learn the
answers that science provides to the questions it asks. The
questioning of such ideas is, however, an academic exercise
which does not impinge on their work, and any proposed change
in their patterns of working must be examined and made sense
of not in such terms but in direct relation to their own and
their pupils' day to day activities and experiences. Will there
be time to cover the given content? How can the interest, or
at least the attention, of pupils be maintained? Can I be
confident of getting the experiments to work? Will there be
enough equipment to go round? How can I ensure that there
will not be chaos in the laboratory? We have clearly noted the
dominance of concerns of these kinds in teachers' arguments
for or against proposed innovations; and similar concerns
were even more clearly dominant when, in another phase of
our research, we asked teachers to talk about their planning
and evaluation of teaching which we had observed.

It is worth noting that it is entirely rational for teachers to
try to make sense of innovative proposals at this level rather
than at the level of the fundamental concepts and principles
on which these proposals are based. For them, priority must
be given to ensuring that they can cope fluently with the
practical situations with which they are faced, meet the criteria
for which they are accountable (coverage of the syllabus,
maintenance of control, pupil safety), and not use all their
energies in dealing with one of the several classes which must
be taught each day. Unless the innovative ideas can be translated into these terms, consideration of such ideas must, for
the teacher, remain an empty and irrelevant exercise.

If, on the other hand, a proposed innovation was translated
into its classroom implications and was consequently considered
by teachers, it seems likely that over a period of time teachers
might also consider modifying their more general ideas in
response to their experience with the new practices which they
had used. While conceptual clarity is necessarily a first priority
in the planning of any innovation, it may be that a clear understanding by teachers of the full meaning of an innovation is
most likely to be attained through their close consideration of

the practical implications of the innovation. We would argue that those wishing to urge upon teachers innovative ideas must consider what it might mean to teachers to have to use those ideas in the classroom. This point brings us to the third section of this chapter, where we consider what might be involved in taking classroom realities seriously into account in planning.

BREAKING THE STALEMATE: CONSIDERING THE COSTS AND REWARDS OF INNOVATION

Breaking the Stalemate: Support for Innovation

We have argued that conceptual confusion on the part of planners is unlikely to be sorted out by teachers; teachers either do not have the time or are reluctant to think about their teaching at the conceptual level unless explicitly provoked to do so. They test the knowledge that they use to order their routines in the classroom by its practicability and they seldom subject it to further conscious, systematic criticism. Routines that are familiar and comfortable may not be abandoned even when they are manifestly unsuccessful in achieving declared aims. The effect of emphasising the practical is to make teachers much more aware of the importance of detailed guidance on appropriate classroom procedures than of the need for conceptual clarification.

Much of the curriculum planning of the last two decades has failed to take into account the nature of the cost and rewards associated with changing classroom practice. In this section of the chapter we explore ways in which support for innovation might be given to teachers that is sensitive to their own concerns and to classroom realities.

The change in the amount of practical work that is carried out by pupils themselves is an example of an effective innovation in science teaching. Twenty years ago, almost all the experiments in science for pupils of 12 to 14 years of age were undertaken as demonstrations by the teacher, but our classroom observation study undertaken recently indicates that now about 50 per cent of the time spent in science lessons is devoted to pupil practical work in groups. In the early 1960s, a great many Scottish science teachers were uncertain about whether they should or could introduce this change, so why did it come about? We suggest that a crucial feature of the exercise was the effort that was made to explain clearly what was involved in classroom terms. The main thrust of this effort was in the production of worksheets. In the few years immediately before the publication of 'Curriculum Paper 7' in 1969, substantial amounts of time and energy were put into worksheet trials: proposed pupil experiments were tried out; problems were identified by teachers, the experiments redesigned and the worksheets written. Although the growth of pupil experimentation did not emerge until the late 1960s, the

development of ideas for good laboratory experiments in
secondary schools was a subject-centred exercise that was
familiar to and enjoyed by many specialist science teachers;
furthermore, the product of the exercise had obvious relevance for classrooms and the worksheets were eagerly received
by almost everyone. That is not to say that the materials were
not criticised; many schools and local authorities subsequently
developed new sets of sheets for themselves. An analysis of the
tasks set and the topics covered showed that some of the more
demanding work had been dropped in order, we suspect, to
respond to the particular circumstances of each school. The
procedure appeared to be one of 'personalising' the materials
for use in a specific context.

The support provided by the worksheets was supplemented
by in-service courses which concentrated on giving teachers
experience with selected experiments; particular attention was
paid to the problems of specialist science teachers having to
teach unfamiliar subject matter within the integrated course.
Considerable efforts were made by local authorities to ensure
that schools had suitable and sufficient equipment for pupil
experiments, and advice on its use was readily available from
the Scottish Secondary Schools Equipment Research Centre.
Within the schools the Heads of biology, chemistry and physics
departments saw their primary role in relation to integrated
science as one of providing help with experiments in their
subject for teachers with other subject specialisms. [28]

We can thus assert with some confidence that where adequate
conceptual and procedural guidance has not been provided the
probability of effective innovation will be slight, and also point
to an example where such guidance does appear to have borne
fruit. So far, however, our argument lacks the support of an
example of effective innovation involving more abstract ideas
than those involved in the development of activity based science

To explore this issue further we used an action-research
approach to develop the innovative 'differentiation of work
among pupils' introduced by the 'New Science Worksheets' for
use by teachers with mixed ability classes. [29] Our task was to
develop an innovation strategy that would lead to effective
implementation in the context in which we were working. The
procedures we adopted involved: an initial analysis and clarification of the innovation (i.e. of the nature of the differences
perceived among pupils and among the differentiated materials);
an analysis of the context into which it was to be introduced,
involving an exploration of the attitudes and practices of nine
teachers and two science departments with whom we worked;
formulation of a hypothesis about appropriate action to take;
execution of this action (i.e. discussions with teachers to
clarify issues, provision of assessment procedures, compatible
with a mastery-learning approach, revision of worksheets to
match the theoretical concepts of differentiation, provision of
suggestions about how to cope with classroom management

problems about which teachers had expressed apprehension);
collection of data to assess the effectiveness of the action; and
reformulation of the hypothesis.

Our strategy had some success: differentiation of work
occurred in 89 per cent of lessons in comparison with 37 per
cent before our intervention, and those teachers who had
previously expressed reservations about mixed ability teaching
all expressed more favourable views after experience with our
scheme. These sorts of findings sustain optimism that the provision of conceptual and procedural guidance that is personalised
(i.e. responsive to the context in which the innovation is taking
place) will facilitate effective implementation. However, in a
second strand of the study we had much less success; we tried
to influence the science departments to provide support for
innovatory activities and, in retrospect, we believe that our
failures on this front can be largely put down to a prescriptive
style that we adopted, unrealistic notions of the time that
departments take to reflect upon ideas and put them into practice and an inadequate analysis of and response to the conventions and attitudes that governed the corporate activities of
these two groups of teachers.

We found that two teachers had very distinctive ideologies
that were in direct conflict with our ideas: the first was opposed
to the use of worksheets and to the basic idea of any differentiation of work and the second was committed to collaboration among
pairs of pupils (our scheme used the assessment of the individual pupil's attainment to determine the allocation of work). There
was no reason to expect that our intervention would be useful
to these teachers, nor that we would see effective innovation
on their part (and we did not).

Even if teachers have examined and reflected on the classroom implications of the proposed innovations (as we believe
these two teachers did) their willingness to introduce changes
in their teaching will depend on whether they perceive those
changes as salient to their own problems and aspirations and
whether they believe that they can adapt the suggested procedures to their own requirements. This, as we have argued,
implies that the sort of information the teacher is looking for
is of a personal type; that is, sensitive to what the teacher
sees as the costs and rewards of attempting the new approach
in their classroom. For example: information that indicates
what is involved in a commitment to guided-discovery in his
or her particular context or that predicts what will be the
effects of taking account of differences among pupils in his
or her class in certain specified ways. The value and relevance of the innovation as perceived by the teacher will be a
crucial factor in determining how it is implemented in that
classroom, and different teachers will have different sets of
values and different problems.

Not only is it important to seek knowledge that is helpful
in specific contexts and for specific individuals, it also seems

to be the case that effective acquisition of such knowledge is
dependent on systems of personal support for the teacher.
Summarising conclusions from research that has attempted to
acquire knowledge about innovative strategies, Fullan and
Pomfret conclude that:

> There is some evidence that suggests that the following
> strategies and tactics are important for implementation:
> inservice training (depending on the type), resource support
> (time, materials, etc.), feedback mechanisms that stimulate
> interaction and problem identification, and participation in
> decision-making (depending on the nature and timing). It
> is important to note that these factors may be interactive in
> the sense that they may be mutually reinforcing over-time.
> The presence of any one without the others would probably
> limit if not eliminate its effectiveness. [30]

They go on, however, to argue that very little is known
about the effectiveness of the different ways in which these
elements might be utilised.

The implication of our argument is that curriculum documents, materials or in-service courses are unlikely to be
effective unless they are used in a way that is responsive to
the teacher's personal context and to what teachers see as
the costs and rewards of innovation. This sort of support
might be provided by outsiders in an action-research approach
of the type we undertook, but it would be unrealistic to expect
that such schemes could be introduced in anything but a small
minority of schools. A more likely source of support might be
the science department within the school. To study the role
of the science department we undertook a detailed investigation
of the science departments of eight Scottish secondary schools. [31]

The Integrated Science scheme, like other curriculum developments in Scotland, made assumptions about Heads of Departments
adopting distinctive, creative, managerial roles to facilitate the
introduction of innovations in the classroom. These assumptions
were not supported by our findings.

There was only very limited evidence from Heads of Departments' descriptions of their own roles, responses to question-
naires by the rest of the science staff, an examination of
departmental characteristics and practices (e.g. materials
used, financial arrangements, guidance for teachers) and an
assessment of the relationships among the attitudes of different
teachers, to indicate that there was specific departmental
policy making, creative management, supervision or support for
teachers in implementing the four innovations central to the
Integrated Science scheme. The Heads of Departments took
very seriously their responsibilities in providing apparatus and
subject expertise for the integrated course (e.g. the physicists
made considerable efforts to familiarise chemists and biologists
with the physics in the course) and in constructing and process-

ing examinations. But it was not seen as appropriate for departments to specify methods for presenting the material, planning and evaluating the lessons, or dealing with the variety of pupils' learning characteristics.

This may reflect distinctions among the teaching activities for which Scottish science teachers are and are not accountable: everyone is expected to cover the prescribed content and practical work and so prepare their pupils for the department tests and examinations, but no one is held responsible for the attainment of the goals, and the ways in which teachers choose to work towards those goals is seen as their own affair. Science teachers value this autonomy but they do so at the cost of the support and creative criticism of their colleagues. This low level of departmental collaboration is reflected in the absence of any significant inter-teacher correlations in attitudes towards classroom innovations such as guided-discovery or teaching towards specified objectives (this contrasted, however, with the relationships that were found among attitudes to administrative change to which we will return later). [32]

The maintenance of classroom autonomy is probably seen by teachers as important evidence of their professional status. As such it is an obstacle to the provision of personal support for the teacher and, together with the pressures of limited time and resources, administrative arrangements within schools and nationally determined curriculum content, it may account for the failure of school science departments to display the management structures that were hoped for.

If specific personal support for teachers is vital for effective innovation, and if it is not feasible to provide this through formalised departmental management systems, then other ways have to be found. One possible mechanism in Scotland is through the activities of Assistant Principal Teachers with special responsibility for integrated science. Of the eight schools in our study, four had no such posts of responsibility, and in two schools the distinctive tasks carried out by the Assistant Principal Teacher were of an entirely routine kind (e.g. duplicating worksheets); but two very enthusiastic and productive individuals occupied the posts in the remaining schools. Both of these teachers had made substantial efforts to give realistic guidance to their colleagues on how they might go about translating the general aims of the course into action. Our observations of teachers' classroom behaviour and the commentaries that teachers provided on lessons they had taught suggested a number of features that distinguished teaching in these two schools from the others. [33] For example, in the other schools the general pattern of teacher activity during pupils' group work is to move quickly around the laboratory, stopping only briefly (i.e. for less than one minute) to make short, practical and often superficial comments on the experiments or to provide quick answers to pupils' questions. In the two schools with enthusiastic Assistant Principal Teachers we noted

that teachers would often stop for more substantial discussions
with pupils, persuade them to think in more depth about what
they were doing and be less concerned about continually checking up that everyone was working and behaving themselves.
These teachers seemed to be more aware than others we observed of what they were trying to achieve beyond just 'getting
through the experiments'. It appears then that these two
Assistant Principal Teachers, through fairly close social
relationships with (rather than hierarchical control over)
other members of the department, were able to influence classroom events by carefully thought out practical suggestions and
by stimulating discussions about these suggestions among
teachers and technicians.

More research on the factors that influence the effectiveness
of an Assistant Principal Teacher in this area is needed. For
example, priority should be given to research on the nature
of the autonomy that teachers value, the kinds of interventions
in their classroom that they would find threatening, the aspects
of their work or relationships that they fear might be destroyed
and the kinds of help or support (if any) they would welcome
(even if they might not normally feel able to admit to such
needs). Data of this kind could inform hypotheses about specific
ways in which Fullan and Pomfret's four elements (in-service
training, resource support, feedback mechanisms and participation in decision making) might be utilised in an effective innovation strategy.

In omitting to clarify for teachers the procedures which they
proposed, the authors of 'Curriculum Paper 7' have assumed
that professionally competent teachers, given the general ideas,
would be able to develop appropriate procedures for themselves. Such a stance is consistent with a common notion that
to specify in detail how the innovation should operate is to
infringe upon teachers' cherished sense of their right to
autonomy in their own classrooms. This notion cannot lightly
be dismissed: teachers do wish to personalise new materials
and plan their own classroom routines.

On the other hand, we also have substantial evidence that
Scottish science teachers are anxious to have detailed suggestions about appropriate procedures for implementing new ideas,
that many see a large degree of uniformity across classrooms
as not only acceptable but desirable,[34] and that what is normally provided as guidance is seen as inadequate.[35] Furthermore,
the provision of detailed guidance and clarification about
pupils' experimental work seems, as we have agreed, to have
achieved its aims, and to have done so without undermining
teachers' sense of their autonomy.

In what circumstances, then, is the provision of guidance
by an outsider inconsistent with teacher autonomy? For teachers,
the crucial distinction appears to be between prescriptions about
what they should do and knowledge or materials which may be
helpful in simplifying their tasks but which they are free to

ignore or use as they see fit. In principle this distinction is
clear, but in practice it can be very subtle: what is intended
as merely a helpful suggestion may, if offered in the wrong
context or with the wrong tone, be experienced as an inter-
fering directive. Perhaps the most important factor is whether
or not the teacher has, implicitly or explicitly, asked for the
advice which is offered.

There is, however, another level at which the issue needs to
be considered. Teachers may willingly accept advice, materials
and equipment which will, they clearly see, simplify their work;
but the effect of this may be that their teaching comes to
involve little more than the use of routines which have very
largely been planned by other people. In our research on the
integrated science course we have noted that many teachers
find it necessary to do very little planning or preparation for
their lessons, since they can rely very heavily on the standard
worksheets and packaged equipment. This helps teachers by
reducing the immediate pressures on them, but it is our strong
impression that it leads teachers not only to show less initiative
and flexibility in their teaching but also to obtain less satisfaction from it. The provision of procedural clarity by outsiders may be acceptable to teachers and a necessary condition
for the implementation of the outsiders' innovations, but it
may also have costs for teachers and perhaps for their pupils.

The previous discussion assumed that teachers are, by and
large, preoccupied with solving the immediate problems of
the classroom and show some reluctance to think at a conceptual
level. This is not to argue that teachers' ideologies do not
affect how they use an innovative idea in the classroom. Some
teachers at least have ideological commitments which are
sufficiently important to them that if innovative ideas are at
odds with the commitments they hold, they are unlikely to
implement them in the classroom even when they have been
clarified and discussed.

We have already reported that two of the nine teachers in
our action-research study had strong commitments of this
type. We had developed a scheme to help teachers to conceptualise differences in attainment, to assess individual
pupils' attainments and to match alternative worksheets to the
individual's attainment. But this sort of scheme has little to
offer a teacher who sincerely believes that mixed ability teaching means that everyone should be offered the same work at
the same time, that worksheets are unsuitable vehicles for the
acquisition of scientific knowledge, or that to assess an individual's attainment is a divisive strategy since comparisons
among pupils will always be made and that the assessment
should be of pairs of pupils in which a high achiever is helping
a low achiever. Support for these two teachers, to be effective,
would have had to develop hypotheses for action that took
explicit account of their personal ideologies and our 'general
purpose' model was not able to do that.

The importance of teachers' commitments to their classroom autonomy suggests that proposals for pedagogical change if presented within a framework of coercion from 'above' (whether within or outwith the school) are likely to be resisted. Such proposals, however, may find more response if they are based on collaborative action-research.

We should not overemphasise the importance of teachers' allegiance to their autonomy as an influence on their classroom teaching. Our research suggests that factors external to the teachers are also important. The uniformity that we found among the strategies used by the 24 teachers we observed was remarkable. Only rarely have we seen what might be a distinctive ideology of teaching reflected in a consistent classroom style adopted by a teacher. In general, distinctions among styles reflected ways of coping with the contexts in which the teachers found themselves. For example, one of the major systematic differences which we found among schools and among teachers was in the amount of time spent by pupils in 'readying' for their practical work; this variation appeared to stem almost entirely from two contrasting strategies for coping used by teachers whose laboratories were less than satisfactory: one group avoiding problems by having apparatus set up beforehand, the other group adopting the time-consuming approach of monitoring the distribution and setting up of apparatus very closely. Another of the systematic differences among teachers and schools was in the amount of time pupils spent on practical work, in contrast to the amount of time they spent attending to the teacher; this variation was closely associated with the timetabled length of lessons. Those teachers who had less time clearly tended to feel obliged to spend more of the time talking with the whole class in order to ensure coverage of the work. There were, nevertheless, two among the teachers who could be distinguished from the others (in general and in their own schools) by their consistent styles which we think stemmed from strong personal commitments. One teacher sustained one kind of classroom activity for much longer periods of time than most: he had extended discussions with the whole class about the entire range of topics pertinent to the general theme of the lesson; he was reluctant to move on from one issue until he was sure that everyone had grasped the crucial points; he deviated markedly from the common pattern in which a single topic was discussed, an experiment on that topic was prepared for and carried out, equipment was cleared and results discussed. His strategy of thorough discussions involving multiple topics was accompanied by considerably less than average time spent on pupils' experiments and almost none on getting ready for, or clearing up after, practical work.

The second teacher's style was in marked contrast to that of the first. In comparison with others, she spent very little time talking or demonstrating to the whole class. More than an average amount of pupil practical work was done, but there was no set pattern of introducing the work. More than any other teacher, she encouraged pupils to do things and find out things for themselves and was prepared to spend substantial amounts of time in discussion with individuals or small groups during practical work: she appeared to have sufficient confidence in her pupils' abilities and sense of responsibility to avoid constant 'checking up' on them and, instead, devoted her attention to exploring more thoroughly the issues and problems that the pupils identified from their own work.

Each of these teachers appeared to us to be an excellent teacher but their styles have different implications for the implementation of particular innovations. For example, guided-discovery methods conceived of as pupils finding out things for themselves would fit closely with the way in which the second teacher already organised her lessons, but the first teacher's greater emphasis on talk and the consolidation of knowledge acquired would not fit with this interpretation of guided-discovery. On the other hand, teaching towards specified objectives would fit with the structured, probing question-and-answer approach of the first teacher, but not with the second teacher's emphasis on pupils' freedom to learn by discovery.

COSTS AND REWARDS OF INNOVATION: THE TEACHER AS 'ECONOMIC MAN'

We have suggested that how teachers make sense of innovative ideas and use them in classrooms depends not only on the nature and quality of the information and support they are offered by outsiders, but also on their own ideas about how their subject should be taught and on the constraints which exist in their day-to-day work.

Where freedom of choice and opportunity to develop alternatives exist, the science teacher may reject the innovation because, for example, it is seen as not practicable, not in the pupils' interests, or too demanding of time or energy. Even if a teacher assimilates an innovation into his or her existing pattern of teaching a commitment to it is not assured; the teacher may accept the new ideas as part of a job to be done but not as a source of personal satisfaction. As our research suggests, where a teacher reacts positively to opportunities to innovate and adopts distinctive methods of implementation, the underlying causes are likely to be complex and to relate to teachers' confidence in themselves, the characteristics of the environment in which they work and their conceptions of what the job of teaching is about.

The fact that teachers operate within science departments influences their actions in relation to the use of innovative ideas. There is considerable variation in the extent to which departments provide support, but these differences appear not to reflect differences in managerial efficiency. 'Management' turned out indeed to be an inappropriate concept for describing the ways in which science departments function. The important differences seemed rather to depend on the enthusiasm of those holding a crucial, but low status post of Assistant Principal Teacher with responsibility for integrated science. The assumptions that have been made about the feasibility and efficacy of departmental management structures in promoting innovations have been naïve and largely unexamined.

A framework that relates teachers' responses to innovative ideas to the <u>personal costs and rewards</u> to them of introducing change seems to us one appropriate way to summarise the arguments and hypotheses that have emerged from our case studies.

On the cost side, an innovative programme may be asking teachers to expend time and effort in developing new ideas and formulating suitable procedures for implementing changes that reflect neither concern for the problems most salient for them, nor the educational aims that they regard as the most important or pressing, nor the aspects of their teaching for which they are held accountable. They may be asked to relinquish familiar and comfortable classroom practices, some or all of their valued classroom autonomy and certain features of their activities or roles that enhance their sense of efficacy and their status in the eyes of their colleagues.

On the reward side, innovations could: take explicit account of teachers' immediate concerns and problems; provide clearly articulated ideas and general procedural guidance that individual teachers could modify to suit their personal conditions, styles of teaching, classroom difficulties and educational aims; and present a context within which teachers could be encouraged to promote their own initiatives and to judge themselves (and be judged by others) in terms of their professional (teaching) competence and creativity.

Most of the evidence that we have accumulated on pedagogical innovations has indicated that, in the past, the balance has tipped towards costs. The difficult task is to identify an innovative strategy that ensures a different balance. Strategic decisions tend to be made at a global level but there may be subtle distinctions among alternative ways of implementing these strategies that can make the difference between an exercise that is 'costly' to teachers and one that is 'rewarding'. Suppose, for example, we consider the decision to provide worksheets to support the implementation of pupils' practical work. There is a tension between, on the one hand, the possibility of reducing the costs of lesson preparation for teachers through the supply of worksheets and corresponding packages of equipment, and, on the other hand, the danger of depersonalising the whole procedure by the prescriptive provision of the lesson 'on the plate' and so of diminishing the rewards.

In anticipating what will be costly or rewarding for teachers
it is probably crucial to take account of what teachers gain
from the teaching process and from immediate working relationships; to disturb these is a costly business and would have to
be balanced by obvious rewards. The prescription of a management role for Heads of Departments, for example, can be specu-
latively justified by rewards expected in the efficient use of
innovative ideas, well organised support for teachers and creative initiative from the top of the hierarchy. But that assumes
that management activities are not only compatible with the
values, sources of satisfaction and expectations of Heads of
Departments, but are also seen as valuable, supportive and
non-threatening by other teachers. If this is not the case, then
the costs of developing a management structure will outweigh
the rewards. The lack of evidence for the existence of such
structures suggests a reluctance to emphasise the Head of
Department role as 'manager' at the expense of de-emphasis on,
say, the 'honours chemist/experienced teacher' image. The
former would tend to set the Head of Department apart from
those with whom he or she works and it could challenge the
autonomy of the other teachers; the latter ensures a position
within the group (albeit a rather privileged one). Our research suggests that science departments appear to operate
within a stable system of implicitly negotiated bargains: science
teachers are prepared to put up with the costs of the global
and administrative decisions that are passed down from the
Head Teacher (e.g. on timetabling) or from national authorities
(e.g. curriculum content) provided the reward of classroom
autonomy is preserved. To introduce a departmental 'manager'
would upset that equilibrium and put at risk the other teachers'
perceptions of themselves as autonomous professionals.

We are not suggesting that the introduction of departmental
managers or other radical changes could not be brought about,
but the success of their introduction would depend on the
establishment of a comparable but different balance of costs
and rewards. Despite science teachers' concern for professional
autonomy, they might be ready to trade some autonomy for
something they value and see as salient to their teaching. At
the moment, autonomy is maintained at the cost of isolation
which denies them collaborative support from their colleagues.
This, together with the constraints on their actions from
externally imposed curricula, the limitations of time, the
attitudes and expectations that pupils bring from their other
school experiences and the decisions taken at school or department level, imply that the autonomy they value may be largely
an illusion.

However, the provision of alternative rewards is of crucial
importance. The introduction of team teaching in open plan
laboratories in Scotland for example involved concessions from
teachers who have had to share decision making at the classroom level. In those schools where teachers saw the new

arrangement as a means of achieving ends that they personally value (e.g. more effective learning by pupils, more coherent schemes for keeping disruptive pupils occupied, greater opportunity for teachers to work creatively and collaboratively on course development), the innovation has been successful. In other cases, where outsiders decide what is 'needed' and, without adequate consideration of the aspirations, sources of satisfaction or expectations of the teachers, as was the case for guided-discovery, the outcome is less likely to be as intended. Under these conditions, as we saw, teachers gain little of personal value in the change to recompense them for the costs involved.

We have found it useful to talk about teachers' responses to innovations as the consequences of the diverse costs and rewards which these innovations hold for them. However, we believe it is also important to recognise the limitations of this way of construing the teacher as 'economic man', innovations as packages which teachers may or may not 'buy' and the outcomes of attempts to innovate as dependent on the arithmetical totals of profit and loss accounts. As we hope our discussion has made clear, the 'costs' and 'rewards' which innovations can hold for teachers may be of many diverse kinds, not obviously or necessarily commensurate with each other: teachers, like other people, are a great deal more complex than the classical economic model suggests. Similarly, both the intended outcomes of innovations and the processes by which they are introduced are so diverse that they cannot adequately be viewed simply as a set of different packages for sale.

This model has, of course, always tended to be more attractive and useful to those who have things to sell than to those who, it is hoped, will buy. We suspect that the same is true when it is applied to educational innovations. For the person who has developed an innovative educational idea, it may seem very reasonable to construe the problem as one of how to sell it to teachers; and we believe that he can usefully approach this task by analysing the costs and rewards which acceptance and implementation of this idea might entail for teachers, and by modifying, concretising, packaging and advertising it, and planning an appropriate after-sales service, in the light of this analysis. Our evidence suggests that this will rarely be an easy task, and that it is unlikely that any theory can be developed to provide definite rules for the aspiring innovator to follow. Instead, he will be dependent on untidy, pragmatic hypotheses extrapolated from studies of the type we have reported here, on detailed analysis of the specific characteristics of the innovation he proposes, and on extensive 'market research' into the characteristics, concerns, failures, achievements and intentions of teachers in the particular contexts with which he is concerned. On this basis, he will have to generate an ad hoc theoretical framework on which to base a 'selling' strategy appropriate for the specific circumstances.

From their own perspectives, however, science teachers are not, first and foremost, potential customers for other people's ideas. Nor can teachers, as a group or as individuals, be encapsulated within any such formula, since like everyone else each teacher is a complex human being whose thoughts, feelings and concerns are constantly changing, are of many different kinds, and are at different levels of consciousness, immediacy and realism. In every teacher there is, inter alia, the 'homme moyen sensuel', the 'person with a job to do', and the person who aspires to some kind of ideal of what a teacher should be. Self-evident as this may be, its implications for innovation are important. Given a well-informed and sensitive selling strategy, teachers will tend to be responsive to being treated as customers, since they do have problems which they want solved, and they do experience needs which can be satis- fied through their work or by reducing some of the demands which their work makes on them. But the more teachers are treated as customers, buying and using other people's ideas, procedures and materials, the less easy it is for them to define themselves as the planners and initiators of their own teaching, and the more their own creative thinking and aspirations are likely to appear superfluous to their teaching work. And this is likely, in the long run, not only to lead to deeper and per- haps less conscious dissatisfaction among teachers, but also to deprive schools of an immense amount of potential creative effort. Thus the notion of teacher as 'customer' is limited.

We have summarised our interpretations of the innovations of the Scottish Integrated Science course in terms of the costs and rewards model because it reflects the way in which these proposals have been externally formulated and then offered to teachers. This model would not, as we have suggested, be appropriate for thinking about how teachers could be better helped to reflect on their own teaching and on existing curricula and organisational structures, and to make and implement plans which would enable them to realise their own developing educa- tional ideas and more ambitious conceptions of their own pro- fessional roles. Although we believe that some of our analyses and speculations in this chapter may be relevant to develop- ments of this kind, the practical exploration and more adequate articulation of such an alternative conception of innovation re- mains, in the context of Scottish science teaching, a task for the future.

NOTES

1. S. Brown, D. McIntyre, E. Drever and J.K. Davies, 'Innovations: Teachers' Views', Stirling Educational Mono- graphs No. 2 (Department of Education, University of Stirling, 1976).

2. J.J. Schwab, The Practical: a Language for Curriculum, 'School Review', vol. 78, no. 1 (1969), pp. 1-23.
3. W. Doyle and G.A. Ponder, The Practicality Ethic in Teacher Decision-Making, 'Interchange', vol. 8, no. 3 (1977), pp. 1-12.
4. Brown et al., 'Innovations: Teachers' Views'.
5. I.W. Williams, The Implementation of Curricula Adapted From Scottish Integrated Science in P. Tamir, A. Hofstein and N. Sabar (eds.), 'Curriculum Implementation and Its Relationship to Curriculum Development in Science' (Israel Science Teaching Centre, Hebrew University, Jerusalem, 1979), pp. 295-99.
6. Scottish Education Department, 'Curriculum Paper 7: Science for General Education' (HMSO, Edinburgh, 1969).
7. Scottish Central Committee on Science, 'New Science Worksheets' and 'Teacher's Guide' (Heinemann Educational Books, Edinburgh, 1977).
8. A.W. Jeffrey, Case study A: Evaluation of the Scottish Integrated Science Syllabus in D. Cohen (ed.), 'New Trends in Integrated Science, Volume IV' (UNESCO, Paris, 1977).
9. Brown et al., 'Innovations: Teachers' Views'.
10. Scottish Education Department, 'Curriculum Paper 7', pp. 10-13.
11. Ibid., pp. 10-25.
12. Ibid., p. 18.
13. M. Ben Peretz, Teachers' Role in Curriculum Development, 'Canadian Journal of Education', vol. 5, no. 3 (1980), pp. 52-62.
14. Scottish Education Department, 'Curriculum Paper 7', pp. 10-25.
15. Ibid., pp. 11-13.
16. Scottish Central Committee on Science, 'New Science Worksheets'.
17. S. Kellington and A.C. Mitchell, 'An Evaluation of New Science Worksheets for Scottish Integrated Science' (Heinemann, London, 1978).
18. Scottish Central Committee on Science, 'Teachers' Guides', p. 14.
19. Scottish Central Committee on Science, 'New Science Worksheets'.
20. Kellington and Mitchell, 'An Evaluation of New Science Worksheets'.
21. B.S. Bloom, 'Taxonomy of Educational Objectives' (Longmans, London, 1956).
22. Scottish Education Department, 'Curriculum Paper 7', p. 22.
23. Ibid., p. 22.
24. Ibid., p. 24.
25. D. McIntyre and S. Brown, Science Teachers' Implementation of Two Intended Innovations, 'Scottish Educational Review', vol. 11, no. 1 (1979), pp. 42-57.

26. M. Shipman, 'Inside a Curriculum Project' (Methuen, London, 1974), pp. 45-6.
27. C. Lacey, 'The Socialization of Teachers' (Methuen, London, 1977).
28. S. Brown, D. McIntyre and R. Impey, The Evaluation of School Science Departments, 'Studies in Educational Evaluation', vol. 5, no. 3 (1979), pp. 175-86.
29. S. Brown and D. McIntyre, Action Research and Curriculum Innovation in a Centralised System of Education, 'European Journal of Science Education', vol. 3, no. 3 (1981), pp. 243-58.
30. M. Fullan and A. Pomfret, Research on Curriculum and Instruction Implementation, 'Review of Educational Research', vol. 47, no. 1 (1977), pp. 335-97.
31. Brown et al., 'The Evaluation of School Science Departments'.
32. S. Brown and D. McIntyre, Influences Upon Teachers' Attitudes to Different Types of Innovation: a study of Scottish Integrated Science, 'Curriculum Enquiry' (in press).
33. McIntyre and Brown, 'Science Teachers' Implementation of Two Intended Innovations'.
34. S. Brown, 'Introducing Criterion-Referenced Assessment: Teachers' Views', Stirling Educational Monographs No. 7 (Department of Education, University of Stirling, 1980a).
35. S. Brown, Key issues in the implementation of innovations in schools, 'Curriculum', vol. 1, no. 1 (1980b), pp. 32-39

BIBLIOGRAPHY

Ben Peretz, M. Teachers' Role in Curriculum Development, 'Canadian Journal of Education', vol. 5, no. 3 (1980), pp. 52-62.
Bloom, B.S. 'Taxonomy of Educational Objectives' (Longmans, London, 1956), vol. 1.
Brown, S. 'Introducing Criterion-Referenced Assessment: Teachers' Views', Stirling Educational Monographs No. 7 (Department of Education, University of Stirling, 1980a).
Brown, S. Key Issues in the Implementation of Innovations in Schools, 'Curriculum', vol. 1, no. 1 (1980b), pp. 31-9.
Brown, S. and McIntyre, D. Action Research and Curriculum Innovation in a Centralised System of Education, 'European Journal of Science Education', vol. 3, no. 3 (1981), pp. 243-58.
Brown, S. and McIntyre, D. Influences Upon Teachers' Attitudes to Different Types of Innovation: a study of Scottish Integrated Science, 'Curriculum Inquiry' (in press).
Brown, S. McIntyre, D. Drever, E. and Davies, J.K. 'Innovations: Teachers' Views', Stirling Educational Monographs No. 2 (Department of Education, University of Stirling, 1976).

Brown, S. McIntyre, D. and Impey, R. The Evaluation of
School Science Departments, 'Studies in Educational Evalua-
tion', vol. 5, no. 3 (1979), pp. 175-86.
Doyle, W. and Ponder, G.A. The Practicality Ethic in Teacher
Decision-Making, 'Interchange', vol. 8, no. 3 (1977), pp. 1-12.
Fullan, M. and Pomfret, A. Research on Curriculum and Instruc-
tion Implementation, 'Review of Educational Research', vol. 47,
no. 1 (1977), pp. 335-97.
Jeffrey, A.W. Case study A: Evaluation of the Scottish Inte-
grated Science Syllabus in D. Cohen (ed.), 'New Trends in
Integrated Science, Volume IV' (UNESCO, Paris, 1977).
Kellington, S. and Mitchell, A.C. 'An Evaluation of New Science
Worksheets for Scottish Integrated Science' (Heinemann,
London, 1978).
Lacey, C. 'The Socialization of Teachers' (Methuen, London,
1977).
McIntyre, D. and Brown, S. Science Teachers' Implementation
of Two Intended Innovations, 'Scottish Educational Review',
vol. 11, no. 1 (1979), pp. 42-57.
Schwab, J.J. The Practical: a Language for Curriculum, 'School
Review', vol. 78, no. 1 (1969), pp. 1-23.
Scottish Central Committee on Science, 'New Science Worksheets'
and 'Teacher's Guides' (Heinemann Educational Books,
Edinburgh, 1977).
Scottish Education Department, 'Curriculum Paper 7: Science
for General Education' (HMSO, Edinburgh, 1969).
Shipman, M. 'Inside a Curriculum Project' (Methuen, London,
1974), pp. 45-6.
Williams, I.W. The Implementation of Curricula Adapted From
Scottish Integrated Science in P. Tamir, A. Blum, A. Hof-
stein and N. Sabar (eds.), 'Curriculum Implementation and
Its Relationship to Curriculum Development in Science'
(Israel Science Teaching Centre, Hebrew University, Jerusa-
lem, 1979), pp. 295-99.

John Olson

INTRODUCTION

One of the statements curricularists make today with some
authority is that efforts to change the practice of schools
through the intervention of curriculum projects have not been
very successful; 'recitation' persists. [1] However, the influence
of curriculum projects has been felt in other ways. Partly as a
consequence of national policy and partly as a consequence of
increased opportunity for research, the presence of innovative
projects in schools has led to increased study of classrooms and
the impact of innovations upon them. As Lortie put it: 'Change
increases the need for accurate reports on the empirical reality
of schools and teaching-representative reports rather than
"news" which is generally unique. . . The prospect of a different kind of future can increase our dependence on understanding the past.' [2] In this sense the innovative activity in the 1960s
has provided a stimulus for the increase in evaluation and research activity in the 1970s.

One of the surprises of increased classroom observation
activity was that methods thought to be antique persisted. For
example, teachers continued to use recitation or, teachers,
considered superior, used unexpectedly 'old fashioned' methods. [3]
Not only was there little evidence that innovations had been
effective, but observers woke up to the fact that classrooms
seemed to have changed very little from the beginning of the
development of the classroom system in the nineteenth century.
Why hadn't classrooms changed? Why did teachers fail to adopt
the many new practices which research in education, or new
subject perspectives, had stimulated? Observers surmised that
there must be something adaptive about the methods teachers
used. In some way teachers were thought to be using methods
that were in fact well suited to the requirements of the classroom situation.

Without an understanding of how teachers view their work,
what problems they consider salient and the nature of solutions
they adopt to deal with those problems, it is difficult to see
how it is possible for worthwhile ideas for changing schools to
influence practice in the classroom. The data presented in this
chapter have been collected with this concept in mind and interpreted with a view to improving our understanding of how
teachers use innovative ideas and why they proceed as they do.
In short, rather than a study developed within the theoretical

140

framework of a social science, this work emerges from problems
associated with the practical field of curriculum change, and is
meant to help improve the policy processes which lie at the heart
of curriculum renewal.

The conceptual framework within which this work was undertaken has been developed from a functional model of the school
used by Taylor[4] and Reid.[5] The model is based on the idea that:
'Since the school functions as a single organization, and its
ability to function depends on keeping dissonance and conflict
within reasonable bounds, an overall determinant of the curriculum is the way in which accommodation is achieved between
technology, task group and theory.'[6] A major assumption of
the model is that how policies are realised in school depends on
the interaction of technology (the means of accomplishing the
tasks of the school), task group (the social systems of the
school) and theory (the theoretical conceptions of the purposes
of the curriculum) in such a way that 'accommodation' is
achieved in practice.

The functions of curriculum policy, however, are realised
as teachers teach. It is the teacher who, in the end, accom-
modates to the sources of conflict and dissonance in his work.
To understand policies in practice we need to understand how
teachers do this, and of particular interest are the dilemmas
experienced by teachers as they are faced with decisions, in
which points of view conflict and not everyone is likely to be
satisfied with the results of the decision. Teaching involves
such dilemmas for teachers, and attempting to implement innovative doctrines increases teacher consciousness of these
endemic dilemmas. This is not to say that teachers are con-
tinuously aware of the dilemmas created by the nature of their
work. They are not. However, when teachers attempt to
implement innovations whose doctrine is, in some respects,
at odds with their own commitments, the opportunity exists
to fathom what teachers perceive to be problematic in their
work and to understand how they deal with such problems;
particularly ones stemming from innovation.

In this chapter, teachers' perceptions, of the dilemmas
created by their efforts to implement 'Patterns', the schools
Council 'Integrated Science Project' (SCISP)[7] are described in
order to illuminate the nature of dilemmas endemic in the
teachers' world and magnified by proposals to change radically
habitual practice. SCISP doctrine, as we shall see, posed a
radical challenge to customary practice and, for this reason,
suits us well as a context in which to study how teachers construe their work, and how their ideas about practice affect
their interpretation of the SCISP doctrine (see Table 5.1).

To gather information, eight graduate science teachers, in
three comprehensive schools, were asked to report on their
science teaching in a systematic way, and various procedures
were provided in the plan to check these reports with others
and to probe behind possible facades that might be erected in

Table 5.1:   The Contrast Between SCISP Doctrine and School
Practice

	SCISP Doctrine	Science Department Practice
Goals	- general education - habits of critical intelligence - goals are tightly related to methods	- career orientation - acquisition of information - goals loosely related to methods
Social relation-ships	- a new partnership between teachers and taught - equality - teacher-teacher co-operation	- teacher authority vested in subject expertise - teachers on their own
Technology	- discovery approach - discussion - science as process - no syllabus - no revision for exams - teacher control of content detail - internal assessment - attitude change assessed - assessment criterion-referenced	- lecture/question-answer - instruction - science as content - syllabus based - revision for exams - mandated content - no internal assessment - no attitude change assessment - assessment norm-referenced

the research encounters. Classroom observation, student interviews and inventories were used in this fashion.

The reports of the teachers are discussed in terms of three
major dilemmas of teaching: the dilemma of conflicting commitments (theory); the dilemma of uncertain efficiency (technology);[8] the dilemma of influence (social relationships). The
main body of the chapter focuses on the dilemma of influence
as it emerges from the use of an inquiry approach to science
teaching. In the final part of the chapter, all of the dilemmas
will be used to support the argument that, instead of policy
makers continuing to urge more and increasingly exotic innovations upon teachers, many of which increase the complexity
of their work, attention ought to be given to helping teachers
become more aware of the underlying nature of their work and
thereby come to terms with the limitations imposed by its complex
nature. By understanding the complexities of their work,
teachers can begin to build the basis for their own more sophisticated assessments of policy proposals coming from outside.

DILEMMAS OF INQUIRY

The SCISP designers urged that a partnership between pupil
and teacher be fostered. This partnership was to be based on
the use of discussion built around investigations in the textbooks dealing with social issues and experimental data. Such
discussions form the central activities of an inquiry approach
in science teaching. However, a discussion runs directly counter
to customary science classroom practice. Normally the teacher
acts as an authority on the subject at hand, and there is usually
nothing at issue. If there appears to be something at issue, it
is only because the point is hidden temporarily, but all the
while the teacher is exercising a controlling function over what
is asked and how responses are appraised. The teacher is in
control of the point of the lesson and exercises editorial peroga-
tives. With nothing at issue, and with the teacher at the helm,
normally it is possible to cover material without interruption
and with dispatch; under these circumstances the job of covering the syllabus can proceed apace. Such is the usual way the
teacher exerts influence.
    In an inquiry lesson, however, all of this is changed. The
point is often elusive to all concerned, and control over what
is significant is relinquished, because it is shared, and to those
involved, 'progress' seems slow. In comparison with more direct
ways of teaching such as recitation, inquiry was seen by the
teachers in this study to be inefficient and they reported
difficulty in handling such lessons. When one considers how
the role of the teacher in the discussion that inquiry involves
differs from more direct teaching, it is not hard to understand
why the teachers had difficulty. In inquiry, and unlike instruction, the parties share an equality of status as they pursue what
is or what ought to be the case. No one holds the answer by
authority of expertise or role, and the answer is 'discovered'
rather than pronounced. [9] The contrast between inquiry and
didactic modes of teaching could hardly be sharper, especially
with respect to the status of the participants and the function
of the activity. In inquiry the teacher cannot claim the right to
impose answers on the group by virtue of status or expertise.
If this happened, then the parties involved would not be
inquiring.
    Two forms of inquiry as a way of teaching can be discerned
in the SCISP Investigations. [10] One, which will be discussed
first, involved the pupils in seeking generalisations, what the
'Handbook' called 'pattern finding'; what is the case is sought
through an assessment of the data. In the second form, what
ought to be the case is considered; in this case controversial
issues rather than experimental data are discussed. In both forms
of inquiry, the teacher and pupils are guided by standards of
inference and argument; no one has the final word by right of
position; the influence of the teacher is indirect.
    Teachers, had they looked in the 'SCISP Handbook', would

not have found much guidance concerning the pedagogy of inquiry; the teacher was offered only this:

> Teachers are often worried about the danger of imposing their attitudes on pupils. It is suggested that class discussion be based on the material provided . . . and that they should not become the basis of disagreement between pupils and the teacher. Direction will sometimes need to be given and the teacher often selects material to be discussed. [11]

Teachers had to work out their own approach to the use of discussion in their classrooms. In doing this they faced - dilemma; to fully implement the SCISP doctrine they had to adopt less influential styles of teaching. Yet teachers saw such styles as inefficient; how were they to get the point across to pupils as clearly as possible if the point of the lesson was at issue; how could one teach and inquire?

The experience of the teachers with an inquiry approach as a way of teaching science will be described first and later this experience will be interpreted using data gathered from probing clinical interviews. We begin with the problems teachers experienced in teaching by inquiry.

Discovering What Is the Case

Teachers spoke of the special language they found in the 'Patterns' books. At first it was hard to understand what teachers meant by the term 'language'. However, it became clear that the direct interrogation of the pupil in the SCISP texts was being referred to, and the teachers were somewhat puzzled by this 'language'; a combination of suggested activity and questions built into the text. As well, the SCISP texts have a vocabulary of their own: 'patterns', 'problem-solving', 'predictions' and 'building blocks' occur in the first four pages of 'Patterns 1'. 'Carbonates fizz' was offered as the 'type species' of SCISP language. It is, in fact, part of the first series of Investigations in 'Patterns 1'. What the teachers were confronting was the SCISP version of an inquiry approach based on the learning theories of Gagné. [12]

James Edwards at Midfield School [13] described how difficult it was for his students to deal with the first investigations in the scheme:

> One of the first experiments in the third year was to find the patterns, the whole of SCISP was to find the pattern. . . Add acids to carbonates; they fizz. Acid plus a carbonate (fizzes), but then (the fizzing) stops (with marble). . . Now in mixed ability groups, or for anybody who is lower ability, they were finding it difficult to change their idea.

The SCISP language posed problems in the sense that pupils

were being asked to generalise immediately, and then they had
to deal with an example which required them to change their
generalisation; all this occured in the first four Investigations.
The generalising to find a pattern and having to modify the
pattern continued to gives James' students problems:

> And in there is an experiment to find what happens with the
> rate of reaction. . . You put in lots of thermometers, which
> we'd managed to get through SCISP, and they'd watch the
> reaction. They can see it goes faster with increasing tempera-
> ture. They'd get a graph which is completely different . . .
> and that was within the realm of the most able. But the
> lower ability, they weren't getting it at all.

Mercia teachers described the difficulties the discovery
approach leads to:

> Carbonates fizz. They can all see this, but when you start
> talking about a pattern, some of the low ability say, 'What
> are you talking about?' (BJ)

> Discovery learning is very good for able kids. But, you
> know I don't think it's the way to do it for less able kids. . .
> It wouldn't work because they just don't have the reasoning
> capacity to move from factual information to mental models.
> This is the difference between the O-level and the CSE
> chap. (TJ)

> Whereas for the lower ability child to do that (look at things
> from different angles) would be confusing. Therefore the
> lower ability child needs to look at it from just one angle,
> and learn it. (RS)

The 'carbonates fizz' example was used by a number of teachers
to describe how the SCISP material was organised. It was the
combination of a find-out-for-yourself approach and numerous
questions in the 'Pattern' books that the teachers called the
'language' of SCISP. James Edwards' comments also suggested
that he preferred direct teaching to pattern finding, because
it is more efficient:

> This finding of patterns is all very well, but it doesn't follow
> into A-level. You're not searching for patterns when it comes
> to A-level. You use the patterns you already know.

Two SCISP students taking A-level physics at Midfield echoed
James' distinction between the inquiry approach in SCISP
and instruction at A-level:

> (It) teaches you to look for patterns. In normal science (they
> say) this is such and such. You are told. In SCISP you look

at information and see what is going on. So it's a good basis for practical work. A-level is quite different. You know what you are looking for. In SCISP it's more 'do it and see what happens'.

There isn't much pattern finding at A-level. (You) read about it rather than finding it out for yourself.

The dilemma Robert Young experienced was that the SCISP methods left him with the feeling that the problems pupils had with SCISP reflected on him:

The level at which they had to discuss and the amount of information required first of all to understand and then to approach from a different point of view was beyond their ability. . . I think possibly one of the reasons why I felt I wasn't being successful teaching SCISP, because I didn't have a sufficiently broad background of teaching experience . . . I was in the situation where you are asking two questions; am I successful as a teacher and am I successful in teaching the material?

James Edwards also felt ill-prepared for the teaching demands of SCISP. He considered that the training of scientists did not prepare them for the inquiry mode:

I'd gone away from traditional chalk and talk. But this now not only asked the teacher to be a leader of pattern finding, but also a leader in terms of discussion. And scientists, by their very training, have been accepters of knowledge, bodies of facts, and they've not found them all by going through discovery learning . . . the pattern of SCISP work was foreign to what they'd received.

Bryan Jenkins echoed James' view that inquiry was not the usual way of teaching science:

The trouble is we don't deliberately use that. I think the teacher tries to short-circuit it. You don't give them the information saying, 'There's a pattern, find it.' We say, 'This is true, this is true. Ptyalin digests starch.' You can tell them, 'That's a fact, then write it down and learn it', or you can give them a lot of different liquids, play with them and say, 'Now, which one digests starch?' . . . You can either tell them or leave them to discover it and I know which is the quickest.

Peter Judge said that he imposed his own structure on the discovery lessons. Ironically, he considered that his teaching had become more didactic to compensate for a lack of structure:

I feel the lessons have become more didactic than the equiva-

lent Nuffield (course). (We) either print the missing material
or tell them about it. They are being talked at more than in
an ordinary course. . . The Nuffield type discovery lesson
became more and more limited as time went on. A cap had been
doffed to it rather than it being the backbone.

Andrew Scott took much the same view:

One should have some idea of where you are going; you don't
want to blunder in the dark. (I) want to tell them what they
are up to in experimental work. I like to show the light at
the beginning and develop it from there. Set the scene
initially. (I) try not to delay getting at the pattern.

These comments suggest that a dilemma exists for teachers
here; unless the teachers put their perspective forward quite
clearly, the pupils might not get the point of the lesson; yet
to do so tends to destroy the 'discovery' experience. The
teachers, I found, modified the inquiry based project material
either to rescue a semblance of structure and purposefulness,
or they abandoned the formal lesson entirely. [14]

Teacher Approaches to Inquiry

Three views about inquiry emerged from the teachers' comments
on their lessons involving discussion. These might be characterised as 'waffle', 'recess' and 'pretence'. The waffle view is
based on the idea that discussions used in inquiry are like
instruction in that they are intended to convey some predetermined information but, because of the background role
of the teacher, are aimless and inefficient. Discussion is seen
as an inefficient method for accomplishing instructional goals.
John Williams' comments illustrate this point:

There were blocks of practical and blocks of waffle. . . It's
a bit badly balanced. In some sections it's all practical, in
other chapters a lot of discussion all together, some of
which can be boring for the students. You can find yourself talking your head off leading the group and you suddenly think, 'Well, they're not offering any opinions!
They're just sitting there!'

John's characterisation of discussion as waffle suggests that he
does not see what the function of a classroom discussion might
be; using the function of instruction as a basis for his assessment of the structure of a discussion, he concluded that it was
nothing but waffle. Because discussion failed to deliver facts,
John found it frustrating; 'I do like the facts. I do think that
you have to get the facts in first. SCISP doesn't seem to agree
with this.'
John is critical of discussions because they seem pointless.

Not knowing how to organise a discussion, he finds himself talking, but accomplishing nothing. Compared to instruction, which is efficient for getting the 'facts in', discussion is inefficient. Getting the facts in is prime; what happens after that is left to the pupil and to the future. Teachers' comments left the impression that there is no second step; getting in the facts is the job; using them in a discussion is not.

Bryan Wilson viewed discussion as the absence of serious teaching. Having a discussion was a form of recess; as his comments suggest:

I just let the argument go. It got very noisy. . . As I say, being near Christmas it was something which they would say, 'Oh, we haven't done any work this afternoon, we had this.' When in fact they probably had to think quite deeply to formulate their arguments. If nothing else, it's been teaching them to argue.

Bryan had the students 'discuss' the Investigation as an impromptu event. No background reading had been done and the students had not prepared in any way for the event. It was not a serious episode, and even if the pupils got out of hand, as a non-serious event, the teacher's authority was not undermined. Bryan saw himself exerting minimal influence in a discussion: 'I say, "Anybody got a suggestion?", and someone will immediately take the viewpoint of the business people, or the worker, or the people . . . You know, eventually the class takes over.'

Other teachers also viewed discussion as a form of recess:

I sit back and let them argue with each other. I emphasise that what I say is my own opinion and they can shoot me down. Quite often they will argue with me. I use my opinion to start a discussion. (JW)

I will give them the mechanics of the problem and then I will throw out an outrageous statement like people with genetic diseases should be allowed to die and then get them going. It takes a lot to get them going. (AS)

The amount of time I can spend on discussion is limited and, you know, in that sense, a free-floating discussion is not on, because you can free-float for twenty-five minutes and not leave yourself enough time for an important practical. (TJ)

The pretence view involved adopting something resembling the form of a discussion for a period of time, after which the teacher took over and explained what the point was.

That's where you have to discuss it and that's where some of them get lost. It becomes so open-ended that a good many

of them don't know where they are going. You have to
direct it very clearly and when you have finished you have
to put up your main points. (BJ)

Essentially the teacher is trying to get them to form their
own ideas independently of his, but he will make sure they end
up with the right idea in the end. (TJ)

The bulk of the lesson would be independent of the teacher,
it's their feelings, but the crunch of the lesson is summing up;
(this) would be the teacher. (RS)

Although a discussion might appear to be taking place in the
classroom, and some aspects of the form simulated, the point
of the lesson was predetermined and imposed by the teacher.

Inquiry and Teacher Authority

Teachers reported a dilemma in controlling inquiry lessons.
Ironically, some of the teachers thought that the SCISP students
were often too critical. Others simply felt that the students
were unable to participate responsibly in discussion because
they were immature or could not grasp the point. John Williams
expressed concern about overly critical pupils:

One (an ex-SCISP pupil in the sixth form) has got the
attitude which makes me see red. When I am telling them
how to find the specific heat capacity of something or other,
(he says), 'Well, if it's a known number, why do we have
to know how to find it?' My point of view is that we might
be on the verge of a great discovery.

John's answer seems to suggest that he had no good answer to
the student's question. The critical stance taken by the
student, one encouraged by SCISP, is not appreciated by
John, who felt that this kind of outcome of SCISP was un-
desirable. What he has taken for granted as being valuable,
the pupil is clearly questioning and this is interpreted by
John as a direct challenge to his authority and therefore
meriting an extravagant answer. Comments made by students
suggested that taking a critical attitude was something they
felt SCISP promoted; typical of the comments made was, 'You'd
get a set of results and you had to think out your own answer
rather than a whole lot of textbook answers.'
  Bryan Jenkins also found that the pupil participation encouraged in SCISP created a dilemma: 'I said, "Look, if you
don't understand, ask me." I regretted it later. They asked
me little points and we were held up . . . I learned to turn
around to the class and say, "Look, what I taught you last
week was wrong." '
  One of Bryan's lessons I observed provided an example of
some of the difficulties in running a discussion that he en-

countered and his desire to 'get on with it'. The class had
been given an exercise from 'Patterns 4', which involved
deciding what criteria to use in designing a new town. Bryan
gave the class a lead in making the first suggestion and from
there the class produced ideas which were not treated in any
systematic way. Ideas emerged, but they were not sorted out,
and most of the flow was between teacher and pupil, rather
than from pupil to pupil. The episode ended when Bryan gave
a lecture on a new town based on some reading he had done.
The shapeless discussion mode was pre-empted by the well
organised lecture. Thus Bryan was able to conclude the lesson
on a note of authority and purposefulness.

Richard Simpson also was critical of the willingness of the
SCISP pupils to question his statements:

> There are some characters in there who are deliberately
> obstreperous. They are supposed to question and some of
> them question for the sake of it . . . the experienced teacher
> can (stop it).

One pupil challenged Richard's marking scheme in relation to a
question taken from one of the 'Teacher's Guides'. The pupils
were asked to explain how a boulder had come to be standing
in a field. The pupils said that it was a glacial erratic, while
Richard claimed that it was there because of differential
weathering. When his answer was challenged strongly by the
pupils, Richard conceded that they might both be right and he
allowed part marks for their answer. How did Richard interpret
this episode?:

> So they were prepared to argue and I was prepared to listen
> and give them credit for argument, and of course for their
> putting over their argument under pressure. It gave them
> confidence in handling themselves . . . . Their knowledge may
> have been better than mine. I had a nagging doubt in the
> back of my mind that they might be right . . . Perhaps it
> showed them that it is possible to have a different answer
> and arrive at the same result, that I was good, fair enough
> to give them justice for it.

At the heart of these comments are dilemmas associated with
the altered authority relationships which inquiry involves.
For example, John Bryan and Richard expressed misgivings
about the increased pupil 'comment' which seemed to be questioning established practices and teacher expertise, and slowing
down the progress of the work. Established relationships
between pupil and teacher seemed to the teachers to be undermined by operating in an inquiry mode.

Teachers clearly had reasons for treating the discussion mode
with caution; first, the teachers did not see how they could
accomplish important tasks in the classroom; secondly, they

were unsure just what role they and their students were to
play in a discussion; finally, the experience they had had with
discussion was viewed negatively. In short, their reports
suggested a lack of understanding and a suspicion of the altered
social relationships that discussion seemed to them to entail. [15]
Why was this so?

In order to probe the views of the teachers about social
relationships in different forms of science teaching including
inquiry, and to understand why teachers thought about
discussion-based lessons the way they did, searching, clinical
interviews were planned. It was clear from preliminary interviews that teachers had misgivings about reducing the amount
of influence they exerted in the classroom; it was clear too
that they had experienced some unpleasant episodes in attempting to operate in a less directive fashion. This meant that,
perhaps, what they might be asked to talk about, would be
seen as being asked to admit failures, or otherwise be seen to
be in some respects unsuccessful. Rather than confront teachers
directly about how they viewed their role in the classroom,
indirect techniques were used, based on the personal construct
theory of George Kelly. [16] These are described briefly now and
the results of these interviews used to interpret the teachers'
reports of classroom experience with SCISP.

TEACHER THEORIES OF INFLUENCE: A KEY TO
UNDERSTANDING PRACTICE

Each teacher was asked to complete a grid in which each of
twenty forms of science teaching was appraised using ten
constructs; five supplied by the person and five supplied by
the investigator (see Table 5.2). Thus, for example, if the
person had supplied the construct 'productive-unproductive',
this construct was used to appraise each of the twenty elements: for example, giving notes, acting as a discussion leader,
pupils on a field trip, and so on. Each of these would be
assessed, for example, as either definitely or somewhat productive or unproductive; or, if the person did not think that it
made sense to appraise an element in terms of productivity
then no appraisal was made. Each person thus made two hundred
appraisals in the process of completing the grid. The grid, it
can now be seen, contains a large amount of information. In
order to see what patterns might exist in the appraisals correlation, matrices of constructs and elements were factor analysed. [17]

Forms of Influence

Bipolarity was taken to be especially useful in interpreting the
nature of the factors involved in the teachers' perceptions of
science teaching approaches (see Table 5.3). An analysis of

Table 5.2:   Science Teaching Events Used as Elements in
Construct Elicitation

---

1. Pupils are making notes during a lesson given by the teacher.
2. At their seats pupils are doing problems.
3. The teacher is asking the class how to control an experiment.
4. The class is watching TV.
5. The teacher is asking pupils to offer hypotheses.
6. The teacher is doing a demonstration while pupils make observations.
7. In class some pupils are helping others who have had difficulty.
8. The teacher is questioning pupils to guide them to a generalisation.
9. On a field trip to a pond pupils are collecting data.
10. The teacher is acting as neutral chairman in a class discussion.
11. The teacher is questioning the class on the homework.
12. The teacher is putting examples of a relationship on the board for the pupils' notes.
13. During a practical pupils are making observations.
14. Three pupils are presenting a seminar.
15. The teacher is pointing out the scientific principles of a model he is demonstrating.
16. A group of pupils are gathering data from students on the sports field.
17. Pupils are writing an essay at home.
18. Pupils are making measurements to verify a law.
19. A pupil who has had difficulty is using a programmed text.
20. Pupils are supplying labels for a diagram.

---

factors exhibiting this feature suggested that an important perception underlying the appraisals of the teaching events was the nature of the influence exerted by the teacher. Two forms of influence could be discerned in the way elements loaded on factors; these have been called high influence or direct teaching; and low influence or indirect teaching. It is in terms of influence that the data from the clinical interviews and the grid analysis are discussed.

The analysis of the bipolar factors suggested that teachers appraised different teaching events in terms of the extent of their involvement in the event. Events which did not involve the teacher directly tended to load together; those that involved direct teaching also loaded together. Table 5.3 shows that when direct or high influence teaching (information giving or teacher guided lessons) appears to characterise one pole, often low influence teaching (self teaching) appears to characterise the

Table 5.3: Teaching Activities Characteristic of Bipolar
Factors Extracted From the Analysis of Grids

Teacher is putting notes on board. (960)* IG	Pupils are gathering data on sports field. (-517) ST
Pupils are supplying label for a diagram. (923) IG	Pupils are gathering data on sports field. (-337) ST
At their seats, pupils are doing problems. (908) IG	Teacher asks class how to control an experiment. (-461) ST
Teacher is doing demonstration while pupils record observation. (899) IG	Pupils are presenting seminar. (-714) ST
Teacher is putting notes on the board. (863) IG	Pupils are presenting seminar. (-893) ST
Pupils are making notes during a lesson given by teacher. (820) IG	In class some pupils are helping others who have had difficulty. (-858) ST
Teacher asks class how to control an experiment. (913) TG	Teacher acts as neutral chairman in discussion. (-485) ST
Teacher asks class how to control an experiment. (867) TG	In class some pupils are helping others who have had difficulty. (-739) ST
Pupils verify law (863) TG	Teacher acts as neutral chairman in discussion (-887) ST
In class some pupils are helping others who have had difficulty. (897) ST	The teacher is questioning pupils to guide them to a generalisation. (-843) TG

Notes: * loading on factor.
   IG = information giving.
   TG = teacher guided.
   ST = self-teaching.

other. The loading on the bipolar factors suggested three forms
of science teaching which might be called: 'information giving'
and 'teacher guided interaction' (involving high teacher influence), and the contrast to these activities, 'self teaching'
(pupils working mostly on their own, or with other pupils).
In the latter case, apparently varied approaches seemed to be
viewed as similar on the basis of the common property of low
teacher influence; their idiosyncracies seemed to have been
ignored in favour of this common property.
   It is not surprising to find that there may exist one or two

fundamental dimensions of role appraisal common to these
teachers. Westbury, for example, has argued that because
of the nature of the organisation of classrooms, teachers face
a set of common dilemmas which evoke common responses. [18]
Now, Westbury's argument is couched in terms of classroom
characteristics somehow shaping teacher responses. He says,
'The classroom . . . modulates the conception of teaching
derived from the tutorial.' A step beyond this formulation is
to ask what the common responses are - how teachers view
their function.

Initiative, Control and Influence

Using coded teacher observation data and cluster analysis,
Eggleston, and his collaborators found three clusters which
were identified as three styles of science teaching. [19] These
styles have similarities with ones identified here. The first
style that they identified involved 'initiative held by the
teacher, who challenges his pupils with a comprehensive array
of questions'. [20] This style is similar to the present 'teacher
guided participation' one. Their second style is characterised
by a relatively high incidence of teacher statements of facts,
and teacher direction to sources for fact finding. This style
is similar to the present 'information transfer' one. Their third
style is characterised as: '(pupils') work is practical, and the
intellectual level of engagement in it is high. Perhaps the
description "pupil-centered inquiry" might not be inaccurate.'
This style is suggestive of the 'self-teaching' style identified
here. Although using quite different investigation methods,
the Eggleston analysis shares considerable similarities with that
suggested by the study of the SCISP teachers.
    Walker and Adelman also developed a typology of teacher
styles based on an analysis of tape records of lessons. [21] Their
conceptualisation of teaching styles also has some similarity
with that of the present study. Their analysis is contained
within two conceptions of control; one involving the nature of
the response required of the pupil, and the other the control
exerted over the lesson by the way the content is organised.
Their low control style is similar in concept to the present
'self-teaching' and their focused style, involving high control,
is similar to 'information giving'. Thus, under high control,
the pupil is asked to give right or wrong answers, and the
content is predetermined according to the logic of the subject.
Under low control, multiple answers are possible, and the
direction of the substance of the lesson not tightly predetermined. Walker and Adelman call this style 'freewheeling'; a
term reminiscent of the way teachers in this study viewed
inquiry lessons. The style is, of course, only freewheeling
with reference to more tightly controlled styles. In their discussion of this style, they refer to the lack of predictability
of the pupil contributions and the direction of the lesson typical

of the freewheeling style. In the present study, teachers
construed low influence teaching similarly.

The two studies referred to, and the present one, centre
the analysis of teaching on the influence of the teacher over
the lesson. In the case of Eggleston's work, the initiative of
the teacher is assumed as a defining characteristic of a style;
in Walker and Adelman's case, the control of the teacher is
evoked.

In the present study the conception of influence is developed,
guided by comments of the teachers, as a way of portraying
how teachers construed social relationships in the classroom.
Influence, as will be discussed below, involves more than
control of the pupils and more than leadership; it is a conception which attempts to capture the complexity of social
relationships in the classroom as seen by teachers. Perhaps in
all these conceptualisations it may well be a case of the ana-
lytical framework driving the data. However, the analysis of
interview data and follow-up probes suggests that interpreting
the teachers' appraisals of the teaching elements in terms of a
conception of influence is warranted. It is to a discussion of
this conception that we now turn.

Forms of Influence

Both the factor analysis of the grids, and the nature of the
constructs elicited from the teachers themselves, suggested
that a consideration of who was in charge in the classroom
formed an important perspective from which they looked at
different forms of teaching. To pursue this, how teachers
construed their influence was examined in a follow-up interview, which took place once the grids had been completed.
Each grid was analysed and a set of probing follow-up questions then was developed, based on how the grid had been
completed, and unique to each person. Teachers were asked
questions about their grid based on: apparent inconsistencies;
empty cells; and surprising appraisals (given what was known
of the person). Each teacher was asked about ten questions
based on their grid in a non-threatening way. The answers
to these questions form the basis for the analysis of the concept of influence. Particular attention was paid to how teachers
appraised low influence situations.

To organise the discussion of influence, all of the elicited
constructs were divided into three categories depending upon
the degree of influence that seemed to be involved judged on
the way the teacher talked about and used the construct. On
the face of it, this might seem a difficult thing to do; but so
pervasive was the concern about influence as a basis for
appraising teaching approaches, and so great the extent of
similarities in the way the teachers construed the science
teaching approaches, that this way of organising the constructs
seemed to be possible without distorting what the teachers had

tried to convey through their use of the grids. Accordingly, the discussion of influence is organised into three parts: forms of high influence teaching (1) teacher as 'prime mover' and (2) as 'navigator'; and low influence teaching (3) teacher as 'referee'. Forms of high influence teaching are discussed first, beginning with the teacher as prime mover.

Prime Mover. Acting as prime mover was seen to serve a number of functions; the main one being that the teacher could ensure that important information was transferred to the student during a process in which pupils paid attention to the teacher. The transfer of information involved was said not to engage the student intellectually, but it did get across facts without which, it was argued, further, more stimulating activity could not occur. The teachers emphasised that it was necessary to give notes and to lecture in spite of the drawbacks. However, their comments intimated that they did not want it thought that this was all that they did, nor that they didn't realise that there was limited intellectual challenge for the student. Information transfer was construed as: menial, not ideal, rote, humdrum, the pupil as a sponge. Robert Young's menial construct captures the 'love-hate' dilemma of information transfer:

> Pupils sitting at their seats doing physics problems - that's menial, but it is essential . . . Pupils supplying labels - you don't really need to understand what it's all about to label a spade a spade sort of thing. You can do that and be successful at it, but have no idea what's going on. It's menial in that sense, but it is essential.

One of the complaints about the approach was that the 'teacher did all the work'. The teachers, by saying this, recognised a dilemma: they were not supposed to do all the work; yet this is how they thought they should teach. Positive appraisals involved such terms as: fundamental, essential, have to have it, quick, economical, valid, necessary, productive.

Robert Young explained how, in this style of teaching, he could be a 'prime mover':

> The teacher is hopefully conveying enthusiasm and liking for the subject knowledge. Hopefully this (knowledge) would also be in their books. Taking down relevant notes which would be useful to them, in the sense of the impending exam. This is productive in the sense of, for the time spent, they will have precise information, from which to learn and gain knowledge. Productive in the sense of getting them through the exam. Since I consider that that's the essentiality of teaching (leading the class), then I consider it (giving notes) productive.

Teacher as Navigator. Teachers construed a number of teaching

events in terms of their controlling the <u>direction</u> and <u>point</u>
of the lesson while allowing students to <u>participate</u>. This function involves the teacher as navigator. The following comments
illustrate why the teachers thought that it was important that
they navigate the lesson:

> I would never like to have a class sort of hung up too high
> and dry (with their) going out of the room thinking, 'Well,
> what on earth am I supposed to make of that one?' (TJ)

> I think the less able pupil relies on the teacher for guidance,
> for information. They tend to believe what the teacher says.
> They lose confidence if the teacher isn't leading them (JW)

> I think it's ideal that a pupil find out the answer for themself.
> But I think it's too long-winded. (JE)

> They've got to believe in what you are saying. If they think
> you are unsure of your facts, they switch off. Do they trust
> you are telling them the right things they need to know, and,
> in fact, is the stuff you are telling them factually correct?
> (AS)

The teachers took it as their task to ensure that the lesson had
a valid point and that the students could trust the teacher to
make sure that the class ended up with the right information and
the correct ideas. Simultaneously, they had to ensure that the
lesson did not go astray. The former might be called the
'editorial' and the latter the 'director' function.
The following comments describe the <u>editorial</u> function with
the key terms underlined:

> The teacher guides the discussion and puts them right if they
> are wrong. He <u>takes out</u> what isn't quite relevant. (TJ)

> Now the teacher is a physiotherapist, <u>putting right</u> any of
> the ills. (JE)

> The <u>final arbiter</u> of what is correct or incorrect is, I think,
> the <u>teacher</u>; unless someone else in the class knows the
> answer. (TJ)

In the editorial function, the teacher lets the students have
their say. He listens to what is said and assesses it in relation
to factual accuracy and relevance to the point. It is the teacher's
job to see that the point of the lesson is established. If the
pupils on their own fail to get the point, then the teacher must
step in. By acting as an editor, the teacher serves three related
functions: students <u>understand</u> the material, they are <u>assured</u>
that there is some <u>point</u> to understanding the material and they
<u>participate</u> in a process which is designed to engage their attention.

Besides acting as editor the teacher steers the lesson to a
desired end; a predictable outcome for the lesson. This is
the <u>director</u> function. Selection of materials was referred to as
a way of directing the lesson. In John Williams' case, doing
problems from a book or labelling a diagram had predictable
outcomes because, through the materials, he controlled what
pupils did. Such activities he saw as necessary and he contrasted them somewhat defensively with 'breaking new ground
every time'; a reference to the supposed discoveries of the
discovery approach which he didn't see happening in his class.
Bryan Jenkins saw practical work and demonstrations as under
his control so that he could ensure that the intended points
would be made: 'If you are trying to get an important point
over, you are going to choose an experiment which <u>will</u> show
it. You don't choose something which <u>might</u> show it.'
The most common way of directing a lesson was to use a
series of questions to alert students to the direction the
lesson was meant to be going. By careful questioning, students
could be made to discover the point. The following excerpts
suggest how this works:

He is taking it bit by bit to build a clear picture of the whole
thing, so that each pupil in the class is contributing a small
part. (RS)

It's a form of guiding which you can give to kids. When the
penny drops, hopefully, for the majority of them, for me
that's gratifying. You have given them information and you
have guided them to the conclusion you wanted. (AS)

The very good teacher is the one that can control the discussion exactly along the lines he wants to go without the
pupils realising it. (BJ)

Low Influence Teaching. Teachers' comments concerning low
influence teaching contrasted sharply with those associated
with high influence teaching. Where teachers were clear about
what they were trying to accomplish and how to go about it in
the latter case, they were unclear about the effects of their
teaching and their role in the former. Where they had been
<u>definite</u>, <u>realistic</u> and <u>evaluative</u> in their comments, they be-
came <u>tentative</u>, <u>detached</u> and <u>unrealistic</u>. All of these trends
suggested that high and low influence teaching are construed
in quite different ways by teachers, and that they represent
<u>quite different forms of teaching</u>. Two main themes emerged
from comments about low influence teaching (which involved
the teacher acting as a discussion teacher, or organising a
student seminar, or field work, or setting essays on social
issues topics). First, teachers found it difficult to talk about
the <u>intellectual</u> activity which they tended to associate with
low <u>influence</u>. Their talk about intellectual goals seemed vague

and loosely related to what they said they did in class. Secondly, teachers had difficulty seeing how they or their pupils were meant to behave. They were not sure where their influence lay.

Pupils' Thinking

Comments about the effects of instruction on the pupils' thinking were either in everyday kinds of language like 'reasoned judgements' or 'powers of reasoning'; in pyschologically derived phrases like 'insight' or 'synthesis' or 'affective'; or in phrases derived from science like 'deduction' or 'inference'. Whatever the origin, they seemed vague. The following examples illustrate the language used by the teachers:

> They are having information fed to them and they are having to <u>churn</u> some information back out again. It has to undergo a <u>wave length change</u>. (JW)

> We then <u>infer</u> from the data. When the pupils are given or have the <u>information</u>, they are asked to <u>deduce</u> what might happen, <u>what is what</u> . . . They have to <u>have</u> various <u>ideas</u> . . . In putting labels (on a <u>diagram</u>) . . . they are <u>using</u> previous notes and previous experiences and <u>reasoning from</u> them. (RS)

> I think many of them will never be good <u>problem solvers</u> because this involves the highest level of <u>cognitive performance</u>. (TJ)

> <u>Psychological strata</u> are, ideally, all being <u>brought into play</u> here . . . They must involve a variety of <u>bringing together</u> all of your different <u>affective</u> and cognitive <u>styles of thought</u>. (PJ)

The teachers described the effects of their instruction with some tentativeness. Andrew Scott used the term 'hopefully' a number of times to signal a statement about the effects of his instruction: hopefully his instruction was relevant, hopefully intellectually stimulating and hopefully interesting. Peter Judge used the term 'ideally' to signal that what he was talking about didn't always occur. The detached style of the talk can be seen in phrases like 'sort of' or 'what is what' or 'your different affective and cognitive styles'. Bryan Jenkins reverted to short, choppy sentences when talking about the effects of his instruction: 'This group is getting the children to think. Getting them to produce ideas. Going deeper into them. Having to verbalise and defend their ideas. Helping to argue.'
   A good example of the contrast between teacher talk about social relations in the classroom and the effects of instruction on pupils' thinking can be seen in the following extracts:

(In discussion) low ability kids just usually aren't prepared
to say anything, given the situation where they can say anything in a ordered way as opposed to making stupid comments
throughout the lessons. (AS)

Getting them to correlate the appropriate information (in
essays) in a coherent way would be asking too much . . .
This is productive in the sense of, for the time spent, they
will have precise information from which to learn and gain
knowledge. (AS)

The picture of unruly 'low ability' kids making stupid comments
whenever they can get a word in edgeways is sharply drawn
and imbued with concern. On the other hand, the effects of
instruction (underlined) come across as vague and offhand.
It is hard to know what is going on in pupils' heads, and it
is not surprising to find teachers vague about this. Yet others
expected them to be able to say just what the effects of their
instruction are and curriculum materials often assume that
teachers readily understand how to improve the cognitive
abilities of their pupils. The comments of these teachers give us
some reason to suspect the idea that teachers talk easily about
the intellectual effects of their work in the classroom.

Authority in the Classroom

The other main theme running through the teachers' comments
about low influence teaching concerned the authority of the
teacher. The teachers found it difficult to understand how
they should behave and how to construe their students' behaviour, and, because of an apparent lack of experience, the
teachers tended to think of low influence teaching approaches
as if they were ineffective variants of more familiar forms.
The following series of comments indicates the nature of the
dilemmas teachers faced in relation to low influence teaching:

It's quite foreign to a lot of science teachers (being a neutral
chairman). They deal with a lot of facts and here we are
asking for discussions which could be very open-ended . . .
It's very difficult to manage (a discussion) with some of
them absent, or some have the facts and some don't . . .
Then you've got pupils at different levels of maturity to discuss something. Whereas some can and they might be mature
enough to put forward certain views, but not in a mature
manner, laughing about it, giving some stupid sort of
view . . . I can remember the one (SCISP Investigation)
which I didn't feel I could mark or give any sort of written
work in books, about the population problem and food. The
question was, what to do about it? and they came back, 'Well,
kill off anybody over the age of 32!' Who am I to say that is
wrong? . . . This (seminar) is difficult to manage, I think,

because the pupils haven't got the facts. They are very
loathe to get up and speak in front of others and it is usually
the extraverts who have got unusual ideas, which are
probably wrong anyway, so this is why it becomes difficult
to manage. (JE)

Robert Young did not see how a discussion could be used to
teach; for him a discussion had a predetermined point and pupil
comments were interruptions:

This is something that came up in SCISP that I found great
difficulty with. (Discussions were) very difficult to do.
This sort of area comes up in a course we call Humanities
where this sort of thing would be discussed at length. If
the teacher isn't competent and skilled at extracting conversation from kids, or if he isn't able to provide the correct stimulus to get the discussion started, and if the
conversation doesn't go quite the way it was anticipated, then
this is the difficulty with it. It's an attitude to teaching. If
you are prepared to accept their comments as you are going
through, even during demonstrations and if you are prepared
to answer their questions although not directly related, then
it's a fairly easy step to go to something like this. [22]

Peter Judge did not see how the teacher could act as a neutral
chairman and at the same time have a useful lesson given the
attributes of his pupils. Like the other teachers, he found the
lack of control frustrating, particularly the fact that many pupils
do not participate as a consequence:

When I have tried to play neutral chairman, it's a pretty lousy
description of the role. You are as much a manipulator as in
guided discovery. It might be possible, but I haven't experienced this myself. (Rather) it's the deliberate management of
ideas (by) inculcating your particular picture of these ideas
by a variety of devices. (I am) an information source and a
source of structure . . . It's very difficult to get genuine
synthesis of thought. My neutral chairman debates have tended
to be the students stating fixed positions; there being a clash
of opinions. You just get contrasting and opposing, not
synthesising. You can open your mouth and dribble away.
(Anyway) the majority in your neutral chairman debate are
(not going to talk), but in the essay, everyone is forced to
put something down. By the fifth (form), a typical group,
I'd say were getting a third of the group capable of fairly
good involvement. I wouldn't put it much higher than that.

What do these comments tell us about how teachers construe
their role in low influence teaching? It is evident that the
teachers tend to contrast such teaching with that where they
are in charge and able to act in familiar ways. In other words

the familiar role becomes a basis for describing and evaluating the low influence situations. These situations tend to be construed in terms of the extent of teacher withdrawal from a central role. Images of retreat and withdrawal, or abdication of the teacher role entirely (technician, librarian) are used. The following list captures the way teachers construed their 're-treat':

> The teacher doesn't seem involved. (TJ)

> The teacher is just a controlling person in the background, if necessary . . . The teacher is a guiding hand. (JW)

> I'm likely to be hovering, guiding, inspiring, ticking off . . . I really don't know how to handle that role (neutral chairman). (PJ)

> If the teacher does stay as technician-librarian, in other words, there's the resource, get on with it . . . (AS)

> The teacher is acting as an observer. (AS)

> The teacher is to some extent merely a technician. (RY)

> The teacher is acting as a referee. (RS)

> The teacher has disappeared further into the background. (JE)

The sense of withdrawal comes through clearly, and words like 'merely', or 'just' suggest a negative appraisal of the role. The term 'technician' is probably used to suggest something less than a professional role for the teacher. The teacher is cast as a referee in a game whose purpose and rules are unclear. It is hard to see how such a position could be acceptable to teachers.

WHY INQUIRY FALTERS IN THE CLASSROOM

The preliminary comments of the teachers seemed to indicate that inquiry teaching was difficult; they seemed to have had little experience with the approach. It is now possible to suggest why: teachers consider low influence teaching as ineffective and unsatisfying. A method of checking this hypothesis was available through the use of the supplied grid constructs. Five constructs of a general evaluative nature had been included in each of the grids. These were: promotes thinking; suitable for less able pupils; provides satisfaction for the teacher; appropriate to science; and difficult to manage. Four of these supplied constructs were used as a basis for assessing the way teachers appraised different forms of influence. Within

each category of influence, the pattern of correlation between
each of the elicited constructs in that category and each of the
four supplied constructs was examined in turn. Thus, for
example, it was found that, of the eleven constructs in the
'prime mover' category, ten correlated negatively with the
supplied construct 'promotes thinking', and the mean value of
the negative correlations was found to be +0.39 (see Table 5.4).
One might conclude from this that the prime mover role is not
seen to promote thinking. On the other hand, ten of the eleven
constructs were found to correlate positively with the supplied
construct 'appropriate for less able pupils', and the mean value
of these correlations was +0.40. Although not seen to promote
thinking, the prime mover role was seen to be suitable for less
able pupils.

Table 5.4: Teacher Appraisals of Forms of Influence in Science
Teaching

Appraisal (Supplied Constructs)	Forms of Influence (Elicited Constructs)					
	High Influence				Low Influence	
	Prime Mover		Navigator		Referee	
Provides teacher Satisfaction	Positive[a] (7/11)[b]	(0.30)[c]	Positive (8/9)	(0.40)	Negative (9/11)	(0.17)
Difficult to manage	Negative (10/11)	(0.46)	Positive (6/9)	(0.19)	Positive (13/17)	(0.33)
Appropriate for less able	Positive (10/11)	(0.40)	Positive (6/9)	(0.34)	Negative (12/17)	(0.22)
Promotes thinking	Negative (10/11)	(0.39)	Negative (6/9)	(0.26)	Positive (15/17)	(0.42)

Notes: a. Sign of majority of correlations.
       b. Number of correlations with that sign.
       c. Mean value of correlations with that sign.

The low influence role was seen to promote thinking, but
teachers were uncertain about the satisfaction to be gained
from working in a less direct way and sure that such a role
was difficult to manage. The most satisfying role was that
of navigator. When taken together, the two forms of high influence teaching are seen to provide more satisfaction, fewer
management difficulties and greater appropriateness for pupils
at the expense, it seems, of stimulating the pupil.[23]
    The data presented in the table fit the general trend of the

teachers' comments, which suggested greater concern about
making sure the point and direction of the lesson were established than with the intellectual stimulation of the student. As
we saw, teachers did not emphasise intellectual benefits of the
approaches they favoured; they emphasised the opportunity
these approaches gave them to exercise influence; an influence
directed towards covering the syllabus and ensuring that the
required material was transferred and understood by the pupils
in the correct way.

The teachers tended to appraise low influence situations
by reference to more familiar roles, and they tended to see these
situations as non-functional variants of teacher dominated ones.
Further, they assumed that low and high influence teaching
both serve common goals; so, for example, inquiry and practical
work were criticised for not being as efficient as more directed
forms of teaching. The teachers assumed that the more 'open'
methods were aimed at information transfer and interpretation;
that is, they assumed a conformity of goals for all methods.
Their influence, as they see it, seems to be directed not towards what happens in their students' heads, but to keeping
a bargain with students by ensuring that accurate, valid information is explicated in such a way as to guarantee its usefulness.
Useful tokens are exchanged.

As Peter Judge, one of the teachers in the study, put it,
teachers strive for a 'Good show, well presented'. A sense of
influence is based on being able to provide the stimulus and
expert guidance and the guaranteed information to help students
obtain the credentials they expect to gain. The teacher authenti-
cates what is transacted and guarantees it. Influence, as the
teachers see it, stems not from an understanding of psychological
principles, nor from the structure of their discipline, but from
their ability to convince the students that what is happening is
well produced and directed and with good 'cash value'. These
are the functions of the high influence role. [24]

By contrast, the teachers were not able to construe the nature
of low influence teaching in the same detailed functional way;
they did not seem able to construe the kinds of social relationships called for when teacher influence is low and they did not
seem able to construe an effective role for themselves, nor for
the pupils. The language they used suggested an imprecise and
vague grasp of the low influence role; for example: 'controlling
person', 'observer', 'referee'. The sense conveyed was that the
teacher had withdrawn in perplexity. [25]

The teachers' descriptions of their teaching, when taken in
relation to the expectations of project doctrine, clearly show how
dilemmas arise in practice. The doctrine promises intellectual
development for students; yet the methods recommended for
accomplishing this require the teacher to cope with increased
role diffuseness. Teachers realise they are expected to use less
direct methods if they are to 'succeed' in implementing the project,
yet they cannot see how that success is to be evidenced in terms

they can understand; thus they persevere with 'the old way' and
risk the opprobrium of those who urge the 'new way'. Fortunately
for them, those who do urge the 'new way' often lack the power
to press for it.
  Teachers are influenced by the expectations of parents,
principals, peers and students. They are expected to be influential in quite direct ways and they are expected to help students
pursue instrumental goals. By acting as energiser, editor and
guide, by identifying a syllabus of content, by seeking career
system goals, the teacher is able to adopt a relatively clear-cut
approach to meeting these expectations. [26] On the other hand, low
influence teaching like inquiry, without a syllabus, and involving
situations like being a chairman of a discussion, or sitting back
during student seminars, or marking essays on social issues,
is a much less clear-cut way for a science teacher to work. The
goals and rules of the game are not at all clear. Well might the
teacher ask, as did one of those in the study: 'What is the use
of my subject matter expertise and my ability to interpret it?'
The teachers in this study used the goals and rules they knew
in order to reconstruct the new game into an inefficient version
of the old, and eventually, tiring of the uncertainty about moves
for which the rules seemed unclear or didn't fit, they abandoned
the project. The low influence teaching that the project promoted
didn't make sense.
  In her contribution to an extensive report on science education
in the USA funded by the National Science Foundation ('Case
Studies in Science Education'), Francis Stevens has noted: 'A
disciplinary curriculum and authoritarian teaching are . . .
easiest for everybody.' [27] The report concluded that teachers
did not adopt inquiry methods because they are unwilling to
risk situations in which they may not know the answer and
suggested that teachers lack experience in dealing with the
questions of thoughtful students on doubtful topics. The report
indicated that, rather than stressing intellectual development,
teachers concentrate on 'socialisation' - preparing students to
progress in their school career. Such a conception of teaching,
it was argued in the report, provides teachers with milestones
to measure progress:

> Some 'milestones' . . . seemed to be necessary if teachers were
> to shepherd their students through the subject matter without
> suffering the complaints of their colleagues. [28]

Seeking milestones in teaching, as a form of coping strategy,
might have a broader application than to just an agreed upon
content - a syllabus. One might hypothesise that teachers seek
to establish in their work, and in their relationships with
students, ways of assuring themselves and others that work is
being done; these are the milestones they seek which function as
part of a system of monitoring and measuring progress which
provide teachers with reflections of their influence. Disturbing

the mirrors which reflect influence makes remote the likelihood
of radical project doctrines like SCISP taking root. That doctrine did not comprehend the subtle interconnections between
goals, expectations and techniques which were protected by
teachers, students, parents and peers at the expense of the
innovative policies. The milestones teachers valued in the study
were: the accumulation of notebooks, the exam rehearsals and
the exam results, the licenced content authoritatively taught and
recorded; these were the familiar markers of their classroom
life.

TEACHER CONCEPTIONS OF THEIR WORK AND CURRICULUM POLICY

The relationship between how teachers balance goals, techniques
and social relationships in teaching forms an important area for
future study. How teachers cope with forces which tend to upset
the balance may have a significant bearing on the fate of innovative doctrines which seek, by definition, to alter the balance. Of
particular importance is the issue of technology. One of the
reasons why teachers had difficulty using an inquiry approach
was due to their lack of experience working in that mode. Given
that lack of experience and the effects of that on the fate of the
SCISP policies in practice, an important question for curriculum
policy is: what is the relationship between the technical capabilities of the teacher and the potential for curriculum change? One
answer worth exploring is that the teachers will avoid approaches
where their technical capacities are weak, especially if the ones
they have are well adapted to institutional goals. We can see how
this works in the case of the pursuit of career goals in the
schools studied here.

By seeking career goals, the teachers were able to use in
support a well elaborated technology, which I call the syllabus
system. The syllabus system is well adapted for promoting
career goals. In support of the technology, teachers use high
influence in the classroom to ensure that there are no ambiguities
associated with the material they transmit to the pupils; material
which they warrant as accurate and relevant to the final examination. High influence is a form of relationship well suited to
passing on things to others which needed to be understood in
no uncertain terms.

Parallelling the syllabus system, is a system run for the
benefit of the science department. This I call the preview and
recruitment system. In this system, the content of the discipline
is used to advertise to the third forms (13-14 year-olds) what
the subjects and their teachers are like. On the basis of this
preview, pupils are recruited into separate disciplines for their
O-level work. The O-level work acts similarly to provide a
preview of and recruits for A-level. Again the teachers possess
an appropriate technology - the syllabus system, and the social

relationships support this preview and recruitment; an influential teacher very definitely teaching his or her subject.

The upset could be seen most clearly in the absence of SCISP of a syllabus. SCISP was, I found, a poor vehicle for operating either of these systems. Preview was difficult, since subjects were submerged, and recruitment uncertain, since pupil expectations about science teachers, classroom activity and subject organisation were not met. As a result, lobbying against the SCISP option by other science teachers began in the schools because its organisation and approved methods upset the smooth interconnections between goals, technology and social relationships that pre-existed. The teachers, in their comments, indicated that covering a syllabus of content was a task they perceived as central. For them, the syllabus defined what was to be done, and in conjunction with it, the previous examinations were used to simulate the examinations and stimulate concern. Both defined how the content of the syllabus was to be used: the syllabus embodied the way specialised disciplines were to be understood in the school, and it was used in connection with an effective technology for passing on the information that pupils needed to recycle into credentials. Associated with the reliance on the task defining function of the syllabus, was the view of the teachers that, generally, pupils lacked the ability to place a valid view upon material they received. By seeing themselves as guarantors of validity, the teachers had a good reason to adopt high influence teaching modes. The underlying conception that teachers have of the pupils supported their preferences for high influence in the classroom. They believed that pupils depended upon them for an interpretation of the point and direction of particular classroom events; unless the teacher was there, so it seemed, the point was not going to be established. What this analysis suggests is that there is a smooth articulation between the elements of the teachers' work; one aspect supports another. To the extent that innovative doctrine disrupts these smooth articulations there are going to be problems for the survival of that doctrine. So, in the case of SCISP in these schools, a central reason why its goals were so largely ignored was because there was a lack of an appropriate technology in the schools to support them.

Perrow has argued for the central role of technology in support change. On the basis of his review of research into forms of therapy in mental hospitals, for example, he noted that many mental hospitals sought 'economical custody' as a goal because there existed a 'technology and body of know how for custodial or housekeeping goals'. Perrow suggested that 'social scientists have had an unrealistic perception of the structure and goals of public mental hospitals because they have failed to see how the available technology influences the structure and goals'. [29]

Now there is a significant formal parallel between what innovators in mental care and SCISP doctrine sought ('client centred

therapy'/'new partnership'), and what the institutions were
able to provide ('custody at low cost'/'credentials'). This is
not to equate the goals of the different institutions but only
to show that in both cases goals were urged for which no
supportive technology existed that would work under the pre-
vailing circumstance. Perrow goes on to show that the technology
also influences social relationships. In the hospitals where
economical custody was the care provided, matters such as who
got how much soap and other scarce resources became bones of
contention between people; and similarly in the schools, who
obtained access to bright pupils, or whose students received
good examination marks; or whose pupils were prepared for
A-level were areas of contention between teachers operating
a syllabus system technology.

What the SCISP designers failed to realise was that, without
a technology in place, teachers would not be able to pursue the
revised goals of science education that the doctrine urged and
the project team paid little attention in their own advice to
teachers to the practical matters of implementing the new ideas;
materials directed at teachers were almost devoid of useful
pedagogical advice although there is extensive application of
psychological theory to the selection and sequencing of materials.
Teachers quite naturally continued to use a familiar and reliable
technology in the absence of anything better; it would have been
surprising had they done otherwise.

Perrow's analysis and the parallel one here stresses that
what happens in institutions is influenced strongly by the
available technology. It is the technology that provides the
possibility of operating day by day, of maintaining an efficient
and satisfying role. Here we join the conceptions of specific
role and technology into one conception. If we think of a
technology as a means of accomplishing certain changes in the
'raw material' which it processes (involving predictable consequences of actions taken and ways of detecting the effects of
action) we arrive at the idea that teachers prefer to operate
with a reliable technology, rather than an unpredictable one.
Teaching is an inherently diffuse task because, for a number
of goals that schools are asked to accomplish, a supportive
technology does not exist, and as a result, such goals are
pursued in rhetoric, rather than in reality. The fate of SCISP
doctrine in the schools can be understood in terms of a central
explanation; no technology existed there for accomplishing the
goals of the scheme. Without an appropriate technology, pursuit
of innovative goals and social relationships was inhibited and
the SCISP doctrine remained yet another rhetoric of possibility
for science education.

This view is, of course, presented as a hypothesis for interpreting the actions of the teachers in relation to their use of
SCISP doctrine. How teachers construe the techniques they use
is a matter for further research. Particularly important is the
way they understand the relationship between technique and

social relationships. This study suggests that both teachers
and students perceive important and often distressing social
consequences attached to methods of teaching in which teacher
influence was low. Is this a general problem, or particular to
science? What affects teacher and student ability to shift into
different social relationships associated with different techniques?
What might happen if teachers were more confident of their
technical capability; would greater tolerance of the diffuseness
of low influence teaching result?

POLICY IMPLICATIONS

We can now turn to the policy implications of the study associated with how those outside schools might collaborate with
people in schools. The case of SCISP is instructive. The SCISP
team adopted what Hall called a 'classical' approach to curriculum
design. By this, he meant what aims, objectives, methods and
evaluation were to be linked together systematically. Hall
emphasised the importance of prior identification of aims and
used a gloss of Gagné's hierarchy of learning outcomes as a
structure for developing and organising aims statements. The
assumed relationship between theory and practice implicit in
the development process used by SCISP has been termed
'logistic' by Reid. [30]
   An analysis of the data of the study suggests there are limitations to logistic conceptions of practice as a basis for curriculum
development policies. Ultimately these limitations stem from an
inappropriate conception of the relationship between practice
and theory. Three problems can be identified in the present
case: the dominance of general theory in the teacher guides and
the lack of sensitivity there to practical issues important to
teachers; the immutability of the theoretical formulations in
spite of repeated criticisms; the isolating effects on the Project
team of their allegiance to a doctrine of practice as applied
theory. These points are discussed first as a basis for assessing
the potential contributions of a more collaboratively based model.

Limitations of Logistic Procedures

The aims of the project which were derived from Gagné's
theoretical formulations were emphasised; these provided the
rallying cry to weld the project group together. The innovative
theory that the temporary group rallied to promote was glossed,
and the practical impediments played down. Success of the
system was measured in temporary conversion, not in long-term
survival. The claim here is not that adopting logistic procedures
will automatically lead to treating theory to the exclusion of
practice, but that given the nature of such procedures, an
emphasis on social science theory is a natural, but limiting
tendency.

The second problem concerns the procedures by means of which SCISP doctrine was formulated and its implementation monitored. The direction that the development of the project took seems to have occurred without serious attention to critical feedback from the schools. The record of the Consultative Committee meetings suggests that there were early warnings about the suitability of SCISP for schools as they were reorganising as comprehensives.

Evidence gathered in the study suggests that the SCISP doctrine was protected from critical appraisal. There are three sources of evidence for this. The Minutes of the Consultative Committee to the project suggest resistance by the project team to criticism; this view is supported by the comments of a Science Adviser, who had played an important role in the development of the project, which indicated that the team had not listened to the criticisms of the Science Advisers. Finally, one of the school teachers in this study argued that revisions in the materials, promised by the team to make the 'Patterns' books more readable, were not undertaken. This had been a matter of concern to him in deciding to adopt the scheme and he had checked trial and final materials. What these points suggest is that the development group, isolated as it was from schools, was not in a good position to subject the ideas, and particularly their technical implications, to testing in the place where they were to be used.[31] Removing the innovative processes from the school, and returning to the school later only to recruit adherents to a completed programme of action, creates the conditions for an excessive focus on visionary aims, and a lack of attention to the technical and social considerations important to teachers. Without understanding the endemic uncertainties - the dilemmas that teachers face in their work - and without understanding the ways the new ideas might affect how teachers normally operate in the classroom, the innovative doctrine runs the risk of remaining just a vision. The SCISP team, shielded by procedure and confident that practice could be derived from theory, had no need to confront the realities of practice. Documents produced by the team were meant to control practice by theoretically based formulations. The 'wisdom' of practice itself was not considered.

Learning from Practice

The collaborative model I wish to propose as an alternative is based on the idea that improvement of curriculum-in-action is to be understood as a consequence of teachers learning how to think better about curriculum problems, and not in terms of various forms of cultural and political levers which outsiders learn to manipulate. By probing the intentions of teachers in a way that does not impose a 'foreign' language, the present study shows how researchers, curriculum developers and teachers might find common ground, both in terms of language and methods of communication for talking about and studying problems of common interest. First steps towards that common language and methods can be seen in the results presented in this study elicited from teachers' views about the dilemmas they face in coping with their work. The way teachers talk about these dilemmas and the way they resolve them provide insight into the realities of teaching which need to be attended to by those who wish to engage teachers in curriculum renewal; the method of communication used in this study suggests a way for those concerned about curriculum improvement to explore the terrain that interests them.

Such collaboration characterises a 'methodic' approach to curriculum problems. As Reid suggests: 'Method . . . starts not from principles, but from problems . . . At every point its use is subject to the judgment of individuals.'[32]

Freire talks about this kind of collaboration in his 'Education for Critical Consciousness'. Although speaking in another context his ideas are appropriate here:

> The prerequisite for this task (problem solving) was a form
> of education enabling the people to reflect on themselves,
> their responsibilities, and their role in the new cultural
> climate – indeed to reflect on their very power of reflection.[33]

There are some important parallels between Freire's analysis of efforts to 'extend' modern ideas to rural communities and new methods to schools via centralised curriculum projects such as SCISP. Freire notes that, as commonly used, extension has 'an unquestionably mechanistic connotation, in as much as the term implies an action of taking, of transferring, of handing over, of depositing something in someone'.[34] Lacking in such a process is dialogue about the meaning of what is being extended – an understanding of its deeper significance for practice. The results of this study point to the possibilities of such dialogue.

Cultural and political barriers to collaboration between insiders and outsiders have been suggested in the curriculum literature. Two examples are taken to illustrate these. Wolcott, for example, characterised the reciprocities between educator moieties (he identified two mutually exclusive divisions of educators: teachers and technocrats) thus: 'Educator moieties display cynical, cautious, constricted behaviour vis-à-vis each other.'[35] He sees in this opposition a basis for integration, paradoxically: a way of surviving the conflicting demands of people outside of education. The teacher moiety, he argues, provides a counterpoise to the over-reaction of the technocrat moiety. The negative interaction, Wolcott argues, stems from cultural difference which 'result from the fact that rather different meanings can be assigned to quite similar behaviors'.[36] The anthropological conception of moiety leads to an emphasis on cultural differences. These differences exist with respect to the curriculum, as matters of common concern, but viewed from diverse perspectives.

Ways of identifying and analysing such matters need to develop
in the culture. There is hope. Traditional societies, Wolcott
notes, created go-between groups that combined ideas and
personnel from each moiety; such groups served the common
interests of both groups. But there is a limit to the usefulness
of such analyses. While they may serve the development of
anthropological theory, it is hard to see how policy relevant
implications can be drawn and, in fact, few are in his book.

Political, as well as cultural, barriers to collaboration have
been mooted. For example, Young notes that one of the effects
of the Schools Council's approach to curriculum development has
been the exclusion of 'any widespread teacher involvement in
the transformation of curricula'. [37] Young suggests that the
reason for this has been the fact that the way the Council is
organised reflects 'deeper hierarchies, not restricted to
curriculum development'. [38] Young's analysis sets teachers
against others who have different perspectives on the curriculum
The curriculum becomes part of larger more general issues of
political debate. From the point of view of dealing with problems
which are curricular in nature, the conception of mutually re-
enforcing hierarchies abstracts complex and diverse curriculum
problems in a selective way so as to fit with general themes of
oppression and class struggle. In this abstraction special
qualities of curricular problems are masked, and in relation to
improving the curriculum, the diversity of perspectives that
exist are over-simplified and polarised. Efforts to probe the
nature of curriculum problems, particularly how these problems
are construed by different groups, are frozen by the political
rhetoric. As Reid points out there is a tendency in the rhetoric
of radical perspectives on the curriculum to assume that the
nature of curricular problems is well understood and solutions
known in advance of careful deliberation upon them. [39]

One may grant that there are political and cultural differences
among the diverse groups interested in the nature of the school
curriculum. Some of the contention among them stems from a
failure to appreciate potential areas of common purpose and to
recognise why differences in short-term goals exist. Collaboration between insiders and outsiders has to be based on an
assumption that there are purposes in common between insiders
and outsiders, and that it is worthwhile for different groups to
try to understand long-term common goals and short-term
differences and to come to understand each other's system of
thought. Such a view is optimistic; it ought not to be naïve.
How are teachers and others to collaborate given that there are
risks involved?

Unless teachers can see that it is worth risking the effects
of role diffuseness to try to develop new technologies for the
classroom, it is hard to see how new visions for schools can
succeed. Role diffuseness, as we saw, is created when there
is a lack of technology for accomplishing certain aims that
people ask of teachers. If there was an effective technology the

role would be less diffuse, because teachers would know what
they were supposed to do and how to tell when they were
having an effect. Teachers would then feel less uncomfortable
about the reactions that others might have to their unexpected
teaching activities.

However, there is a vicious circle operating here; if the
teacher innovates, the risk exists that the efforts will be seen
as unexpected and 'odd'. These perceptions will be reflected to
the teacher, who will become even more uncertain about the
innovation. This uncertainty is compounded by the uncertainty
of the <u>methods</u> being used and the acceptability of the goals of
the <u>innovation</u>. The teacher is thus placed at the mercy of
forces which are difficult for him to understand and which tend
to inhibit change by engendering powerlessness and confusion.

The circle has to be broken somewhere and might be broken
by people outside the school helping teachers to develop new
technologies, while at the same time helping them to cope with
the effects such development has on social relationships in the
school. Those outside the school who have ideas about how the
curriculum might be improved might join with teachers in considering the technical and social implications of innovative ideas
at an early stage of their development, whatever their source.
Matters of importance to teachers would be discussed <u>in a language teachers understand</u>; that is, discussed in terms of how
teachers systematically construe the dilemmas they face in their
work in order to clarify for teacher and developer the theoretical
significance of these dilemmas, particularly the potential consequences of innovative resolutions. [40]

Collaboration implies a further requirement. New techniques
have to be practised in a supportive environment. As the reports
of teachers in this study indicated, such an environment was
lacking in the case of SCISP in their schools. Rather than re-
move teachers to sheltered environments where new techniques
can be practised, yet founder in the schools, teachers, through
a better understanding of what happens when they innovate,
may be able to withstand the consequences of their efforts. In
other words, if teachers can increase their awareness of how
goals, technology and social systems interact in their own situation, they may have a basis for surviving as innovators. To
increase such an understanding is an important function of the
collaborative model. In the end the process is one of education
through collaboration in curriculum development involving
reflexive consideration of one's own teaching situation. In this
way teachers can become involved in a process which holds
potential for increasing the power of the language they use
and the control they can exert over their professional activities.

NOTES

1.   J. Hoetker and W.P. Ahlbrand Jr., The Persistence of

Recitation, 'American Educational Research Journal', vol. 6 (1969), pp. 145-67.

2. D. Lortie, Observations on Teaching as Work in R.M. Travers (ed.), 'Second Handbook of Research on Teaching' (Rand McNally, Chicago, 1973), p. 478.

3. L.M. Smith and W. Geoffrey, 'The Complexities of an Urban Classroom' (Holt, Rinehart and Winston, New York, 1968).

4. P.H. Taylor, W.A. Reid, B.J. Holley and G. Exon, 'Purpose, Power and Constraint in the Primary School Curriculum' (Macmillan, London, 1974).

5. W.A. Reid, 'Thinking About the Curriculum' (Routledge & Kegan Paul, London, 1978).

6. Ibid., p. 87.

7. W. Hall, 'Patterns Teachers' Handbook' (Longman, London, 1973).

8. The term 'technology' is used here in the sense of a means to accomplish ends and not in the more common sense of apparatus or complex equipment.

9. J. Wilson, 'Practical Methods of Moral Education' (Heineman, London, 1972).

10. R.T. Hyman, 'Ways of Teaching' (Lippincott, Philadelphia, 1970).

11. Hall, 'Patterns Teachers' Handbook', p. 60.

12. R.M. Gagné, 'The Conditions of Learning' (Holt, Rinehart and Winston, New York, 1965).

13. Pseudonyms are used in place of teacher and school names.

14. Schwab's analysis of the 'eros' of discussion reveals discussion to be affectively complex in nature and requiring great skill on the part of the teacher. The threats to their judgement that worried the teachers in this study are shown to be a natural part of discussion by Schwab. Schwab draws a similar distinction between the nature of discussion and instruction: 'The roles of taskmaster and inquisitor, of giver and withholder of marks, not only adulterates the quality of the experience of conjoint action, but makes it virtually impossible.' See J.J. Schwab, Eros and Education: A Discussion of One Aspect of Discussion, 'Journal of General Education', vol. 8 (1954), p. 62.

15. Young notes that teachers have been unwilling to 'engage in enquiry with their pupils or students'. He attributes this to a failure to appreciate the social context of knowing and urges a greater teacher awareness of the politics of knowledge. Another reason may be that teachers find it difficult to know what role to play in enquiry; that is, to know how to proceed. Rather than lack of theoretical awareness, the impediment might be more fundamentally technical in nature. See M.F.D. Young, Notes for a Sociology of Science Education, 'Studies in Science Education', vol. 1 (1974), p. 58.

16. G.A. Kelly, 'The Psychology of Personal Constructs',

2 vols. (Norton, New York, 1955).
17. The analysis was done using the SPSS subprogramme
Factor with Varimax rotation. See N.W. Nie et al.,
'Statistical Package for the Social Sciences' (McGraw Hill,
New York, 1975).
18. I. Westbury, Conventional Classrooms, 'Open' Classrooms
and the Techology of Teaching, 'Journal of Curriculum
Studies', vol. 5 (1973), pp. 99-121.
19. J. Eggleston, M.J. Galton and M.E. Jones, 'Processes and
Products of Science Teaching' (Macmillan, London, 1976).
20. Ibid., pp. 66-7.
21. R. Walker and C. Adelman, 'A Guide to Classroom Observation' (Methuen, London, 1975).
22. Elliott and MacDonald reported a Humanities Curriculum
Project teacher saying that students 'couldn't conceive of
talking as work and thereby a worthwhile educational
activity'. See J. Elliott and B. MacDonald, 'People in
Classrooms' (Centre for Applied Research in Education,
Norwich, 1975), p. 140.
23. Taylor, Christie and Platts, in their study of how teachers
perceive effective science teaching, found evidence of
'face-to-face' and 'pupil-autonomy' factors in teachers
appraisals. They concluded that the former, more valued
by teachers than the latter, would not lead to 'understanding science as a system of thought having human and
technological implications'. See P.H. Taylor, T. Christie
and C.V. Platts, An Exploratory Study of Science Teachers'
Perceptions of Effective Teaching, 'Educational Review',
vol. 23 (1970), p. 30.
24. The concept of influence goes beyond simply 'control' of
the pupil. While there are control functions exercised
through influence, other important functions also exist.
For example: mutual trust; emotional impact; assurance
of lesson validity and reliability are served through the
exercise of teacher influence. The teachers had difficulty
seeing how these functions could be served through low
influence activities. See also W.K. Hoy, Pupil Control
Ideology and Organizational Socialization: A Further
Examination of the Influence of Experience on the Beginning Teacher, 'The School Review', vol. 77 (1969), pp.
257-65.
25. Barnes notes that: 'At the heart of teaching as we know
it in our culture lies a dilemma . . . There is an implicit
conflict between the teacher's responsibility for control
and his responsibility for learning.' See D. Barnes,
'From Communication to Curriculum' (Penguin Books,
London, 1976), p. 176.
26. The effects on students of a lack of an agreed-upon
syllabus has been noted by Hudson: 'They (students)
had no authoritative guidance about what to concentrate
on, and what to ignore. At school exhaustive coverage

had been possible; now there was just too much to read –
and hence an inherent risk of being examined on material
for which they were unprepared.' Students who were thus
bound to the syllabus Hudson called 'sylbs'. SCISP
teachers also encountered difficulty in assuring the 'sylbs'
that they were not at risk. See L. Hudson, 'Frames of
Mind' (Methuen, London, 1968), p. 12.
27. National Science Foundation, 'Case Studies in Science
Education' (Centre for Instructional Research and Curriculum Evaluation, University of Illinois at Urbana-Champaign,
1978), p. 16:6.
28. Ibid., p. 16:22.
29. C. Perrow, Hospitals: Technology, Structure and Goals
in J. March (ed.), 'Handbook of Organizations' (Rand
McNally, Chicago, 1965), p. 930.
30. W.A. Reid, The Practical, the Theoretic, and the Conduct
of Curriculum Research (paper presented at AERA Annual
Meeting, Los Angeles, April 1981).
31. For a more extended discussion of the development of the
SCISP doctrine see J.K. Olson, Innovative Doctrines and
Practical Dilemmas: A Case Study of Curriculum Translation, unpublished PhD thesis (University of Birmingham,
1980).
32. W.A. Reid, The Deliberative Approach to the Study of the
Curriculum and its Relation to Critical Pluralism in M. Lawn
and L. Barton (eds.), 'Rethinking Curriculum Studies'
(Croom Helm, London, 1981), p. 171.
33. P. Freire, 'Education for Critical Consciousness' (Seabury
Press, New York, 1973), p. 16.
34. Ibid., p. 99.
35. H. Wolcott, 'Teachers vs. Technocrats' (Centre for
Educational Policy and Management, Eugene, Oregon,
1977), p. 191.
36. Ibid., p. 236.
37. M.F.D. Young, The Rhetoric of Curriculum Development
in G. Whitty and M.F.D. Young (eds.), 'The Politics of
School Knowledge' (Nafferton Books, Driffield, England,
1976), p. 197.
38. Ibid., p. 197.
39. Reid, 'Thinking about the Curriculum', p. 11.
40. Similar arguments for a collaborative approach have been
made by others. See, for example: W. Harlen, A Stronger
Teacher Role in Curriculum Development, 'Journal of
Curriculum Studies', vol. 9 (1977), pp. 21-30; A.M. Bussis,
E.A. Chittenden and M. Amarel, 'Beyond Surface Curriculum' (Westview Press, Boulder, Colo., 1976); F.M. Connelly
and M. Ben-Peretz, Teachers' Roles in the Using and
Doing of Research and Curriculum Development, 'Journal
of Curriculum Studies', vol. 12 (1980), pp. 95-107; G.
Fenstermacher, A Philosophical Consideration of Recent
Research on Teacher Effectiveness, 'Review of Research

in Education', vol. 6 (1978), pp. 157-85.

BIBLIOGRAPHY

Barnes, D. 'From Communication to Curriculum' (Penguin Books, London, 1976).
Bussis, A.M., Chittenden, E.A. and Amarel, M. 'Beyond Surface Curriculum' (Westview Press, Boulder, Colo. 1976).
Connelly, F.M. and Ben-Peretz, M. Teachers' Roles in Using and Doing of Research and Curriculum Development, 'Journal of Curriculum Studies', vol. 12 (1980), pp. 95-107.
Eggleston, J., Galton, M.J. and Jones, M.E. 'Processes and Products of Science Teaching' (Macmillan, London, 1976).
Elliott, J. and MacDonald, B. 'People in Classrooms' (Centre for Applied Research in Education, Norwich, 1975).
Fenstermacher, G. A Philosophical Consideration of Recent Research on Teacher Effectiveness, 'Review of Research in Education', vol. 6 (1978).
Freire, P. 'Education for Critical Consciousness' (Seabury Press, New York, 1973).
Gagné, R.M. 'The Conditions of Learning' (Holt, Rinehart and Winston, New York, 1965).
Hall, W. 'Patterns Teachers' Handbook' (Longman, London, 1973).
Harlen, W. A Stronger Teacher Role in Curriculum Development, 'Journal of Curriculum Studies', vol. 9 (1977), pp. 21-30.
Hoetker, J. and Ahlbrand Jr., W.P. The Persistence of the Recitation, 'American Educational Research Journal', vol. 6 (1969), pp. 145-67.
Hoy, W.K. Pupil Control Ideology and Organizational Socialization: A Further Examination of the Influence of Experience on the Beginning Teacher, 'The School Review', vol. 77 (1969), pp. 257-65.
Hudson, L. 'Frames of Mind' (Methuen, London, 1968).
Hyman, R.T. 'Ways of Teaching' (Lippincott, Philadelphia, 1970).
Kelly, G.A. 'The Psychology of Personal Constructs', 2 vols. (Norton, New York, 1955).
Lortie, D. Observations on Teaching as Work in R.M. Travers (ed.), 'Second Handbook of Research on Teaching' (Rand McNally, Chicago, 1973).
National Science Foundation, 'Case Studies in Science Education' (Centre for Instructional Research and Curriculum Evaluation, University of Illinois at Urbana-Champaign, 1978).
Nie, N.W. et al. 'Statistical Package for the Social Sciences' (McGraw Hill, New York, 1975).
Olson, J.K. 'Innovative Doctrines and Practical Dilemmas: A Case Study of Curriculum Translation', unpublished PhD

thesis (University of Birmingham, 1980).
Perrow, C. Hospitals: Technology, Structure and Goals in
  J. March (ed.), 'Handbook of Organizations' (Rand McNally,
  Chicago, 1965).
Reid, W.A. 'Thinking About the Curriculum' (Routledge & Kegan
  Paul, London, 1978).
——. The Practical, the Theoretic and the Conduct of Curriculum
  Research (paper presented at AERA Annual Meeting, Los
  Angeles, April 1981).
——. The Deliberative Approach to the Study of the Curriculum
  and its Relation to Critical Pluralism, in M. Lawn and L.
  Barton (eds.), 'Rethinking Curriculum Studies' (Croom Helm,
  London, 1981).
Schwab, J.J. Eros and Education: A Discussion of One Aspect
  of Discussion, 'Journal of General Education', vol. 8 (1954),
  pp. 51-71.
Smith, L.M. and Geoffrey, W. 'The Complexities of an Urban
  Classroom' (Holt, Rinehart and Winston, New York, 1968).
Taylor, P.H., Christie, T. and Platts, C.V. An Exploratory
  Study of Science Teachers' Perceptions of Effective Teaching,
  'Educational Review', vol. 23 (1970), pp. 19-32.
Taylor, P.H., Reid, W.A., Holley, B.J. and Exon, G. 'Purpose,
  Power and Constraint in the Primary School Curriculum'
  (Macmillan, London, 1974).
Walker, R. and Adelman, C. 'A Guide to Classroom Observation'
  (Methuen, London, 1975).
Westbury, I. Conventional Classrooms, 'Open' Classrooms and
  the Technology of Teachers, 'Journal of Curriculum Studies',
  vol. 5 (1973), pp. 99-121.
Wilson, J. 'Practical Methods of Moral Education' (Heineman,
  London, 1972).
Wolcott, H. 'Teachers vs. Technocrats' (Centre for Educational
  Policy and Management, Eugene, Oregon, 1977).
Young, M.F.D. Notes for a Sociology of Science Education,
  'Studies in Science Education', vol. 1 (1974), pp. 51-60.
——. The Rhetoric of Curriculum Development in G. Whitty and
  M.F.D. Young (eds.), 'The Politics of School Knowledge'
  (Nafferton Books, Driffield, England, 1976).

Sally Brown is a Senior Research Fellow at the University of Stirling, Scotland, and is currently on secondment as a Research Adviser to the Scottish Education Department in Edinburgh.

Donald McIntyre is a Reader in Education in the Department of Education, University of Stirling, Scotland.

John Olson is an Associate Professor of Science Education and Curriculum Theory at the Faculty of Education, Queen's University, Kingston, Ontario.

Neil Sendelbach is Group Manager, Manpower Planning and Development, for the Micro-electronics Division of General Instrument Corporation.

Edward Smith is an Associate Professor of Science Education in the College of Education at Michigan State University.

Rob Walker is a member of the Centre for Applied Research in Education at the University of East Anglia, Norwich, England.

INDEX

Accommodation 141
Adelman, C. 154
Advice: in curriculum guides 22; rules for 22-3; useful to teachers 25
Assistant Principal Teacher 128-9
Atkin, M. 37

Berlak, A. 14
Berlak, H. 14
B.S.C.S. 6

Carlson, Richard 7

Case Study: and bias 68; and communication 20-2; and context 14, 40-5, 68-71, 76-7, 121-2; and ethnography 170; and generalisation 19-20; and preferred metaphors 19; and problems of time 63; and role of informants 43; and self-deception 18-19; and story telling 68; formulating questions for 46; methods of 28-9; reporting 38-9; role of co-ordinator in 38, 44, 68; selecting issues 54-5
Change: as a form of collaboration 171-3; as communication 26-8; as rational 8-9; as reorientation 7; as variation 7; cultural barriers to 171-2; deliberation about 110-11, 172-3; humane perspectives on 11-13; logistic approaches to 171; mechanistic conception of 6-10; methodic approaches to 17; political barriers to 172; reasons for lack of 72; role of outsiders in 173; unrealistic expectations for 4, 6, 167-8
Churchland, Geoffrey 27-8
Classroom: and innovation 118; authority of teacher in 160-2; culture of 62-3; ecology of 9; management of 130; organisation of 77-8; routines of 77-82
Curriculum development: and lack of time 121; recruitment for 113; teachers role in 113
Curriculum documents 22
Curriculum policy 141; and teacher perspectives 166-9

Curriculum translation 25-6

Desegregation as an example of context 47-53
Dilemmas: logical 14; of control 12; of implementation 164-5; of inquiry 144; of teachers 11-12, 62-3; resolutions of 14-16; sources of 164-5; teacher awareness of 141
Discovery 7; effects on teacher role 62-3
Discussion: effects of time on 131; in SCISP 22; use in inquiry 143-4
Doyle, W.A. 108
Dreeben, Robert 8
Dumas, F.M. 20

Ecology: of classroom 9
Egan, K. 14
Eggleston, J. 154
Ethnography 75
Explanations: role in teaching 24

Fenstermacher, G. 23
Freire, P. 171
Fullan, M. 127

Gagné, R. 169
Goals of Science education 143; teacher perspectives on 111
Guided-discovery: and learning theories 110; and the status-quo 121; in SCISP 145-6; meaning of 119-20; role of worksheets in 120: teacher hostility towards 112

Hermeneutics and research 16-20
Heron, Marshall 6
House, E. 17
Hudson, Liam 17

Influence: and preview and recruitment system 166-7; and syllabus system 166-7; contrast between high and low 158-9; forms of 151-62; functions of 164; high 155-8; low 158-60; nature of 155; teacher 27; teacher appraisals of 162-4
Informants, check on reliability of 68-9

For Product Safety Concerns and Information please contact our
EU representative GPSR@taylorandfrancis.com Taylor & Francis
Verlag GmbH, Kaufingerstraße 24, 80331 München, Germany